NEW YORK UNBOUND

New York Unbound

The City and the Politics of the Future

Edited by

Peter D. Salins

Basil Blackwell

Copyright © Manhattan Institute 1988

First published 1988

Basil Blackwell Inc.
432 Park Avenue South, Suite 1503
New York, NY 10016, USA

Basil Blackwell Ltd
108 Cowley Road, Oxford, OX4 1JF, UK

Library of Congress Cataloging in Publication Data

New York unbound.
 Includes index.
  1. New York (N.Y.)—Politics and government—1951–
2. New York (N.Y.)—Economic policy. 3. New York (N.Y.)
Social policy. 4. Political culture—New York (N.Y.)
I. Salins, Peter D.
JS1230 1988   361.6′1′097471   88–24252
ISBN 1–55786–008–4

British Library Cataloguing in Publication Data

New York Unbound: the city and the politics of the future.
  1. (City) New York. Local government
I. Salins, Peter D.
352.0747′1
ISBN 1-55786-008-4

Typeset in 10½ on 12 point Sabon
by Photo·Graphics, Honiton, Devon
Printed in the United States of America

CONTENTS

CONTENTS

PREFACE

Why do we need another book about New York? Given the growing cottage industry of New York based books, studies, reports, monographs and even novels, it might appear that this market niche would be saturated. There are two reasons, however, why the world might welcome this particular New York book. First, New York as a phenomenon is a subject of almost limitless interest and fascination for New Yorkers and non-New Yorkers alike because of the sheer prominence and grandeur of the city on the national and international scene. New York is America's largest city and its premier commercial center; New York is the world's most important financial marketplace; New York is the nation's cultural lodestar; New York is a paradigm of both the best and worst aspects of late twentieth-century urban life.

Second, there is an entire point of view regarding New York's problems and prospects that has not found expression in the New York literature to date. Most recent studies combine lamentations over the city's dismal conditions with prescriptions requiring more doses of failed government policies to remedy them. The biases of the prevailing wisdom call out for the publication of a qualifying, if not outright contradictory, orientation.

New York Unbound has been conceived as a book in which some of the most prominent, insightful and engaging commentators on the New York scene look at the city and its all too familiar problems in a profoundly different light. Their perspectives combine an appreciation of New York's enormous natural vitality with an understanding of the many ways in which existing public policies have stifled it, with the result that old problems don't get solved

vii

and new ones arise. Their remedy, expressed in different ways and concerning different facets of New York's public life, is: let us consider solving the city's problems by harnessing rather than repressing its dynamism and energy; hence *New York Unbound*.

The completion of *New York Unbound* has been a highly collaborative effort. As sponsor of the project, the Manhattan Institute has, from the beginning, furnished the essential encouragement and financial support to make the book happen. William Hammett, the President of the Institute, and Larry Mone, Vice President and Research Director, embraced the project with enthusiasm from the outset and they wholeheartedly continued their commitment and help in countless ways to the very end.

I am deeply appreciative of the effort made by the contributing authors. While one could hardly fail with such an eminent group of scholars and experts, the book was enhanced by the high degree of cooperation they displayed with respect to its central design, and in their patient and sustained work during the process of several editorial iterations. I would also like to acknowledge the critical role of my editorial assistant, Betty Greenfield, who was immensely helpful in working with the contributing authors in organizing and unifying the final manuscript.

Finally, I would like to thank Peter Dougherty, our editor at Basil Blackwell, for his faith in the project, for his editorial assistance, and for his efforts to assure that *New York Unbound* emerged as such a handsome and well produced book.

Peter D. Salins
New York
May 1988

ABOUT THE AUTHORS

Louis Winnick is Deputy Vice President of the Ford Foundation and former Director of Research of the New York City Housing and Redevelopment Board.

Mark A. Willis is Deputy Commissioner for Development of the New York City Department of Housing Preservation and Development.

Nathan Glazer is Professor of Education and Sociology at Harvard University and co-author of *Beyond the Melting Pot* (with Daniel Patrick Moynihan) and of *The Lonely Crowd* (with David Riesman and Reuel Denney).

Jose Gomez-Ibañez is Professor of Urban Planning and Public Policy at the John F. Kennedy School of Government at Harvard University and co-author of *Autos, Transit and Cities* (with John R. Meyer).

Harold Hochman is Professor of Economics at Baruch College of the City University of New York.

E. S. Savas is Professor of Management at Baruch College, former Assistant Secretary of the United States Department of Housing and Urban Development and author of *Privatizing the Public Sector*.

Paul Goldberger is architecture critic of the *New York Times*.

Blanche Bernstein is former Commissioner of Social Services of the City of New York and author of *The Politics of Welfare*.

Roger Starr is the author of *America's Housing Challenge* and is on the Editorial Board of the *New York Times*.

ABOUT THE AUTHORS

Frank J. Macchiarola, former Director of the New York City Partnership and former Chancellor of the New York City Board of Education, is Director of the Academy of Political Sciences.

Andrew Hacker is Professor of Political Science at Queens College of the City University of New York and author of *The End of the American Era*.

INTRODUCTION

Peter D. Salins

New York Unbound is about the future of the most interesting and complex city in the world on the eve of the twenty-first century. No other American city presents such a checkered pattern of successes and failures. On the plus side is the city's unexpectedly strong comeback from virtual municipal bankruptcy in 1975, its commercial revival, and the increasing vitality of its changing population. On the minus side, most of the city's best-known problems are still with us, and some have gotten worse.

There is every reason why New York should be the most prosperous city in the country. It is the premier city of the United States, and indeed the world. Its strengths are greatest in those areas—finance, communications, services—that increasingly dominate the postindustrial economy. As the nation's intellectual capital, and as a powerful magnet for energetic and ambitious young people from around the country and the world, the city is well placed to lead a "knowledge economy" based on the increasing primacy of mind over muscle in production. Its economy is the most diverse in the nation and has been less affected than most by the problems afflicting the manufacturing and farm sectors. With such natural advantages, one would expect the city to enter the next century on a crest of sustained economic growth, with its citizens enjoying a high standard of income and a gratifyingly cosmopolitan quality of life, and with no more than its share of governmental problems.

Yet in spite of its stunning commercial success, New York is a paradigm of urban failure. None of the urban pathologies that afflict New York is unique, but in this city they have reached alarming proportions: the sheer number of homeless men and women lying

1

about in public places; the intensity with which citizens perceive danger from assault and robbery in their homes, as well as in the streets; the shambles of an education system that does not even make daily contact with one-third of its school-age charges and barely educates many of the other two-thirds; the squalor of much of its housing, even in the "better" neighborhoods; the nation's largest and fastest-growing cohort of AIDS-afflicted—one could go on and on.

The mere existence in larger numbers of typical big-city problems in New York should occasion neither surprise nor excessive alarm. What is surprising and alarming is for a city with such a vibrant economy, and one that sustains such a vast and costly infrastructure, to suffer these problems so disproportionately.

As they analyze and discuss why New York should be at the same time the best and worst of places, the authors of *New York Unbound* reveal the tendencies operating at the highest levels of the city's civic culture as well as in its government to both restrain New York's vitality and exacerbate its problems. These tendencies are, of course, not unique to New York. In greater or lesser degree they operate in every large city in the nation, and with the same general consequences. So the lessons *New York Unbound* draws for New York are apt ones for San Francisco and Boston and Minneapolis—and perhaps in the long run for such currently untrammeled places as Dallas and Phoenix.

BOUND BY WHAT?

Of the tendencies and processes that bind New York, five stand out. One of the most debilitating in its impact on the city's economy is *fear of the marketplace*. It is ironic, indeed, that the center of world capitalism has so little faith in the free market. That this is so is evident above all in the myriad public policies that aim to circumvent the processes and prices that might result from a free exchange of goods and services. But it is also manifest in that less tangible realm, the civic culture, as articulated by the media and the local academic community. It is taken for granted that prices must be set on a wide variety of goods and services, not only to assure that they do not rise too high, but also that they do not fall too low. Few question the wisdom of obstacles placed before entrepreneurs trying to start new businesses which aim to "protect" the public from a wide variety of harms. In the view of too many in these opinion elites, market activities can rarely be trusted to operate in the interest of the individual or collective good. To believe otherwise is to betray naiveté at best, or to be part of a conspiracy of greedy businessmen at worst.

A second tendency, one that is fed by the pervasive dislike of market activities, is the average New Yorker's pursuit of a *free lunch*. Not only the poor—perhaps least of all the poor—clamor for discount prices on all manner of urban goods and services. Too many of New York's middle- and upper-income tenants not only cherish the rent discount windfall that keeps their housing bills far below those of the average American (be this a product of rent regulation or "middle-income" subsidy programs)—they are convinced they are entitled to it. The major beneficiaries of the transit subsidy, which pays half the average fare, are middle- and upper-income New Yorkers, who enjoy subsidized mass transit even though unsubsidized transit travel would still be cheaper than the auto-related expenses of the average non-New Yorker. When the City University was pressured by the federal government, as a condition of receiving assistance during the fiscal crisis of 1974, to introduce modest tuition charges, the middle-income constituents of the system were the most outraged, even though CUNY at that time was the last free public university in the country. Under a variety of rationalizations, New Yorkers are convinced that to pay the going rate for almost anything is a serious tax on their standard of living. An ongoing mini-example of the tendency is Mayor Ed Koch's leading the charge against "outrageous" increases in the price of movie tickets. Whenever possible, of course, middle- and upper-income New Yorkers refer to the harmful impact of market prices on the poor. It remains the case, however, that in both average and aggregate terms the poor receive much less benefit from the city's regimen of subsidies and price regulations than do the middle classes and the rich.

A third tendency, again related to the antimarket bias prevalent in New York, is the *propensity to regulate*, because "there oughta be a law." In a large and complex city such as New York, many things are bound to go wrong every day. When things go wrong there usually is an immediate media analysis of the etiology of the disaster and a new law or regulation is born. No other city in the country has so burdensome a web of building, land use, development, and general business regulations as has New York. Some regulations are born out of the self-serving efforts of vested interests to limit competition, but many represent well-intentioned efforts to prevent rare or occasional harms. The irony is that the very size and

3

complexity of the regulatory rubric ensures that few regulations will be enforced, making New York at one and the same time the most regulated and most anarchic of cities.

The overlapping effects of subsidization and regulation, combined with the fact that the city and state governments employ over 500,000 New Yorkers (members of perhaps over 1 million households) make the city an ocean of *vested interests*, the fourth of the binding tendencies. Rare is the New Yorker who hasn't one or another vested interest to protect, be it a discount rent, a larger-than-deserved salary, an overly generous pension, inefficient but prized working conditions, protection from business competition or unwanted institutional neighbors, or access to a free parking space. The accumulation of such a large array of vested perquisites, distributed across such a large proportion of the voting and vocal population, imposes serious constraints on public- or private-sector efforts to introduce greater efficiency and cost effectiveness and hampers the physical and economic evolution of the city to accommodate new housing, new businesses, or needed public improvements.

Of course, there are prices to be paid for the operation of these various tendencies that bind New York. One of them is the need to pay for the city's subsidies and its inefficiencies with taxes. New York has the highest taxes of any municipality in the United States, and it deploys the widest variety of taxes: personal income tax, corporate income tax, sales tax, real estate tax, capital gains tax (apart from capital gains as part of the income tax), property tax, commercial occupancy tax, unincorporated business tax, taxes on parking garage use and hotel occupancy, etc. Both the size of the tax bite and the intrusive nature of the taxes make New York a less attractive place to do business for all but those who need the city's indisputable advantages of size and access. So we must number, as one of New York's binding tendencies, its *indifference to the impact of taxation* (both in general terms, and with respect to its peculiar mix of taxes) on its economic well-being.

In taxation, as in every other aspect of New York's civic life, we see the role of the free-lunch and vested-interest syndromes. Because, as high as New York's taxes are overall, they fall very lightly on some citizens and very heavily on others. The two basic axioms of the city's tax system seem to be: "milk Manhattan" and "spare the affluent." Containing only 20% of New York's population, Manhattan pays 61% of its taxes, from all sources. There are a number of tax rubrics making this happen. New York depends heavily on business taxes (having the nation's lowest property tax

4

share among large municipalities), and most of the city's business is in Manhattan. Among business taxes, New York depends heavily on those that afflict big business, such as the corporate income tax, the financial corporations tax, and the commercial occupancy tax. Among other business taxes of the narrow-gauge nuisance variety, New York depends heavily on those that impact Manhattan businesses: taxes on hotels, parking garages, theater tickets, etc. That New York's tax burden relative to other American cities is so high and so unfairly distributed is testimony to the power of the vested. The outer boroughs, with more votes, conspire to shift much of the burden on Manhattan. The affluent conspire to shift much of the burden on business and the nonaffluent. As a result, the average New Yorker does not feel especially heavily taxed and the system and its antieconomic and inequitable effects continue.

All of these tendencies are mediated and enforced by a *debilitating political culture*, the fifth of the forces that bind New York. It used to be that big cities, including New York, had political machines that, while corrupt, delivered municipal services fairly effectively, built great civic monuments, and expanded the infrastructure of roads, transit and utilities. The political machine in New York has been replaced by a web of neighborhood groups, public employee unions, and government vendors and contractors that is equally corrupt but delivers neither efficient services nor great public works. The political culture of the city, dominated by an "entente cordiale" among the two parties, is designed to deliver an unending series of logrolling deals on small issues, and complete stalemate on large ones. During the fiscal crisis of the mid-1970s, which was above all a *political* crisis, the system rose briefly to the occasion and the public interest prevailed. Since then, it has been political business as usual.

Each of the essays in *New York Unbound* touches on one or another of these themes. Mark Willis, in Chapter 2, documents the vital wellsprings of the city's economy but also points out where New York threatens to kill the economic goose that lays its golden eggs. Nathan Glazer, in Chapter 3, describes the role and contribution of immigrants to the city's economic and social life, but makes us aware of the barriers to mobility and economic integration that arise from some of New York's constraining rules. Jose A. Gomez-Ibañez, in Chapter 4, tells us that New Yorkers must pay the true cost of their trips within the city and the region if traffic is not to grind to a halt. Harold Hochman, in Chapter 5, lays out the grim reality of an overregulated city, and E. S. Savas, in Chapter 6, discerns areas in which public burdens could be devolved to the private sector in the interests of lower taxes and better municipal services. Paul Goldberger, in Chapter 7, conjures a vision of New York returning to its grand architectural tradition under a more rational regulatory regime. Blanche Bernstein, in Chapter 8, and Frank Macchiarola, in Chapter 9, advise us on how New York, if it could shed the constraints of rigid bureaucracies and stale conceptions, could integrate the city's "underclass" into its economic and social life. Roger Starr, in Chapter 10, shows how all the tendencies discussed above, have eroded the quality and quantity of New York's housing stock. Finally, Macchiarola, in Chapter 11, gives us the anatomy of a failed political system but also shows the pathway to reform that goes beyond mere checks on graft.

In outlining the tendencies that need to be curtailed if New York is to thrive, the authors make no representation that these tendencies are unique to New York. It just happens that the size of this city, coupled with some unique historic and cultural circumstances, has made them so much stronger than elsewhere. There is also no representation that they can all be undone.

New York would be much better off, however, if the harmful nature of these tendencies were at least recognized and some modest effort were expended to reverse their most egregious manifestations. We may not soon get rid of rent regulation, but land-use regulation might be reformed. The city may not relinquish the municipal hospitals, but many lesser public services could be turned over to the private sector. The city and state may continue to subsidize the subways but might be more hospitable to private buses and imposition of tolls on the East River bridges. The city may not reduce taxes significantly but might eliminate nuisance taxes and spread the overall burden more fairly. And perhaps, in small increments, the average New Yorker will abandon his attitude of exceptionalism and entitlement and be willing to trade higher prices and the loss of some perquisites for the privilege of living in a more vibrant, more amenity-laden, and above all, more civil city.

Chapter 1

NEW YORK UNBOUND

Louis Winnick

A CITY OF DIVERSITY

New York is a museum of contrasts, a locus for the exhilarating and the harrowing, a place that joyously and communally celebrates the Tall Ships and the Statue of Liberty not far from the burned-out hulks of the South Bronx. Generations of photographers have been enthralled by its skyscrapers looming over modest brownstones. The nation's most expensive city for those in condos on the Upper East Side who satisfy their needs in the area's pricier shops it is among the least expensive for those who don't need a car and who live in rent-controlled apartments in Brooklyn and Queens near keenly competitive supermarkets and discount stores. Twenty-five-dollar power breakfasts at exclusive hotels are balanced by decent $1.50 breakfasts at any number of fast-food counters.

New York is the city of youthful achievers convening nightly at scores of fashionable trysting places for drink and encounter, and of ghetto youths sharing brown bags on stoops. It is the city of schools that are not much more than holding pens and of schools that carry away, with astronomic regularity, the nation's most glittering scholastic prizes. It is the Queens of Archie Bunker and Howard Beach, and also of Jackson Heights-Elmhurst-Corona, one of the most polyethnic settlements on earth. It is the city of prosperity and of poverty; the city that lurches between the unbridled capitalism of Singapore and the benevolent paternalism of Sweden.

The play of one extreme against another yields the most vivid colors and dramatic tensions for writers and the media, but not a whole lot of truth. The mode of contrasts also risks falsehood and

7

caricature. The fact is, most New Yorkers occupy the wide spaces between the highly publicized extremes. They are neither rich nor poor, live neither on the Upper East Side nor in rent-controlled apartments, are neither yuppies nor underclass, dropouts nor National Merit winners. The city's dominant social group comprises its working-class and middle-income population (though the latter has been stretched to allow those with $48,000 to enter a subsidized housing project and others with $75,000 or more to remain in continued occupancy). Accurate renderings of New York by social scientists usually are dull reports based on frequency distributions and time series that are irregular in amplitude and periodicity. Valid generalizations usually must be backed up by platoons of qualifiers and squads of footnotes.

Though the practice of defining the city by its extremes is almost always inaccurate, New York is especially vulnerable to one set of extremes: its socioeconomic highs are matched by its socioeconomic depths. The threats to its economy and civic order are the predations of its large and dangerous underclass. If a prevision of New York's future detects rays of sunshine, the light filters through thick layers of clouds.

The city faces conflicting pulls between dynamic economic growth forces that promise vitality and prosperity, and cancerous social pathologies that threaten fear and stagnation. Although New York's economy is carried to a large extent on national and international tides and currents, policy choices can slow or accelerate its movements and push it closer to or farther from the shoals.

THE CITY DYNAMIC

New York's economy, employment, office construction, and retail sales are nestled in the curl of a wave carrying the city to levels approaching or surpassing its greatest boom periods. Public treasuries are brimming over with prosperity-generated revenues of unprecedented size. The ambitious young flock to New York to pursue careers in its financial houses and law firms, to study in its professional and graduate schools, to follow their muse in the performing and pictorial arts, or to test their creative itch in publishing, advertising, and the media. Immigrants pump new vigor into its economy and new life into depleted neighborhoods, displaying a work ethic beside which the vaunted Protestant ethic shrinks to limp indolence.

8

A heightened morale, a new spirit refreshed by the 1976 Bicentennial, expresses itself in exuberant street life, packed sidewalk cafes and office plazas at lunchtime, and good-natured movie lines and jogging courses on weekends. The Saturday bustle on Steinway Street in Queens or Montague Street in Brooklyn Heights and the Sunday parade of hand-holding couples on a saunter to or from brunch recall an earlier time.

The indexes of confidence are higher than they have been in years. The principal bond-rating houses, who, perforce, gaze beyond tomorrow to the quality of debt that will not mature until well into the next century, have significantly upgraded the City's standing; and the collective judgment of trading markets has ratcheted the standing of New York bonds to levels above those of the rating services. Bond insurance companies have underwritten the city's credit risk past the year 2010, and Japanese investors purchase New York real estate at extraordinary price/earnings ratios; their magnitude can be justified solely by supreme confidence in New York's underlying long-term strength, and discounts whatever wounds will be inflicted by intervening downturns during the life of the investment.

FOUR GROWTH SECTORS

The city's future economy is dependent on four growth sectors. The first is the market for financial products and exchanges of extraordinary complexity—a market that draws upon the capital and skills of the city's major banks, investment houses, and law firms, the certified grandmasters of this hotly competitive game. Adjunct to that market is New York's role as central depot for a global flow of instant information. The city has enormous resources for collecting, configuring, and transmitting prodigious quantities of data through sophisticated electronics communication systems. Equal in importance are the primitive communications systems. Body language, the lift of an eyebrow, a wave of a hand, the wink, the nudge, the whispered confidence constitute a subtext for elaborate transactions and nuanced deals. Such elemental modes of information transfer place an extraordinary premium on face-to-face contact, rendering much of New York's economy resistant to the powerful dispersive pulls of modern communications technology. The executive dining rooms of the city's financial houses, at which every party to a transaction can be swiftly assembled, represent a quintessential component of New York's financial system. In these strengths, only London is a rival, with Tokyo a distant, albeit rising, third.

The second growth sector derives from today's affluent sumptuary world, with its steadily rising demand for high fashion, interior decoration, jewelry and diamonds, art and culture, tourism, gourmet restaurants, and the sundry amusements of the leisured. In these expanding markets New York claims a more-than-proportionate share.

The third growth market is rarely so categorized: the burgeoning welfare state, with its immense outlays for health care, social services, and income transfers. New York's matchless medical facilities and teaching hospitals, along with its large dependent population, make the city a prominent participant in the social welfare market. Substantial employment is found at every occupational level for those engaged in health care, social service, and the transfer of purchasing power to the nonemployed. But while the welfare economy is primarily a system of redistribution, it may also contribute to economic growth. Federal food stamps and Section 8 housing subsidies form part of the city's export base—as much as, for example, the U.S. Navy base does in Norfolk, Va.

Crime and drugs, the fourth growth market, are part of a vast enterprise of worldwide dimensions. In the illicit drug trade— the import, processing, and distribution of mind-altering substances—New York claims its "unrightful" share. The diseconomies of this polluting industry threaten the city's public order and impose on it heavy expenditures for law enforcement and rehabilitation.

Against those costs, double-entry accounting compels us to recognize, as partial offset, substantial unrecorded employment and income. Official statistics on poverty and joblessness are manifestly overstated, as the officials who collect them concede. Economists and social scientists consistently and understandably limit their research to a data base of official and documentable data—a practice recalling the tired saw about the man who searched for his wallet a block from where he lost it because only that street had a light. Descriptions of reality, however, must account for the observable, nor merely the measurable. What drops out of the universe of statistics need not drop out of the universe of thought. Without analysis of error factors, research findings are dubious guides to public policy. Omissions and understatements are germane to conclusions. The fact is that unrecorded dollars spent for consumer goods, housing, real estate, and bearer bonds have the same power as recorded dollars. The illegally employed are gainfully employed.

THE NEW IMMIGRANTS

Approximately 30 percent of the city's population is now foreign-born, and that proportion is certain to rise steadily. By the turn of the century, as the native-born population thins out and the flow of newcomers maintains its pace or accelerates, the percentage of foreign-born in the city's population may well surpass its historic peak of 40 percent. Everything important to New York's destiny—the quality of its labor force, its neighborhoods, and its schools; the size of its welfare caseloads; the incidence of its crime; its politics—depends on how soon and how well new immigrants and their children climb the social and economic ladder.

Recent waves of immigration are invalidating the city's traditional ethnic classifications. New York's ethnicity can no longer be divided into conventional majority and minority or white, black, and Hispanic compartments. The white population, on top of its base of native and old immigrants, has gained substantial numbers of Soviet, Israeli, and Hasidic Jews, Poles, Greeks, Italians, and Middle Easterners. The minority base has been augmented by broad streams from the English-speaking, French-speaking, and Hispanic Caribbean. Blacks have been drawn from the West Indies, Trinidad and Tobago, the Bahamas, Haiti, and elsewhere; a thin but continuing stream arrives from several West African nations. Large numbers of Hispanics flow in from the Dominican Republic and Central America, and in smaller but substantial numbers from several South American countries, especially Colombia. Among the fastest-rising groups are the Asians, once confined in racial tabulations to the catchall category "other." They too are ethnically diverse, divided into Chinese, Koreans, Filipinos, Indians, and Indo-Chinese and further subdivided by language and religion.

Traditional classifications no longer have much consequential significance. The reality is that New York is becoming a city without a genuine majority—an assembly of minorities that can be combined or regrouped in different ways for different purposes and by criteria other than race or ancestry. The latter attributes are coming to matter less than class, an elusive characterization defined by measurable traits such as income, education, and family structure;

11

and by other traits such as values and behavior, words that contain a large residue of the unknown and perhaps unknowable. The value affinities of New York's multiminorities, rather than their ethnicity per se, are likely to be the major shaping force in New York's future.

There is little evidence of significant interethnic political solidarity among the new minorities. Hispanic–black alliances periodically form, but they rarely penetrate below the leadership level to the mass of people. The new West Indian and Haitian immigrants regard themselves as wholly separate groups, and both take pains to distinguish themselves from indigenous blacks. Except for illegals attempting to "pass," Dominicans do not relish being taken for Puerto Ricans, and Cubans and South Americans hold themselves aloof from other Hispanics. Mayor Koch scores impressively across the entire ethnic spectrum, other white candidates do equally well in neighborhoods dominated by blacks and Hispanics, and the City Council remains heavily white-dominated as ethnic competitors split the vote.

But ethnic politics is a marvelous thing that defies the demographer's counts. The Jewish ascendancy in New York's electoral system arrived long after their numbers significantly dwindled; there has been a Jewish mayor in City Hall for nearly 15 years, and five of the eight members of the Board of Estimate are Jewish. And based on numbers alone, one would not have predicted so utter a fadeout of Irish Catholics, for so many generations New York's political overlords. Now, it has been said, it is easier for an Irish-American to achieve sainthood than a seat on the Board of Estimate.

Though they may not have achieved much in the political arena, the new immigrants have entered the city's economy in full force and with every manner of positive result. Two patterns are dominant. One is entrepreneurship—a strong proclivity for small businesses and self-employment that has led the new immigrants to replace older Jewish and Italian storekeepers whose children have spurned the parental enterprises. The second is occupational specialization, under which various ethnic groups have gravitated toward particular types of employment.

Asians have a conspicuously high rate of self-employment, many times higher than that of the base population. According to a Confucian saying, it is better to be the head of chicken than the tail of an ox. The epitome of the immigrant as entrepreneur is the Korean greengrocer. Korean-owned stores are spreading as fast as sites and purchase opportunities permit, and they are being upgraded in size and products diversity. There is also evidence that the Koreans are mounting the hierarchy of food distribution to wholesaling and processing. Korean business is highly co-ethnic, each store serving as an employer of other Koreans and as a training ground for the next cohort of owners. In Los Angeles, it was found that 80 percent of employed Koreans worked in Korean-owned establishments. The bulk of investment capital of Korean businessmen comes from individual savings; many Koreans arrive with substantial capital, supplemented by co-ethnic mutual pools known as *ryes*. The pathway from Seoul to business ownership in the receiving country is so well-trod, involving one-fifth of all Korean immigrants, that the South Korean Overseas Development Corporation deems it productive to provide orientation and additional start-up capital collateralized by assets left behind. The backflow of remittances to South Korea is estimated at $1 billion per year.

The Chinese have shown an equally extraordinary rate of entrepreneurship in the restaurant and retail sectors, as well as, increasingly, in manufacturing. They are a notable force in the garment industry, wholesaling, banking, and real estate, many by now having graduated from the speculator's and rentier's role to that of developer and builder. East Asians dominate the city's newsstand business as the major concessionaires of the Metropolitan Transit Authority, the Long Island Rail Road, and city-owned sidewalk kiosks, and they seem to be expanding into greeting card and stationery shops.

Many non-Asians are also instinctive microcapitalists. Three-quarters of the 30,000 self-employed drivers of New York's 11,700 medallion taxis are foreign-born, with Soviet Jews, Israelis, and other Europeans being increasingly replaced by Caribbeans and Africans. The immigrant proportion is reportedly even higher for the estimated 35,000 nonmedallion taxis, with West Indians predominant in that work pool.

The new ethnics have turned the city streets into a Third World bazaar, hawking everything from trinkets and toys to incense and brand-name watches, electronics, and clothing; by some magic a legion of umbrella vendors appears at the first drop of rain. Greeks and Italians are prominent in sidewalk food vending, pizza stands, and small restaurants. Dominicans are rapidly acquiring the bodegas and houseware shops of Hispanic neighborhoods. To stroll on a summer Saturday along Fifth Avenue in Brooklyn's Sunset Park is to be a tourist in a semitropical marketplace.

Candor forces even the warmest celebrants of immigrant achievements to concede, however, that the newcomers do not altogether spurn illicit activities. Chinese extortion rings, the "Odessa Mafia" of Brighton Beach, the Jamaican "Posses," and the Latin American *hidalgos* of cocaine all testify to the historic role of immigrants in the underworld economy.

The new entrepreneurs work exceedingly long days and weeks—a reincarnation of prior generations of immigrant small businessmen. A survey of retail stores in Jackson Heights found that 54.8 percent of the Korean establishments were open on Sunday, compared with 47.6 percent of the Hispanic stores and 35.4 percent of white-owned stores. The total number of hours open per week was 76.6 for Koreans, 63.8 for Hispanics, and 68.7 for whites. The longer work week is reflected in weekly sales: $2,543 for Koreans, compared with $1,165 for Hispanics and $1,656 for whites. One hundred percent of the Koreans reported a profitable year, compared with 50 per cent of the Hispanics and 66 percent of the whites.

Wage and salary employment of new immigrants is as ethnically differentiated as entrepreneurship. Among the more conspicuous specializations are Chinese and Dominican women in the garment industry, West Indian and Philippine women in health care and nursing, Greeks in fur manufacturing, and East Asian doctors in the city's hospitals, mental wards, and nursing homes. Chinese and other Asian professionals are prominent in architecture, in engineering, and in high-tech occupations. The lower end of the service sector, home care and household domestics, depends heavily on Caribbean and Central American female immigrants, many of them doubtless undocumented.

As with prior waves of migration, there is ethnic differentiation by neighborhood, though with two distinctions. First, an abatement in racial prejudice has given Asians access to virtually any neighborhood they choose and can afford. Second, most of the new immigrants have bypassed Manhattan, settling directly in Brooklyn or Queens, often in middle-class neighborhoods; for older generations of immigrants, such a move usually required a second or third progression.

On New York's ethnic landscape, one now finds concentrations of Koreans in Flushing and several adjacent areas. The Chinese concentration in Flushing is second only to Chinatown's; the latter has exploded from a tight enclave of 25,000 people in 35 small blocks to over 100,000, preempting much of the Italian and Jewish Lower East Side. It has been said that if Flushing and Chinatown were independent cities, they would be among the fastest-growing urban areas in the United States. East Asians are also in Flushing but are more widely dispersed than Koreans and Chinese, many of them having settled in the suburbs. West Indians can be found in Brooklyn's East Flatbush and southeast Queens, especially in Laurelton, Springfield Gardens, and parts of Jamaica; Haitians in Brooklyn's Crown Heights and East Flatbush, and parts of Manhattan's upper West Side; Dominicans in parts of Manhattan, Queens and Brooklyn; Greeks in Astoria, Queens and Bay Ridge, Brooklyn; South and Central Americans in Queens' Jackson Heights and East Elmhurst; Soviet Jews in Brighton Beach, Brooklyn, Washington Heights, Manhattan, Rego Park and Kew Gardens in Queens; Poles in Brooklyn's Greenpoint and Bushwick; and Irish in northern Manhattan's Inwood.

A skein of many colors has been woven into a remarkable polyethnic configuration that flanks the route of the Number 7 subway line in Queens. It has no parallel in previous waves of migration. Even the much-venerated Lower East Side, the historian's exemplar of polyglot New York, was a microcosm only of Europe, plus a sliver of China. The Flushing-Elmhurst-Corona-Jackson-Heights corridor is a microcosm of the world.

THE CITY RENEWED

The settlement patterns of new immigrants and the pushout of younger professionals from Manhattan are jointly responsible for the astounding diffusion of neighborhood revival throughout the city. Virtually every area now contains at least some, if not many, foreigners. What once was true only of a few places, like the Upper West Side, can now be seen in dozens of neighborhoods: side-by-side coexistence of yuppies, Asians, blacks, and Hispanics.

Few neighborhoods in New York are not now undergoing some degree of rejuvenation, and many are bursting at the seams. Even the least promising areas are currently exhibiting spotty signs of new life, and the spots are proliferating. To the extent that land prices and retail vacancies are sensitive indicators of market expectations, even much of the Bronx is now undergoing a significant, and unexpected, investment recalculation.

Among the marks of neighborhood rejuvenation have been the sharply rising prices for homes and cooperatives, even more sharply rising retail rents, the unboarding of vacant stores and buildings, a faster redemption of *in rem* buildings, livelier bidding at real estate auctions, and increasingly competitive claims to the city's residual inventory. New construction has been far less evident than rehabilitation, largely because of high development costs but also because of the scarcity of sites and the impediments to construction approvals. There is no doubt that in hot spots such as Flushing and Chinatown many more high-rises would be built were permit authorizations to match market demand.

New York's attenuated construction rate has contributed to a steep repricing of the capital values of existing housing and derelict structures, accompanied by heightened appreciation for older neighborhoods. It is doubtful that neighborhood rejuvenation would have attained its current force had there been massive production on vacant land—historically, a sine qua non for high-volume building rates. The gigantic Co-op City project accelerated rather than retarded the decline of the Bronx's mature neighborhoods, and in Brooklyn, Starrett City had a comparable effect on Brownsville and East New York. Since it is unlikely that there will be a mass building boom in the foreseeable future, one may confidently predict continued intense exploitation of existing structures: the reclamation of abandoned buildings, the split-up of existing one- or two-family houses, and the recapture of obsolescent nonresidential structures. This so-called SoHo phenomenon will continue to spread to the outer boroughs, to New Jersey, and into neighborhoods formerly bypassed.

The pressure on existing neighborhoods is intensified by rent regulation, which continues without significant modification as interest groups seeking relief from controls and those seeking to widen and deepen them remain at a standoff. Tenant lobbies press for a "means test" to be applied to landlords as predicate to rent increases but vehemently refuse to be means-tested themselves. No common tenant–landlord language exists. What is rational investment strategy to landlords—a time schedule for the marketing of their product—is labeled "warehousing" by tenant spokesmen, who would make it illegal and a punishable offence. The term is not applied, however, to the much larger quantities of preempted shelter space—more than all the subsidized housing the city proposes to build in the next ten years—found in large numbers of grossly underoccupied regulated apartments. In a real sense, the shortage of rational occupancy policies is as serious as the shortage of shelter space itself. Barring some radical and unlikely action by the courts, the impasse is likely to be resolved only by the slow passage of time, as regulated units are gradually lost through casualty or conversion.

At some undated time in the very far-off future, there will be so little inventory left to regulate and the political protectorate of tenants will have so diminished that regulation will expire of natural causes.

Absent substantial relief from rent restraints, building rates will be insufficient to accommodate new households and replace losses. The gulf between average regulated rents for existing housing and the minimal level of rents for unsubsidized new housing is simply too wide to provide the private builder with a mass market. Unsubsidized apartment builders have reconciled themselves to a small volume of high-priced units, mostly condos and co-ops. Were rates of absorption to increase, builders would be happy to accommodate them, as they stand ready to do in hot spots such as Chinatown and Flushing. But a saturation of full-page newspaper ads and expensive marketing campaigns suggests that unsubsidized producers are now approaching the limits of effective demand. Their main competitors are not each other or the builders in the suburbs, but the extremely low-priced units in which so many of their potential customers are comfortably housed. Were rent levels of older regulated housing allowed to drift upward at a more rapid rate, more-affluent tenants would be stimulated to reassess the merits of their old regulated units versus new housing. The calculus of choice between the old and the new is fundamental in every market for durable goods.

Under the circumstances, public subsidy constitutes virtually the only device for increasing the building rate. But this is an insufficient and undependable tool. In the first place, the grant of a housing subsidy to a private builder is necessarily accompanied by a lengthy chain of slow administrative procedures whose outcome is not always predictable. Moreover, the availability of a subsidy immediately ignites fiery policy debates over priorities: What share of the resources should go to the middle class through shallow subsidies and what part to low-income families who require deep subsidies? Given the present cost of new housing, even shallow subsidies are anything but trifling and deep ones are genuinely staggering. Though New York is far more prone to redistributive housing programs than any other municipality in the nation, that generosity has yet to yield an impressive rate of housing construction. A subsidy of $1 billion will not produce a lot of new housing when development costs of more than $100,000 per apartment require capital write-downs, gifts of land, and tax abatements equal to half or more of that amount.

17

Unfortunately, the political rhetoric of the housing crisis is not matched by the political will to escape the dead hand of business-as-usual, the embellishments of zoning, the broad and sometimes capricious outreach of preservation, the tripwires of environmental impact statements, and the community land-use review process known as ULURP. Each of these regulations has a purpose and a constituency, and no doubt all have merit. But the test of a genuine crisis, personal or societal, is a broad political consensus to subordinate customary habits to its resolution. Except for larger budget allocations from fiscal windfalls, thus far sluggishly spent, there is no real evidence that housing has any standing ahead of a hundred other priorities for city government. Continuing housing stress, an actual crisis only for the homeless, appears inevitable.

The extent to which housing-market stress will affect the city's economic growth is a question, however. The move-out of corporate business is often ascribed to the housing difficulties of employees, but that complaint is surely only one item in a long array of other "pushes" such as taxes, rents, utility costs, corporate restructuring, and market shifts. New York's startling economic expansion between 1976 and 1987 occurred in the teeth of plummeting construction rates and gargantuan housing losses. The fact is that New York's new professional and management cadres have found accommodation by extending the "status threshold" in the outer boroughs and by reclaiming erstwhile nonstatus neighborhoods. Others settle in the outer metropolitan areas, a decision alleged to be injurious to New York. But save for transportation congestion, that injury has never been satisfactorily documented, whereas compensatory offsets can be readily identified. Were the quality of transportation to be improved, much more incremental housing demand could be satisfied by exploiting underdeveloped sections in outlying areas, both within and outside the city. To an unappreciated degree, transportation policy is housing policy.

THE DYNAMIC ECONOMY

New York was hoisted from the pits of the 1970s by the astonishing growth of its financial and business service sectors. World trade and capital transfers exploded and the financial, legal, and other business services generated by the explosion funneled massively into the New York economy. New York's resurgence depended as much on the expansion of the international economy as on that of the national economy, possibly more so. The city fared much better than did the nation during the recession of the early 1980s, a fluctuation scarcely noticed here. And the city has prospered despite a continuous exodus of national corporate headquarters. New York now has many fewer *Fortune* 500 corporate headquarters than it did in the 1960s, and still fewer than in the 1950s. It is important to emphasize this because of the media's propensity to adopt a "grass will grow in the streets" attitude every time a large corporation such as Mobil or J. C. Penney bids farewell to Manhattan.

The economics of location are in endless flux, constantly adjusting to new markets and costs, new technologies and structural shifts. With the ascendancy of national government, Washington, D.C. has attracted a multitude of national trade associations, many of them from New York, as well as law offices and public-relations activities whose primary market is the federal establishment. On the other hand, every major international bank has opened one or more offices in New York and so has virtually every law firm with a financial clientele. New York's financial houses, in turn, have branched out extensively to London and Tokyo and are hiving off back-room operations to other rings in the metropolitan area, including Brooklyn and Queens. New York, in large degree, has displaced Paris and London as the world's art and fashion center; and for world-famous retailers New York is a peerless showcase. In this locational sorting-out process, New York has fared quite handsomely.

A sacred tradition assigns manufacturing a higher status than the services partly because the former is an "export" or "base" industry, but mainly because it is presumed to provide employment opportunities singularly suited to new entrants in the job market, with few skills or little education. But economic history has its phases. There is no more reason to canonize manufacturing than there was for the Physiocrats to bestow transcendental status on agriculture. Financial, business, tourist, and health care services are now not only major "export" industries, they are also relatively more productive and rewarding per employee.

Nor is it true that the service sector provides high-level jobs only for the talented and educated. The service industry employs a good deal more than MBAs at Merrill Lynch or copywriters at McCann-Erickson. It includes the porters, chambermaids, and handymen at the big hotels and hospitals, those who clean the office buildings at night, the messengers in the mail rooms and on bicycles, the keypunch operators in the computer rooms, and myriad other low-skill positions. Many of these jobs pay as well as or better than manufacturing, which except for printing and publishing and a few other specialties, has been a notoriously low-wage sector in New York. The West Indian nurse's aide at Sloan-Kettering is as attached to the export base as she would be in manufacturing, earns at least as much in wages and fringe benefits, and has at least as much chance to determine whether the job is dead-ended or the first rung on a ladder. Domestic service, as every career mother ruefully concedes, pays as much to immigrant women as a seat at the sewing machine. And recent "workfare" demonstrations by women transferring from dependency to the job market indicate that not only the opportunities but the preferences favor office and service jobs.

As Thomas Bailey and Roger Waldinger, specialists on New York's low-skill labor markets, wrote in a recent article,

> The weaknesses of the mismatch hypothesis are two-fold. First, its guide to the shifting job requirements of urban employers exaggerates the extent and nature of skill changes. . . .[T]he transition from manufacturing to services tends to alter, not eradicate, low-level skill requirements. The new growth sectors contain both higher and lower-level jobs; and the diffusion of new technology into white-collar fields seems to upgrade some activities and reduce the requisite skill level of others simultaneously.
>
> Secondly, historical dependence on manufacturing is not directly related to current labor market distress; the various groups that compose New York's low-level labor force have differed greatly in their adjustment to the economy's transition. Neither youth nor blacks were overdependent on manufacturing in 1970, and the sector's decline of the 1970s produced small job losses for both groups. Immigrants were overdependent on manufacturing in 1970, and equally so a decade later. Yet they emerged from the 1970s with labor market indicators that were no worse, and in some cases significantly better, than those of the average New Yorker.

It would be going too far to assert that the massive decline in manufacturing jobs—down by two-thirds since the postwar peak—has been good for the city. It is regrettable that many more manufacturing establishments could not be induced to relocate to the outer boroughs. However, a case can be made for the proposition that manufacturing's displacement from Manhattan has made room for more-productive activities. It is unimaginable that Manhattan's growth in the finance, business, restaurant, and tourist industries would have occurred had manufacturing employment remained at its postwar peak. Consider the SoHo experience. The land uses that replaced the factories—artists' studios, boutiques, restaurants, and, increasingly, commercial offices—add to New York's unique elan in ways that the fabrication of plastic handbags would not. As a tourist attraction and the locus of the art industry, SoHo has not only enhanced the city's urban texture, but has probably contributed as much in income as the manufacturing that was lost.

THE UNDERGROUND ECONOMY

There can be no genuine understanding of New York's economy without assigning analytic weight to the underground economy, even if only notionally, as a reflective addendum in published studies. Analytically and empirically, the criminal industry is the keystone of a large illicit economy. Only those confined to an isolation ward can fail to note that it is getting bigger all the time.

Writers traditionally divide the underground economy into two sectors, licit and illicit. The licit sector comprises transactions whose primary motive is to keep transactions and income off the books, mainly to evade taxes, often to hide from immigration authorities, and sometimes to avert a reduction in welfare benefits or surcharges on subsidized housing. That sector is well populated by those who deal in cash, such as taxi drivers, waiters, domestics, and street peddlers, and those who deal in high-value transportable luxuries, principally gold, diamonds, and other precious gems and jewelry.

The illicit sector ranges from chain and pocketbook snatchers, auto radio thieves, prostitutes, pimps, numbers runners, and drug peddlers at the low end, to organized crime, the aging Mafia, and new phalanxes of mostly younger Hispanic and Chinese syndicates engaged in importing, processing, and wholesaling drugs at the high end. The licit and illicit sectors together generate huge if incalculable amounts of income, doubtless running into the billions. According to one estimate, reported property theft alone amounted in 1982 to nearly $1 billion. New York surely accounts for more than a proportionate share of the $100 billion the Internal Revenue Service reports to be missing.

Underground income—that not reported to census enumerators

21

—accounts in large measure for the substantial shortfalls in census income totals compared with those compiled by the Internal Revenue Service, itself a victim of very large shortfalls, or to an even greater extent, with other economic indicators. The shortfalls tend to be most evident at the lowest and highest ends of the income distribution scale and are quite pronounced in poverty areas and among the self-employed. For example, income from Social Security as reported by census respondents is substantially below what the Social Security Administration pays out, and according to a Rand Corporation study in the early 1970s, payments by New York's Welfare Department substantially exceeded those reported in census tabulations of poor neighborhoods.

The illegal sector of the underground economy generates employment as well as income. A drug or numbers runner has a job. So do those who process drugs and carry suitcases with cash on the long trade routes between Jackson Heights and South America. Because few of the illicit jobs are likely to be captured by Bureau of Labor Statistics collection techniques, it is impossible to measure accurately the employment effects of crime.

According to some academic authorities, 100,000 persons in New York were employed in the 1970s either full or part time in the numbers and gambling industry. The crucial role of gambling in the Harlem economy was brought to light when protests by community groups sought to close down newly legalized municipal Off-Track Betting offices that would have placed control of gambling operations in the hands of indigenous groups who, presumably, would have retained the jobs for local residents. When the employment generated by drug traffic and gambling is added to that provided by prostitution, burglary, shoplifting, and hijacking, the same authorities say, it is possible that over 250,000 people are regularly deriving income from underground sources in New York City.

Unreported income may also account for the fact that in spite of frequent and public reports of an increasing incidence of poverty, the number of welfare-dependent people seems to have stabilized during the past decade. There has been a net *decrease* of 114,000 in the Aid to Families with Dependent Children (AFDC) welfare caseload; and in spite of an offsetting increase in the number of people on General Assistance, some of whom were transferred from AFDC, there has been no upward momentum in the size of the overall welfare caseload.

It may be true that very large numbers of the unenrolled are too proud to apply or suffer from some special disbarment. It is also true that the official poverty standard is higher than the standard for admission to welfare. But judging from the Rand study, many of the census-counted poor actually have resources exceeding eligibility standards, a hypothesis consistent with the fact that the error rate in New York's welfare rolls, extraordinarily high in the past, steadily declined as verification procedures tightened, partly in response to federal insistence.

THE UNDERGROUND ECONOMY AND CRIME

The illegally employed are not simply chiselers and cheats who slip through statistical nets and elude revenue collectors, or the street dwellers whose behavior, however bizarre, is not directly threatening. Members of the underground economy are all-too-frequently predatory and almost always addicted, habitual criminals. The most menacing element of this group, the young male predators once labeled "feral animals" by a renowned police official, are social deviants, prone to capricious vandalism and violent crime. They constitute a real and serious threat to New York's future.

The criminals of today seem to be habituated to the calamitous nature, the "banality" of violence. In the inner city, weaponry has escalated. In the early years of the juvenile delinquency plague, the switchblade knife replaced the club and fist. Now the handgun has displaced the knife, and that handgun is increasingly often an automatic. In the killing fields of the ghetto, death comes early. One funeral director reported that he rarely buried anyone over 40.

Claude Brown, 20 years after *Manchild in the Promised Land*, found Harlem's streets frighteningly meaner. "Manchild 1984," said Brown, "is the product of a society so rife with violence that killing a mugging or robbery victim is now fashionable." Brown then recounted a conversation he had had:

> "That's what they do now," the 16-year-old Harlemite said.
> "That's what who does now?" I asked, not understanding.
> "You know, you take their stuff and you pop [shoot] 'em."
> "You mean shooting the victim is in style now like wearing a pair of Pony jogging shoes or a Pierre Cardin suit?"
> "Yeah, it's wrong to kill somebody. But you gotta have dollars, right?"

For more than a year, Brown said, he was thoroughly baffled by the apparent senseless, and often maniacal, rampant killings of

23

mugging and robbery victims. According to news reports and victims who had survived, it was as though shooting the victim had become an integral part of the crime. Sometimes, it seemed to occur with the incredible casualness of an insignificant afterthought, an "Oh, I forgot to shoot him" bang. Talking to young men in the prisons and on the ghetto streets, Brown wasn't comprehending what he was hearing. "Perhaps what I was hearing was too mind-boggling, too ghastly to understand," he wrote. "Murder is in style now."

New York is actually far from the most crime-prone urban area in the United States. In per capita ranking, it generally falls in the middle of the nation's largest cities, consistently outranked by Detroit, Boston, Washington, Los Angeles, Houston, and in most years, even Seattle. That statistic, however, conveys little to ordinary old-time New Yorkers who remember the way things were, and even less to non-New Yorkers who judge the city through the eyes of sensationalizing media. To ordinary mortals, New York is an atrociously crime-ridden city that seems to be getting worse all the time. The number of criminal incidents, save for a recent and apparently transitory decline, has been on a steady rise since 1960 and has spread remorselessly throughout the five boroughs.

Adaptations to crime, actual or perceived, are deeply embedded in New York City's culture and have a severe impact on both the public and the private sectors. Never before has the criminal justice system been so overwhelmed, notwithstanding continual and costly expansions, by the offensive and defensive engagements with crime; there are unmanageable burdens at each step in the law-enforcement cycle, from arraignment through trial, imprisonment, and probation. Moreover, the defense against crime has become a heavy charge on the private sector, as much of the cost of crime prevention has been internalized. Few households and business firms do not take special precautions against the omnipresent threat of predation against person or property. The full economic costs of security, including surging budgets for police, courts, prosecuting and defense lawyers, prisons, and probation as well as the costs of locks and gates, guard dogs, electronic surveillance, private security police, antishoplifting devices, and insurance, form a significant and rising fraction of the city's gross domestic product.

In addition to the economic burden, heavy noneconomic costs are manifested by adjustments in the average citizen's lifestyle: the amount of cash carried; the early closing hours of shops, some opened only by buzzer by day and most steel-shuttered at night; the routes taken at night between subway and home, which often differ from those taken in the morning; cautious positioning on subway platforms; the extra glance at an approaching disreputable-looking stranger or any band of lurking youths. Defensive measures against crime are an equal-opportunity activity, practiced ever more strenuously by minorities who are, by a wide margin, the likeliest victims.

Between 1975 and 1984 the incidence of crime in almost all categories leveled off, and actually decreased in several of the worst categories. Murder and manslaughter declined from 1,690 cases to 1,450, and even more sharply from the 1980 peak of 1,821 cases. Though reported rape cases remained quite stable, it is generally acknowledged that rape is more frequently reported than in the past and that its incidence was actually on a downward trend. Robbery and burglary decreased significantly, as did motor vehicle theft. Between 1979 and 1984, all FBI Index crimes taken together, including all of the above categories plus larceny and assault, went down nearly 6 percent.

Those gains were a brief interlude in a long-term trend. Since 1984, crime rates have resumed their historic rise. The crime category with the steepest increase is sale and possession of controlled substances, principally a wide variety of abusive drugs, including cocaine and its deadly derivative, crack. The director of the National Institute of Justice reported that between 1984 and 1987 the proportion of arrestees who tested positively for drugs substantially increased; in New York, rising cocaine use pushed the drug-positive rate to 80 percent for people arrested in April 1987. Crack is a relatively new substance; we are only now beginning to discover its pharmacology and its terrifying potential for destructive behavior. No drug that is so cheap and easy to buy brings on so quick a high. No other drug leads to such rapid addiction and to such unpredictably violent paranoid reactions. Nothing in the hundred-year history of the use of cocaine, the drug of the middle and upper classes, had given any indication of the chemical properties manifest in crack. It is a species of social dynamite.

Increased crack use probably accounts for the recent upswing in the crime rate. The figures since 1985 indicate not only sharply rising arrests for possession and sale, but also an increase in assault, a common sequel to crack addiction. Moreover, the attraction of crack will probably increase as the attractions of marijuana and heroin dwindle. Marijuana cannot produce the same kind of high and is now regarded as a sissy drug. Heroin is not only more expensive, but unlike crack is most effective when taken intravenously.

The AIDS epidemic, in which shared intravenous needles are deeply implicated, may be producing some substitution of crack for heroin—though not much, judging from the extraordinary increase in needle-inflicted AIDS.

The problem of underclass pathology and crime has no answer or visible end. Its perpetrators may be excluded from public housing or displaced from this neighborhood or that. But like a squeezed balloon, the problem will show up somewhere else. Whether it has the potential, as pessimists believe, to obliterate the sunshine—to topple New York by discouraging business entry and tourists, accelerating the outflow of existing households and firms, imposing a kind of curfew on nightlife—is conceivable but not probable. A growing underclass did not thwart New York's post-1975 renascence any more than did a falling residential building rate. Vital cities have amazing coping powers and manage to survive despite every manner of "hopeless" problem; witness Mexico City's suffocating smog or Tokyo's awful twice-daily commute. Between the impossibility of solution and the unlikelihood of disaster lies the *tertium quid* of coexistence, just plain muddling through. Proposed remedies such as workfare would at best take a thin slice off the problem and there are ironclad legal and moral constraints on draconian remedies.

GOVERNMENT'S ROLE

For the city's policymakers, there is a continuous tug of priorities between those that nourish economic growth and those that advance uncompromising claims for social services, the redress of poverty, and the compensation demands of the civil service. A commanding question in New York's future is whether the city encourages, through its regulatory and tax policies, the entrepreneurial energy that has reinforced the current upswing, or whether it crumbles under the pressure of powerful redistributive lobbies and reverts to the taxing/spending, disguised deficit practices that contributed so calamitously to its downfall in the 1970s.

No municipality, even one as large and rich as New York, has the fiscal capacity to serve as a principal engine for redistributing income and wealth. The city must leave much of that to the state, which has a greater capacity, and the state must leave most of the burden to Washington, which has the greatest capacity of all. It would be folly for New York to consider redressing the national government's incapacities, particularly when mounting national and international deficits indicate that Washington will continue to offload rather more than less.

A hopeful sign is the unusual political consensus that seems to have emerged in recent years in favor of private investment. After an era of unbroken tax increases, an unprecedented reduction in state and local income and business taxes (albeit one that still leaves New York more heavily taxed than all of its neighboring states) has demonstrated a striking reversal of tradition. The program to reduce electricity costs for major business users, by relieving the extent to which Con Edison serves as a tax farmer for the city, has been another step in the right direction. The critical question is whether this new and positive disposition to champion business investment, this present appreciation that New York's private sector is its lifeblood, will last, and how far it will go.

The badly-skewed real property tax, for example, still imposes an extraordinarily heavy burden on office buildings to offset the peppercorn taxes paid by home owners and owners of co-ops and condos, who include some of the city's most affluent people. The effective property tax on a typical home in Brooklyn or Queens is typically 0.5%, and in many cases less than that. The result is that office buildings subsidize a large share of New York's housing—and not necessarily its poorest share. The magnitude of this cross-subsidy dwarfs anything proposed by even the most zealous proponents of housing trust funds and inclusionary zoning. The exaction is not based on ability to pay or on any known standard of fairness or effectiveness. It helps keep rents in newer office buildings, already the highest in the nation, at a level that not only cannot be indefinitely increased but, as is rediscovered in every recession, cannot be sustained. A restructuring of the property tax burden, including the commercial occupancy tax, is necessary to keep the city competitive.

Record tax receipts have permitted New York recently to improve services. An expanded capital budget is compensating for decades of brutal undermaintenance of the infrastructure. Enlarged budgets are now also paying for a wide and increasing array of social costs, for strengthened law enforcement, for low- and middle-income housing, for the homeless, for foster homes, for AIDS treatment, and for a sufficient complement of teachers and schools to assure proper development of the next generation of young people. All that is to the good. One cannot overemphasize the degree to which a New York redux depends on the progress of its new immigrant children and how much better the city would function with a high-performance mass-transit system.

But these recently-assumed budget obligations will not long survive a significant slackening of economic growth and tax receipts. A bitter clash of priorities would ensue, and programs that nourish economic progress, lightened taxes, capital improvements, improved law enforcement, and quality education might give way to programs for redistribution. There would be heavy pressures to return to the credo of the 1960s and 1970s, when the city, so counterproductively, tried to mimic a national welfare state.

To a considerable extent, the city's future will depend on its internal policies—the degree to which it creates the City Unbound or the City Bound, whether it slouches, so to speak, toward Singapore or toward Sweden. Given New York's history and ethical values, it will always be a compassionate city that does more for its disadvantaged than any other city in the nation. But the city has paid a heavy price for the lesson that public revenues must be earned before they can be redistributed.

THE RISKS OF FORECASTING

The city's policy choices will only partly determine its future. As a world city, whose central business district is the core of the economic planet, New York's economy will to a large extent be conditioned by national and international events, by policies enacted in Washington, Tokyo, Bonn, and the Common Market. The size and composition of its population and labor force will largely depend on what the People's Republic of China does about Hong Kong and Taiwan, on whether the Soviet government unlocks its gates to the emigration-prone, and on whether there is violence and terror in Central America, South Korea, India, the Philippines, or the Middle East.

The gods of uncertainty mock the long-term forecaster. Over the last 40 years, economic prognosticators have buried New England at least twice; but booming Boston and Portland now look back in wonder at the funereal soothsayers. The St. Lawrence Seaway failed to transform Duluth into a world port, as had confidently been expected. The Cassandras of the Club of Rome are yet to witness our free fall to perdition in a nature exhausted and barren.

It is quite possible that everyone—Moody's, Standard & Poor, the bond-insurance companies, foreign investors and all other full-throated optimists—will prove wrong about New York. It is no great imaginative feat to sketch out a variety of bleak scenarios featuring defaulted foreign debt, collapsed banks, shrinking world trade, or a devastating and uncontrollable AIDS epidemic. Such scenarios surface regularly; any one of them may eventuate, exposing today's writers to the scorn of tomorrow's readers.

The likeliest scenario, however, is that New York will muddle through; it will be neither the City on the Hill nor the doomed San Francisco of *On the Beach*. It may be marginally more populous and well-to-do, its services better-functioning, its subways perhaps graffiti-free and on time. But it will still be extensively pockmarked by flaws and failures. It is a good bet that its streets will remain strewn with potholes, that more prison cells will still be needed, and that linen and rug merchants will still be trumpeting going-out-of-business sales. The city may be incrementally poorer and more rancorous, with more locks on its doors, and with certain neighborhoods that are now on the brink of recovery falling back to dereliction. But though muddling through is neither a dazzlingly successful outcome nor a hopelessly failed one, New York is still likely to remain the nation's primary business and cultural center, a proving ground for the creative, and magnetic north on the compass of the world's emigrants.

Chapter 2

NEW YORK'S ECONOMIC RENAISSANCE

Mark A. Willis

New York is energy. Cities are often spoken of as great machines, engines of business and commerce. But the metaphor of the city as machine is outmoded, a conception of the nineteenth century and the Industrial Revolution. A machine wears out and its product may become obsolete. But envisioning the city as energy—indestructible but constantly being transformed—provides an appropriate model for a twenty-first-century New York. This energy translates daily into new ideas and enterprises that fuel the City's economy.

New York's energy is not simply a function of its size, although the numbers are large indeed: 3.6 million jobs, an over $200 billion economy, over $1 trillion in dollar payments electronically transferred on an average day. Nor does it stem solely from the diversity and drive of its population, over 25 percent of whom were immigrants according to the 1980 census. Rather, it is New York's compactness, its physical density that concentrates the forces, that gives the city its competitive edge in an increasingly global and information-based economy. At the intersection of 47th Street and Fifth Avenue, as many as 12,000 people may pass by in an hour. Among them will be advertising executives refining new marketing concepts, investment bankers and lawyers closing on new stock offerings, financial printers delivering offering statements, researchers nailing down details at the Public Library, and many others producing and plugging into that energy for which the city is celebrated. This productive density exists throughout the city—at Wall Street, the Garmont Center, Madison Avenue and elsewhere. This opportunity for face-to-face contact is New York's key advantage in a world where so much of our information is perishable, its freshness sometimes lasting only

30

seconds and its transferability often limited to personal contact.

The unique density of New York's business population also allows it to provide an unparalleled set of specialized services and a wide breadth of business activities. As the diffusion of technology and productive capacity and the advances in telecommunications link New York's fate more closely to worldwide competition and the vagaries of world trade, the depth and diversity of the city's economy give it the adaptability and resilience essential for survival. This density helps to ensure New York's long-term survival, and provides a strong competitive advantage, particularly during periods of rapid change, such as those caused by the recent deregulation of financial markets. This ability to prosper and thrive on change, however, appeared to have been lost just a few short years ago.

DECLINE AND TRANSFORMATION: AN OVERVIEW

The turmoil that beset the city's economy in the late 1960s obscures its inherent resilience. Employment declined precipitously and the prognosis seemed poor. Six hundred thousand jobs were lost between 1969 and 1977. Beneath the statistical surface, however, the economy underwent a massive transformation from one based on manufacturing and large corporate headquarters to one based on business and financial services. By 1977, growing sectors of the economy began to outweigh those in decline, and total employment began to rise. By 1982, the explosive growth of domestic and international banking and security trading pushed total employment in the financial industry above that of the manufacturing sector.

Changes in sectoral composition are not new to New York. Throughout its history, even during periods of growth and prosperity, some sectors have stagnated or even withered away while new ones have emerged. New technologies have caused one sector to replace another—such as international airplane service based in Queens replacing transatlantic passenger ship service based on Manhattan's Hudson River waterfront—or have allowed firms in existing sectors to seek greener pastures in the suburbs or more-distant destinations, as when the book and magazine printing industry moved to the Midwest earlier this century. Over time, only firms that successfully developed new markets or new products for old markets have survived; while firms that failed to revamp their product mix fell by the wayside. As long as change was gradual enough to allow new sectors and products to establish a foothold, the economy's

31

overall growth continued unabated. For most of New York's history, save for interruptions caused by national recession, the winning sectors have prevailed.

In the late 1960s and early 1970s though, something seemed to go terribly wrong. The cumulative impact of technological change and shifting national and international trading patterns caught up with the city as a long period of sustained national growth was interrupted by a recession in 1969 and another one in 1975. Many previously strong or relatively stable sectors showed unexpected weakness. Corporate headquarters, which had been viewed as both the backbone of the city's economy and the symbol of its power, started to exit in search of cheaper space and labor. Manufacturing employment, which had been falling slowly since 1949, dropped precipitously. The decline was widespread, encompassing garment, textile, furniture, and other manufacturing activities. The financial sector as a whole also declined, but its smaller losses left it in a more dominant position. No sector showed sufficient strength to counter the employment decline among the losing sectors.

In retrospect, what had gone wrong was a loss in the degree to which the city's competitive advantages could offset the higher costs of doing business. Years of dominance of the national economy had left New York with a cost-and-wage structure significantly higher than that of the rest of the nation. The market reacted in classical fashion, producing a weakened local economy that in turn led to a dramatic drop in the relative cost of doing business in the city. During the 1970s, wages and prices rose less rapidly in New York than elsewhere in the nation, improving the city's relative competitiveness in all sectors. As unemployment soared from 4.8 percent in 1970 to over 11 percent in 1976, wage rates came under increasing pressure. Similarly, the general weakness in the local economy slowed the growth of costs relative to those of the nation as a whole both for housing costs (average housing costs fell after adjustment for inflation) and for personal services. In the early 1970s the huge surplus of vacant office space peaked at over 30 million square feet or enough space to accommodate 120,000 to 150,000 workers. This backlog weakened commercial rents, which declined only slightly in nominal terms, but dramatically in real terms.

As a consequence of these market forces, from 1977 to 1982 the cost of living in New York rose at only four-fifths the national rate, and wages rose less rapidly locally than elsewhere. For example, from 1977 to 1983, wage increases for office clericals and electronic data processors were smaller in New York than in any other of the twelve largest metropolitan areas for which data are available. Increases in the city lagged over seven percentage points behind the U.S. average.

The improvement in relative costs helped the remaining firms survive and prosper as their markets grew nation-wide; yet the savings were not sufficient to lure manufacturing back to the city, since occupancy rates rarely amount to more than 5 percent of a firm's overall production costs. In fact, the recycling of many of the older manufacturing spaces allowed the city to absorb the growth in employment and shift to a service, office-based economy without rents spiralling up before new construction geared up again.

Since 1976, the turnaround in the local economy has been dramatic, as some 400,000 jobs have been regained. Many factors made this recovery possible. In addition to the restructuring of the economy and the relative decrease in costs, public policy changes helped to reduce the government's drain on the economy. Before the changes, a growing tax burden combined with the neglect of city services, particularly the maintenance of the infrastructure, had been signaling a fiscal system out of control. New York first imposed corporate and personal income taxes in 1966 and then proceeded to increase rates, as well as the effective rates of property taxes on business, through the mid-1970s. Per capita state and city revenues grew to well over 50 percent above the national average in the late 1960s. With at least 26 different types of levies, New York's tax burden, unrivaled among cities, even exceeded that of most states. Nevertheless, annual budget deficits soared, exceeding $1 billion by the end of this period. Meanwhile, the deterioration of the city's infrastructure was dramatic, made infamous by the collapse of a portion of the West Side Highway under the weight of a truck. Funds to repair and rebuild the city's roads, bridges, sewers, water, and mass-transit systems were virtually nonexistent.

The specter of fiscal chaos, added to the decline in the quality of public services, made businesses reluctant to expand or even to stay in the city. By inhibiting the birth or growth of firms—new and old alike—this lack of state and local fiscal discipline hindered the ability of the economy to adjust. The emergence of winning sectors was slowed, helping to ensure that the declines in losing sectors would dominate the statistics.

A brush with bankruptcy was necessary to galvanize the city's efforts to restore fiscal order. It achieved this mainly through controlling expenditures. Although tax rates initially shot up as a result of the fiscal crisis in 1975, the city managed to cut its payroll and balance its budget by 1981—one year earlier than expected. By the mid-1980s the city was running surpluses of more than $500 million; at the same time it cut tax rates. By 1988 the corporate income tax rate had fallen from its peak of 10.05 percent to 8.85 percent; the stock transfer tax was effectively repealed; the commercial rent tax was trimmed, with special relief provided outside of Manhattan; and the taxes on energy were substantially reduced. The shift in the property tax burden away from home owners and toward businesses was constrained by the formal establishment in 1981 of four classes of property. The rapid growth of personal income and the less-than-proportionate increase in property taxes has led to a dramatic turnabout in the city's tax burden, measured by revenues as a percent of personal income. From a high of 11.7 percent in 1977, the burden has remained near 10 percent since 1982.

In addition to a balanced budget the city also instituted four-year operating plans, and ten-year capital plans. The days of papering over huge deficits by overestimating revenues and paying operating expenses with capital funds were over. Even in the face of dramatic cutbacks in federal aid in recent years, the city has maintained a balanced budget, while undertaking a massive program to rebuild its infrastructure, currently forecast at nearly $50 billion over the next ten years. The annual debt service of the city has fallen steadily as a percent of expenditures, from a high of almost 19 percent in 1976 to just over 8 percent in 1987.

The return to fiscal sanity by government was insufficient by itself, however, to produce an economic rebound. Self-correcting changes wrought by market forces were essential to the recovery. But New York, like many other governmental entities, was subject to political pressures from those being hurt by the changes, and so in some cases, state and local government tried in vain to defeat these market forces. But while experience has demonstrated that state and local government actions can accelerate or delay change, they cannot altogether overcome the market. Inevitable sectoral declines have to be accepted even when individual businesses are hurt and even when the pressures of the political system to help them become enormous.

The impact of New York's efforts to freeze the status quo was limited, although no precise estimates have been—or for that matter, can be—made. It does not appear that these efforts have reversed any sectoral declines, although they may have slowed the emergence of winners, thus slowing the overall recovery of the economy. An example of such a misguided, though well-intentioned policy to reverse a market trend occurred when the city tried to use its zoning power to preserve manufacturing jobs in the garment and flower districts. Prohibitions against use of land for residential purposes may have moderated the decline of manufacturing, but the proliferation of open-air parking lots in these districts provides ample evidence of misallocation of strategically located land in the central business district.

Fortunately, governmental action designed to counteract market forces has not stopped the shift of the local economy toward sectors in which it has natural strength. In fact, the city has also taken actions that have helped smooth the transformation of the economy, for example, the establishment of a new flower district in Queens. It has begun to rebuild its infrastructure, improve the education of its work force, and disperse economic activity beyond its traditional borders through a combination of incentives, penalties, and improved mass transit.

THE TRANSFORMATION PROCESS AT WORK: A SECTORAL ANALYSIS

To understand how the city's economy works, it is essential to focus on the evolution of winners and losers rather than on swings in overall employment. The decline in employment that took place from 1969 to 1977 was not spread uniformly across all sectors of the economy, but rather was concentrated in certain industries. While some industries remained competitive, the birth of new firms and expansion of existing firms was insufficient to offset declines elsewhere in the economy. Even after recovery began in 1977, some sectors continued to decline. However, the city's growing role as a center for national and international finance and as a provider of specialized business services began to dominate the aggregate statistics. The overall trend turned upwards, further aided by the increasing share of the national economy devoted to services and international trade (imports of goods and services doubled over the last two decades as a percent of the country's gross national product). Old firms expanded and new ones started up. By 1986, New York City had more business starts annually than Houston, Chicago, or Los Angeles.

The city's overall economic performance during these years reflected relative changes in the rate of decline in the manufacturing sector relative to the growth of the service sector. Since 1969, the decrease in manufacturing employment has been almost continuous, falling from 22 percent of total payroll employment to 11 percent in 1987. During the same period, the share held by the service sector, including financial, insurance, and real estate firms, has increased steadily, from 33 percent to over 45 percent. These aggregate numbers tell only a part of the story. Business and legal services have grown faster than either banking or securities firms, and even within each of these sectors the relative fortunes of different activities have varied widely.

The Decline of Manufacturing

Manufacturing, once the bedrock of New York City's economy, peaked in 1949 at over 1 million jobs. Even during its growth years the composition of this sector was never constant. Manufacturing firms began moving out of the city when railroads, then trucks, made it possible to serve both local and distant markets from decentralized locations. Cheaper land, lower wages, and proximity to raw materials, such as iron ore, coal, wood pulp, and foodstuffs, drew many operations to rural areas, as did the advantages of the horizontal rather than vertical movement of goods allowed by sprawling, single-story factories. Factories that remained in the city along with the new ones that started up there, were the ones with the most to gain from the size, diversity, and ready availability of its labor force, the specialization of its suppliers, and direct contact with customers located in the city.

The loss of manufacturing was slowed through the 1960s because strong economic growth allowed local and multilocational firms to remain profitable, even in their older, multistory, and often obsolete city facilities. The onset in 1969 of the first national recession in almost a decade, however, left many firms and industries with excess capacity. Operations least able to compete were the first to go, and New York was particularly hard hit. Good quality space was much more expensive than elsewhere in the metropolitan region or in other areas of the country. As a result of advances in telecommunications, operations that had previously been centralized could be scattered across the region, the nation, and the globe. In some cases, America's loss of international competitiveness particularly hurt New York, as in the case of garment and textile manufacturing, which was concentrated in the city.

Many of the large, mass-production operations still in the city in

1969, such as breweries, furniture makers, and garment manufacturers, left in the following years. Those that did stay faced increased competition that required belt tightening and further shedding of jobs. Only rarely did increased competitiveness from increased productivity produce sufficient sales growth to maintain overall employment. Thus, even among manufacturing firms that remained in the city, employment tended to fall. An exception was the printing industry, which, with strong local demand from advertising and financial firms, nearly held its own. Similarly, the arrival of an energetic labor force from abroad allowed the rapid growth of the garment industry in Chinatown, where employment grew in just a few years from 8,000 in 1969 to some 20,000 in the 1980s even while overall garment employment fell roughly by half.

Although the attrition continues, the future for manufacturing today looks less gloomy, as the firms remaining in the city tend to be the stronger ones, having survived the earlier shakeouts. For the third time since 1975, the job decline has slowed, creating some hope for long-term stability. New technologies may reduce the manpower needed to produce the same output, but manufacturing clearly retains a place in the city's economy. The combination of the incomparable size and flexibility of New York's labor market and the city's proximity to customers and suppliers will continue to prove singularly inviting to certain manufacturing operations. For example, while local garment-manufacturing firms cannot produce as cheaply as mass-production operations abroad, their ability to get the latest styles to market rapidly ensures them a market niche. Locally based designers who see the need for modifications only after a mockup is on the model, or when a buyer sees the line, also ensure a market for local garment firms. No facsimile machine or other form of telecommunication can replace this direct interaction between designers, manufacturers, and buyers.

Corporate Headquarters

The exodus of corporate headquarters of manufacturing companies, as well as drastic reductions in the size of many that remain, has contributed to the decline in manufacturing employment. Many experts had thought that the improvements in communication and transportation technology that made possible the separation of production from administration would strengthen New York's role as a center of corporate headquarters, and for a while, this was the case. From 1969 to 1977, however, the number of *Fortune* 500 firms with headquarters in the city plummeted from 125 to 80, and remained at that level fairly steadily into the early 1980s. Since then, the decline has again resumed, although at a slower rate, with mergers and acquisitions replacing moveouts as the major cause. The current number of 53 (106 in the region) has no rival. Chicago is second with only 21.

By 1977, the corporate headquarters sector, traditionally viewed as underpinning the postindustrial economy of New York, looked quite fragile. Even firms that remained in the city cut their employment to improve their competitiveness, especially vis-à-vis foreign rivals. Efforts to trim back middle management pervaded the industrial sector. In addition, many firms found that they could save money by contracting out for services, thereby allowing them to further reduce their headquarters staffs. For many of those that moved out, the opportunity for constant exposure to competitors and close contact with specialized professional services no longer seemed worth the higher occupancy and labor costs, even for the relatively small staffs that a headquarters operation required. The lure of the tranquil suburbs, with their untapped female labor force and longer standard work week, was enhanced sharply by the difficulty of attracting middle managers to the city and the fears of continued urban violence and blight following the urban riots of the 1960s.

The blow to New York's confidence from the mass exodus of headquarters now seems over, and the fear of damage from further losses is now reduced. The level of employment in these operations has already dropped by more than half from its peak of 86,000 in 1969. Exxon, for example, has reduced its headquarters staff from a peak of 2,300 in 1976 to under 400 today. Even the threat by AT&T to move its headquarters to New Jersey, although perhaps psychologically important, paled in comparison to the tens of thousands the company had already transplanted across the river. AT&T's expensive postmodernist headquarters on Madison Avenue is largely symbolic, with only some 300–400 jobs. While some recent mergers and highly publicized moveouts, such as those of J. C. Penney and Mobil, have again focused attention on this sector, the city seems well positioned to weather these losses.

Among the many headquarters operations that emigrated, most found that it paid to leave some activities behind to provide continuing direct contact with either local services or local customers. For example, J. C. Penney plans to leave a fashion-buying group behind, and General Motors still maintains a large staff in the city many years after it officially moved its headquarters. In some cases the number of jobs transferred out of the city was far smaller than the number left in financial or marketing offices. For example, the headquarters operations of Deloitte, Haskins, and Sells, which is being moved to Connecticut, employs only a small fraction of the firm's regional office, which remains in the city. Even those corporations that included as part of their move internal operations (for example, routine legal work) have found that specialized services could still be best purchased in the city.

Other threats of moveouts seem to be motivated, at least in part, by an effort to bargain for concessions from the city and from local developers. Dreyfus Corporation's threat to move to New Jersey to escape what it considered an onerous provision of the corporate tax law, like NBC's much-publicized search for space, may well have been a bargaining ploy. Although the drive to save on occupancy costs may have reflected the policy of NBC's new owner, General Electric, the search for another location took on a life of its own. In the end, NBC remained in New York, and the proposition as to whether a company so closely tied to the city's entertainment, advertising, and communications industries can prosper beyond walking distance from Midtown remains untested.

Not every firm that moved to verdant pastures found the move to have been in its long-term interest. In many cases, the countryside these firms sought has been turned, by their own actions, into a landscape of clogged arterials and endless corporate parks. The short-term savings or profits from the sale of buildings may in the long term be outweighed by the costs of lost competitiveness. A study by the Regional Plan Association found that firms with headquarters in the suburbs have lower profit margins than those in the city. A comparison of increases in stock prices from 1977 to 1986 tells a similar story: market values rose less for firms that moved out of the city than for those that stayed. It may be that isolation dulled the movers' competitive edge; alternatively, it may be that those that moved were more vulnerable to the lure of cost savings because they already had weak bottom lines. In any case, firms continue to establish or move their headquarters back into the city, among them such *Fortune* 500 firms as Triangle Industries and Inspiration Resources. Others, such as Sterling Drug, have canceled their plans and remain in the city. And even others (e.g., IBM) maintain huge headquarters-type operations even though technically their head offices are elsewhere.

Services

In sharp contrast to the manufacturing sector, the city's service sector (encompassing, for this discussion, so-called business, personal, and financial services as well as retail trade) increased its share of local employment over the past two decades. The absolute number employed in the service sector actually dipped slightly in the early 1970s before turning upward in the later half of that decade. As employment increased, so did the number of headquarters operations; for example, the number of *Fortune* 500 service firms headquartered in the city grew from 62 in 1983 to 70 in 1987.

Although convenient as a catchall phrase, reference to the service sector as if it were a single entity obscures important differences among firms and the functions they perform. Separating the sector into subcomponents reveals the wide range of roles service firms play in the growth of the local economy. For example, major advertising firms, law firms, accounting firms, financial firms, hospitals, and many other types of firms export their services, drawing money and resources from outside the city into the local economy. Through specialization, these firms offer unique services to customers and clients located either outside or within the city but serving national and international markets. In these cases, the concentration of people and companies in New York creates a pool of highly skilled labor and a competitive environment that together keeps these business service firms performing at peak levels. New York City's increasing ability to compete in such markets, aided by the growth of these markets, has provided the impetus for growth over the last decade, even in the face of increasing deindustrialization of the local economy and the loss of corporate headquarters.

At the other end of the spectrum, some service firms cater only to the needs of local residents. These firms provide what are often viewed as "personal" services, although services provided directly to individuals for their own use can also be exported. For example, services provided to tourists (over 17 million a year) who come to the city to shop, dine, and be entertained, are, in an economic sense, exported. The well-being of firms that service exclusively the local market depends solely on the health of the local economy. Thus, the status of these firms provides a barometer of current economic conditions, while the outlook for service firms that export is crucial to the city's future prosperity.

Unfortunately, although these distinctions are conceptually appealing, they are all but impossible to apply to available employment statistics. For example, there is no way to distinguish restaurant employment generated by the demand of the local populace from that generated by tourists. In fact, many restaurants serve both types of clientele, as do many retail, educational, and health service firms. Similarly difficult to categorize is employment in the city's specialized business and financial services. Some of the firms in this sector serve only the local market, but many serve national or international markets. Even when the client technically is locally based, e.g. in a local corporate headquarters, the demand for the service may be far from local and the impact on the local economy of providing that service may be essentially equivalent to the direct exporting of the service to a customer located outside the city.

The overall strength of the service sector is a testament to New York's attractiveness as a place to locate part or all of the operations of these types of exporting firms. Employment growth, however, has resulted and will continue to result from the dynamic interplay of a divergent set of forces. While new firms or branches of noncity firms have started up over time and many existing firms have expanded, others have contracted in size. Within firms, some divisions have grown while others have moved or have been phased out. Firms that invent new products and develop new markets expand. Meanwhile, other firms or parts of firms follow the path of mass-production manufacturing. As products and processes mature, becoming routine and susceptible to management without direct oversight and interaction from the head office, these operations can and do often move to the suburbs or beyond. Even though these operations often start in the city to take advantage of access to the best lawyers, accountants, advertising executives, they become free to benefit from the lower labor and occupancy costs offered by other locations. Such a maturation has characterized, for example, the processing of credit card transactions. Many banks and other financial firms that initiated these operations in the city have now moved them out, setting up these services in places as close as the nearby suburbs and as far away as South Dakota and Utah. Yet, as is true for the service sector as a whole, bank employment in toto has grown as the constant generation of new products and markets has more than offset the effects of this natural outmigration.

Business Services

Few cities rival New York's specialized offerings of business services. New York claims the headquarters of many of the nation's top advertising, accounting, and law firms, and most large firms not headquartered in the city maintain large representative or regional offices there. As a center of publishing, law, broadcasting, fashion design, architectural design, advertising, and medical services, New York's economy offers experts in areas of such narrow specialization that people travel from around the world to seek their counsel. These experts and their firms draw strength from each other as well as complementing each others' skills and competing for the same clients.

The ties of business service firms to New York are a function both of the amount of specialization and of the city's central role as a processor of information vital to the national and international economy. Business service firms depend not simply on information, but, on that information's timeliness; yesterday's idea may be just that. As information technology advances, information loses its freshness more quickly, forcing those dependent on it to cluster more tightly so as to shorten and multiply the number of lines of communication. Although telephones and computers permit the rapid exchange of information over long distances, nothing can replace the efficiency of face-to-face contact, whether at formal meetings or at power breakfasts. Firms such as advertising agencies, which thrive in the New York environment, need proximity to keep tabs on each other's latest ideas and innovations and to profit from each other's mistakes. With no immediate challenge to these linkages in evidence, the business services sector looks likely to continue to grow faster than the economy as a whole and even faster than the financial sector. As measured by the Labor Department's narrow definition of "business services," the increase in employment has been over 50 percent, from 195,000 in 1977 to just under 300,000 in 1987. Law firm employment grew even faster, almost doubling over the same period, to nearly 70,000.

Financial Services

Technological advancements and deregulation here and abroad have greatly affected employment levels in the financial services sector, comprising securities, insurance, and banking. On balance, this industry grew by about one-third from 1977 to 1987 after falling in the prior eight years, mostly because of weakness in employment in securities firms. Increased computerization allowed for the automation of back-office operations, which reduced the number of staff needed and initially cost jobs. Meanwhile, improved telecommunications eroded the ties to the central city for routine operations, allowing them to be moved out at little or no loss in efficiency and at substantial savings. On the other hand, improved communications also allowed firms within the city to manage larger and more far-flung operations, resulting in larger headquarters.

In contrast to conventional wisdom, deregulation of the financial industry made a New York location essential for many firms. Those observers who had feared deregulation would lead to the dispersion of the New York financial industry failed to foresee how much the parts left in the city would expand. Deregulation, combined with rising interest rates in response to an outbreak of more rapid inflation, caught up the formerly staid world of banking in a whirlwind of competition. The invention and marketing of new products can nowhere be done better than in New York, the locus of the top accounting firms, lawyers, and advertising firms. While routine operations can be located anywhere, dynamic and innovating operations demand the energy and specialization that New York alone offers.

Deregulation also led many non-New York banks to establish operations in New York. Freed of the absolute strictures of interstate banking laws, such institutions as the Mellon Bank and Bank of America opened substantial operations in New York, using such vehicles as loan production offices, Edge Act corporations, and nonbank banks. Despite the growth of regional financial centers, banking employment grew rapidly in New York in the late 1970s, at times outpacing growth at the national level. The development of worldwide credit markets also strengthened employment in the financial services sector. To compete in these markets, banks from around the world found that they needed a presence in New York. By 1986, over three-quarters of the assets in the Federal-Reserve-Board-created International Banking Facilities were in New York, and 356 foreign banks had opened branches or representative offices in the city, with over one quarter of a trillion dollars in assets. Today, more than 90 out of the 100 largest banks in the world have a New York office.

The securities industry, another part of the financial services sector, after booming in the late 1960s faltered in the early 1970s as increased trading volume buried back-office operations under tons of paper and trading hours on the stock exchanges were reduced. The combination of a bear market and computerization took its toll, as employment fell by nearly one-third from its 1969 peak of 105,000. But as trading volume soared in the late 1970s, employment began to rise again, and by 1985 it surpassed the 1969 record level. New York continues to maintain its dominant role in this industry, but its share of national employment continues to fall. The decline has abated during the recent period of enormous expansion, dropping only from 39 percent in 1977 to 35 percent in 1987.

Of all the financial services, only the insurance industry failed to recover its previous levels of employment after the decline of the 1960s. Part of the reason was that some insurance firms moved out of the city, but the main reason for the decline appears to have been the substitution of computer power for clerical power. Because of this trend, the proportion of jobs going to clerical staff fell significantly.

Locally Dependent Services

Many of the firms engaged in personal services, retail trade, and construction depend for growth on the prosperity of the local economy. For example, retail trade employment fell by nearly one-sixth from 1961 to 1977 and only started to recover in the early 1980s, when the city's population started to increase again after declining by almost 1 million persons during the previous decade and its per capita personal income growth ran above that of the nation as a whole.

In the construction industry, changes in local business activity do not translate immediately into changes in employment. Increasing office employment spurs development activity only after a lag during which preexisting vacant space is absorbed or made obsolete through technological change. The time required from the start of planning to the start of construction and then to building completion further causes building cycles to lag behind employment cycles. With the recession of 1969, construction employment did not begin to decline immediately, but kept climbing through the early 1970s as the buildings from the boom of the 1960s reached completion. Between 1971 and 1972, almost 40 million square feet came on the market, including 10 million square feet in the World Trade Center alone. The supply of office space in major buildings increased by almost 25 per cent at a time when the local economy was weakening. As

44

a result of this surplus, and of a declining economy, the construction industry went into a deep and prolonged depression. By 1977, construction employment was little more than half its 1971 total. The following year, employment began a slow climb, and it has regained its 1971 peak. In spite of current economic prosperity and office space absorption in excess of office completions, the construction industry may experience another period of cyclical decline as the inventory created by the recent building boom is worked off and land prices adjust to the reduced tax benefits for real estate under recent federal tax reform.

Government Employment

Government employment—city, state, and federal—was initially unaffected by the downturn in the early 1970s because the local government continued to increase spending despite a faltering economy and falling tax revenues. But the bond market eventually refused to continue financing the deficits and closed its doors to the city. This move, which precipitated the fiscal crisis in 1975, caused local government employment to fall by some 60,000 in the following two years. Total employment for all three levels of government fell from a 1974 high of 584,000 to just under 507,000 in 1977. Since then, local government has expanded its work force in step with its fiscal recovery, and employment now exceeds its pre-fiscal crisis peak. In 1981, the city balanced its budget under generally accepted accounting principles and reentered the long-term bond market to finance a capital plan that now anticipates funding approaching $50 billion in the next ten years.

GEOGRAPHIC DISPERSION OF THE EMPLOYMENT GROWTH

The city's economic recovery, initially evident only in Manhattan, has now permeated all the boroughs. From 1983 to 1986, in fact, employment grew at a faster rate outside of Manhattan than within, as manufacturing operations that were no longer viable in Manhattan found homes in other boroughs. The service sector—particularly firms that service reviving residential neighborhoods—continued to expand citywide. New centers for offices and showrooms and renewed interest in old ones, such as downtown Brooklyn, should help to ensure continued strength.

SPURRING ECONOMIC DEVELOPMENT: LOCAL GOVERNMENT'S ROLE

The economic twists and turns of New York City's economy over the last two decades provide new insights and confirm old ones, suggesting some basic principles that should shape local government development policy. The aim of such a policy is to build upon and strengthen the forces that contributed to recent growth. The vitality of the city's economy has led to a sharp decline in the local unemployment and a slowing, if not reversal, of the previously dramatic increase in the poverty rate. Economic prosperity has helped fill the local coffers, allowing restoration of many city services to their prefiscal crisis levels, while even allowing some modest tax cuts. Although certainly no panacea for all of the urban ills besetting the city, continued economic growth seems critical to efforts to maintain a low unemployment rate, to draw more of the adult population into the labor force, to ensure that jobs exist for those who need them, and to help sustain the high level of energy that gives New York its competitive edge.

The most basic principle demonstrated by recent experience is that New York's economy is resilient and fundamentally sound. It is not an old machine, obsolete and wearing out. New York has shown itself capable of revitalizing itself and maintaining its unique role as a large, dense urban environment, full of energy. Just at the point when many observers of the local scene were convinced of the inevitable and permanent—if not continuing—reduction in the size of the city best symbolized by the term "planned shrinkage," the economic upturn and subsequent employment growth of recent years had already erased more than half of the earlier losses.

Another principle that stands out clearly is the formidable strength of market forces. During the period of economic decline, the market acted powerfully to reduce wages and prices in New York relative to those in the rest of the country and produced a striking shift in the sectoral composition of the local economy, from manufacturing to business and financial services. These shifts played to New York's competitive advantages and provided the basis for the upturn.

The third principle is the creative and fundamental role played by change, both within and among sectors. Without the sectoral changes, the economy likely would not have grown at all. In fact, it probably would have continued to decline, as major parts of the manufacturing sector lost the ability to compete with suburban and urban locations, as manufacturing declined somewhat nationwide in response to foreign competition, and as manufacturing employment fell due to rising productivity.

The fourth principle is the difficulty of predicting winners and losers. Even if government could have a major impact on the fortunes of specific sectors or firms, the challenge of choosing the appropriate targets is formidable, if not impossible. To suggest that the most prescient economist or investment banker—let alone an economic development official—could have predicted which firms and industries would grow is absurd. To do so would have required foreknowledge of the directions of the world and national economies as well as of the city's competitive advantages.

The last principle is the dampening influence government has on economic activity when it fails to carry out its basic responsibilities and, in particular, seems incapable of putting its house in order. When the future of public services, basic infrastructure, and tax burdens is in doubt, business is reluctant to remain, let alone expand, in the city.

From these principles, local government's responsibilities in nurturing economic development become clear: efficient and effective provision of basic public services; stabilization or reduction of the tax burden; promotion of flexibility of the labor force and business sectors to adjust to continually changing market conditions both locally and around the world; and mitigation of the hardships caused by sectoral change. Only in those limited cases where markets cannot work well—as in the generation of a sufficient critical mass of activity to create satellite business centers—is direct intervention desirable.

Effective Provision of Basic Public Services

Given the city's limited resources and the damage caused by the neglect of basic services in the 1970s, the first priorities for the city must lie in its traditional areas of involvement: education, mass transit, water, sanitation, police, fire protection, and other services that local government must organize, if not provide, on behalf of the whole city. Inadequacies in the provision of these services increase costs for firms doing business in the city: for example, by increasing the debilitating and demoralizing travel delays for employees trying to get to work on time or the need for the private sector to provide its own security personnel or systems.

Requiring special attention is the city's educational and social services system. New York has a great resource in its abundant working-age population, but not all of these people are working or even considered part of the labor force. New York's record is very poor in this regard. The proportion of its working-age population holding a job or looking for a job is significantly below the national average. Even with major improvements in education and socialization, the city, along with the rest of the nation, can expect to be hit by a labor shortage over the next decade, when the 16- to 25-year-old age cohort falls dramatically below recent baby-boom levels. Without effective programs to bring into the mainstream the so-called underclass, particularly through reductions in alarmingly high dropout rates, this labor shortage could cripple the city's major industries even as it fails to draw the underclass into the work force. Even low-skilled jobs today are requiring higher and higher levels of literacy, as services replace blue-collar trades. Translating increasing job opportunities into higher levels of employment requires an educated work force. Here, the schools are the first line of defense.

Stabilizing or Reducing the Tax Burden

The high tax burden imposed by New York, combined with a comparably high burden at the state level, spurs repeated calls for a reduction in taxes. The first aim of local government must be to guard against increasing the tax burden (measured as a share of the local economy). Rising taxes, especially when combined with deficit spending and declining public services, signal a government in trouble. Individual citizens and businesses have little direct control over government expenditures and taxation, and they show their concern by investing in other locations. They seek a place where the tax burden is at least predictable, if not reasonable.

Although steadily increasing taxes may well have hurt the local economy, in the late 1960s and early 1970s, one must note that high but stable taxes did not prevent its resurgence. The recent drop in the tax burden as a percent of personal income seems to have been more a product than a cause of the economic recovery. Even with stable local tax rates, however, the effective local tax burden can rise, as has happened as a result of recent federal income tax reforms that lowered federal tax rates while broadening the base of income that is taxable. Tax savings from local tax deductions—sales taxes are no longer deductible—have been reduced, thereby increasing the net after-tax effect of local taxes. While New York City and

State have reduced their tax rates so as not to collect any more revenue as a result of the base broadening, the effective burden of local taxes is now much higher than it was before.

Disproportionately high taxes on individual industries do not necessarily prevent growth. For example, although until recently the highest business-tax rate fell on the banking sector, its employment growth has been among the best in the economy. In contrast, the insurance industry, unburdened by any local income or premium taxes, has continued to decline slowly, even during the upturn in the overall economy during the last decade.

City policy, therefore, should be to stabilize tax rates and seek whenever possible to lower them. Because of its vast array of taxes, the city should also look to eliminate whole sets of taxes, thus simplifying what has become a very complex and, to some, intimidating tax system. Although few would quarrel with the desirability of lower taxes, the import of any consequent revenue reductions on city services must also be considered.

Promoting Flexibility of Business and Labor

Another area suitable for government involvement is ensuring that everyone who is able to work has the skills necessary not only to find a job, but also to find new jobs as the economy adjusts in response to external factors. In addition to improving basic educational services, job training and literacy courses for adults are essential.

To maintain the flexibility of the businesses themselves, and their ability to adjust to changing market conditions, government also should allow active competition among companies and sectors and eliminate any unnecessary barriers caused by excessive regulations. Companies used to dealing with market pressures will develop tight and flexible management structures; those protected from such pressures will be least able to adjust to change.

Regulation by government of health and safety is essential to protect its citizenry. Economic regulation may sometimes also be justified to restrain the predatory aspects of monopolies, monopsonies, and oligopolies. But regulations that limit the effectiveness of economic forces without strong evidence of countervailing benefits, as Harold Hochman points out in Chapter 5, should be continually reexamined, as the conditions that originally required them may change. Zoning, for example, which may have started out as a tool for preserving light and air, and then have become a vehicle to separate residential, manufacturing, and commercial uses, may now be used primarily to stop needed development. In fact, the City Planning Commission, recognizing this change, has moved a long way toward accepting the viability of mixed-use neighborhoods and even buildings. However, the boundaries defining manufacturing districts no longer make sense. Although the desire to preserve manufacturing employment at current levels is admirable, the reality is that zoning is at best a weak tool for combating market forces. It results in empty lots, as along the Brooklyn waterfront; in nonconforming uses, as in the residential and artist lofts in old manufacturing buildings; and in underproductive uses, such as the parking lots along Avenue of the Americas in Chelsea. Mixed-use districts and buildings offer some solutions, but the Planning Commission needs to be more aware of and responsive to changing market pressures. Other areas of regulation need similarly constant reevaluation.

Another important policy to ensure flexibility is protection or creation of the "level playing field." All types of businesses—new or old, large or small, front or back office, manufacturing or financial, banking or insurance—and all legal forms of organization, partnerships, corporations, and sole proprietorships should have an equal opportunity to survive and prosper or to fail. Government policies that discriminate among businesses or firms are bad for the city's economy. First of all, attempts to pick winners or losers are more often wrong than right. Second, with regard to tax policy, even though economic theory calls for taxing most heavily "captive" industries (those that cannot easily move or be started in other locations), changing technology and economic conditions can quickly turn part or all of a captive industry into a footloose one. Such has been the case with the banking industry, as deregulation has opened it to competition from securities and investment firms within the city and advances in telecommunications and computers have permitted it to relocate some of its operations outside the city. Third, the impact of most tools available to local governments is at best marginal. For example, in the case of preferential tax treatment, it must be noted that taxes are only a small part of the cost of doing business and the net effect of any tax differential is reduced by the deductibility of local taxes in computing taxable income for federal income purposes.

Examples of discriminatory treatment still abound, but the city has recently taken three important steps to level the field. First, in the area of commercial banking, bank taxes have been reduced to the level paid by other corporations for the first time since the fiscal crisis. Without the lowering of the tax rate, banks would have been hobbled in their efforts to hold their existing markets and to gain new ones. Eventually, to ensure equal treatment, taxation of banking institutions should be brought under the General Corporation Tax that covers banks' competitors in the securities and investment banking fields. Second, an increase in the exemption under the Unincorporated Business Tax has eliminated the double taxation of small partnerships and sole proprietorships. For larger firms, however, the choice of these forms of organization means higher taxes than for corporations carrying out the same business activities. Third, the city is eliminating both the gross receipts tax and the regular sales tax as they apply to sales of energy to businesses. In the past, the taxation of energy was viewed as a harmless and hidden way to collect revenue, since the costs were passed through to customers by the utilities in the form of higher energy bills. But the heavy taxation of utilities disproportionately hit firms and processes that use energy intensively.

Mitigating Hardships Caused by Change

Any discussion about the benefits and importance of change must acknowledge that change does not come without negative side-effects. Changes can cause radical redistributions of income and capital among individuals. While the economy as a whole may gain from change, individual businesses and their employees may suffer greatly. This personal hardship can produce intense pressure on the political system to preserve the status quo. Although this pressure must be resisted, the government should work hard to mitigate the negative impacts of change. One obvious route is to offer retraining to employees who cannot find alternative opportunities to use their skills.

Creative approaches are needed to deal with these hardships, since the pace of change is likely to accelerate. For example, rather than protecting the status quo by zoning out other uses, the city should find other ways to assist firms no longer able to survive in open competition for space at their current locations through such programs as the Business Relocation Assistance Corporation (BRAC), which captures some of the profits from the residential conversion of manufacturing space and uses them to compensate firms who relocate within the city for moving costs. Similarly, the Industrial Retention and Relocation program has helped firms to move out of the central business district and a few other hotly contested areas—as when the flower market relocated to College Point and the produce market to Hunt's Point—without blocking or reversing market pressures. Requiring new waterfront development to include space permanently set aside for manufacturers, with preference for local firms, offers another way to ease the pain of change.

Ameliorating Compactness

New York's success as a place to live and work is a function of its compactness—the immense number of people who live in the metropolitan area and work and interact in the centrally packed business district. Density imposes costs, however, in complicating aboveground and underground transportation and in creating very high land prices. To ameliorate these costs, government should work to ensure efficient mass transportation as well as to expand the boundaries of the main business districts. The enlargement of Midtown to the west around Times Square and the creation of critical masses of back offices in downtown Brooklyn are positive public land-use policies. The more dispersed the areas of commercial development, the more jobs can be accommodated for those with different levels of skills.

THE OUTLOOK

The last decade has once again demonstrated the resilience and vitality of New York City and its economy. Its compactness facilitates access between people and businesses, giving it an unrivalled energy level and a singular competitive advantage. As the largest city in the world's largest economy, New York's place as a world business and financial capital should be assured. This is not to say that short-term declines are a thing of the past, especially since the recent evolution of the city's industrial mix makes New York particularly vulnerable to any events that lead to secular declines in the financial sector. The shrinkage of the municipal bond market due to federal tax reform and the October 19, 1987, crash resulted in thousands of layoffs. Obviously, any national recession will almost inevitably cause a local slowdown, although New York's lower dependence on manufacturing may cushion the impact.

This optimistic long-run forecast depends, of course, on several important assumptions about the rest of the world. First, it is essential that the United States keeps its economy open regardless of changes in technology and world trading patterns; any international trade war would impinge directly on New York's economic health. Similarly, re-regulation of financial markets (as is being proposed) could reduce the importance of New York's position on the cutting edge of the latest market innovations.

Under these circumstances, city government must resist pressure to preserve the status quo and pursue policies to facilitate the economy's ability to adjust to changing market conditions. It must continue, within the confines of a balanced budget and stable if not declining tax rates, to mitigate the negative aspects of its otherwise beneficial density, provide basic public services, maintain the infrastructure, and ensure health and safety. In general, however, the city should limit its involvement and interference in the local economy. Such an approach will help to ensure the city's economic prosperity. The city government should do no more—and no less.

Chapter 3

THE NEW NEW YORKERS

Nathan Glazer

If the United States remains the permanently unfinished country, to an even greater degree the same is true of New York City. Depression-era forecasters were clearly wrong in predicting that the American population would stabilize at about 150,000,000—now a ludicrous figure. Equally wrong were projections of the 1950s and 1960s that led to alarm at an environment-destroying overpopulation and gave strength to the zero-population-growth movement. We have been taken by surprise by great new waves of immigration from Asia, the Caribbean, and Latin America. Our assumptions and expectations regarding New York City have been continually upset by the decisions of hundreds of thousands of individuals, inside and outside the United States, whose movements are constrained only by what is possibly the least constraining set of laws and regulations on the face of the earth.

These reflections are motivated by consideration of the contrast between the present population of New York City and that of 25 years ago, when I was working on a study of the ethnic groups of New York titled *Beyond the Melting Pot*.

I took it almost for granted then that the relevant categories for examining the population of New York were those of race and ethnic extraction, rather than those of class. Because of the city's history of migration and social mobility, any type of class—lower class, working class, or middle class, business class or home-owning class, occupation or any other economically based category—inevitably would consist of some specific ethnic groups, one or two or three of which dominated each socioeconomic category. Thus, class and ethnic factors were inextricably mixed in considering each group's self-interest. When an explosive conflict over community school control broke out, one could say "low-income Brooklyn parents of public-school children" were pitted against "middle-class teachers," and that would be true enough. But the more sharply felt reality of the situation was that blacks were pitted against Jews—and that aspect of the conflict was more explosive than the purely socioeconomic one.

In evaluating what has happened to New York's population in the last 25 years, then, we must consider, in the first place, ethnic and racial change. The 1960 census showed that in a city of 7,783,000, there were 300,000 immigrants and their children from Germany, and about the same number from Ireland. But because the Germans and Irish had been the dominant immigrant groups of the latter half of the 19th century, with their grandchildren and great-grandchildren—not distinguished statistically by the census —taken into account, it could be assumed that they made up much more than the 4 percent of the city's population comprising immigrants and their children alone.

The census also recorded 953,000 immigrants and their children from Russia and Poland (mostly Jewish) and 859,000 from Italy, 1,088,000 Negroes and 588,000 Puerto Ricans and their children. The most recent elements in the population—Puerto Ricans and blacks—were still growing, the German and Irish elements were declining, and Jews and Italians demographically dominated the city. Scores of lesser ethnic groups also contributed to the population of New York City.

In the early 1960s, no one believed there would be any great resumption of European immigration: the immigration laws forbade it, and Europe was entering a period of prosperity that made emigration less attractive. Jewish groups and other ethnic organizations still fought for changes in the immigration laws, as they had since World War II, but quota restrictions remained in force. Emigration from Central and South America, unlimited by quota, had not been great to the United States as a whole, and certainly not to New York City. Asians were a tiny minority of a few tens of thousands, and few expected there would ever be many more.

THE GATES ARE OPENED

Even with the change in the immigration laws that came into effect in 1965, in that burst of revolutionary legislation that accompanied the first few years of President Lyndon B. Johnson's presidency, little change was expected. National quotas favoring Britain, Ireland, and Germany were eliminated, and all nations were given quotas of 20,000. But consider what two attorney-generals of the United States, testifying before congressional committees, had to say about the impact of the proposed new law on immigration from Asian and Latin American sources. Testifying before a House subcommittee, in 1964, Robert Kennedy said,

> I would say [the number of immigrants to be expected] for the Asia-Pacific triangle. . .would be approximately 5,000, Mr. Chairman, after which immigration from that source would virtually disappear; 5,000 immigrants would come in the first year, but we do not expect that there would be any great influx after that.

And in 1965, Nicholas Katzenbach testified,

> If you look at the present immigration figures from the Western Hemisphere countries there is not much pressure to come to the United States from those countries. There are in a relative sense not many people who want to come.

Despite these forecasts, the immigration reform act of 1965 (which came into effect in 1968), combined with political, economic, and social changes in various countries of the Caribbean, Latin America, and Asia, had enormous effects. Emanuel Tobier has estimated, on the basis of statements by legal immigrants as to where they live or plan to settle, that 80,000 immigrants a year came into the city during the 1970s, and 86,000 a year in the 1980s. Simple multiplication suggests that 800,000 immigrants came in the 1970s, and that 880,000 may have been added by the end of 1986. And nothing has happened (including the new immigration reform law, which came into effect in 1986) to reduce that number. Admittedly, these crude figures tell us little about the changing population of New York. Many of the new immigrants have already moved to the suburbs or to other cities, and others have returned to their native countries; many have already had native-born children; many others have entered the city illegally (the figures above are for legal immigrants); many native-born have left the city; and many others have entered from other parts of the country. What is unquestionable is that the cast of ethnic and racial characters that made up New York in the early 1960s has undergone as substantial a change as that caused by any of the great migratory streams that have swept into the city again and again in the past.

Those who fought for the radical changes in federal immigration laws in 1965 did not expect them to have any substantial effect on the pattern of immigration to the United States. In the early 1960s, immigration ran at a rate of under 300,000 a year and was predominantly European. The complaint with the immigration act then in effect, the McCarran-Walter Act of 1952—which set quotas for each European country on the basis of its contribution to the makeup of the American population and provided only tiny token quotas for Asia—was that it discriminated against Eastern and Southern Europeans, Jews, Italians, Poles, Greeks, and other groups. The aim of the revisions of 1965, for which Jewish and Catholic groups had fought energetically, was to increase the number that could come from those countries. The expectation of those who fought for revision—such as Senators Herbert Lehman, John F. Kennedy, and Edward Kennedy—was that it would permit constituents eager to bring family members to the United States to do so. These were expected to be *European* family members; there were at the time few Asian constituents, and they played no political role. Neither did the Hispanics in the Northeast, who in the early 1960s were almost entirely Puerto Rican, concern themselves with immigration restriction, for as citizens they had no immigration problems. Nor did black groups concern themselves much with immigration, even though West Indian blacks had established substantial communities in New York and Boston.

But the pattern of immigration changed very rapidly. The pool of family members and others interested in coming to the United States from older European ethnic groups was soon exhausted (except for Russian Jews, whose emigration is strictly controlled by the Soviet government). By the late 1960s, the Caribbean, Latin America, and Asia were the dominant sources of immigrants for New York, and they continue to be the dominant sources today.

How could an act based primarily on family and relative preference serve groups who had few of their number in the United States, as was the case with Asian groups and most Latin Americans? One reason was that another priority of the act was to make it possible for those with skills and talents in short supply in the country to come in. Thus, Jamaican nurses, Korean doctors, and Indian and Chinese engineers were all able to immigrate as the act came into effect. And shortly after, on the basis of resident alien status and later, citizenship, immigrants from these groups were able to bring in family relations, regardless of whether or not *their* occupations were in demand and could be filled by resident Americans.

We are still far from the 1 million legal immigrants who came into the country in each year of the first decade of the century—and into a country less than half its present size. But the steady immigration of 500,000–600,000 legal immigrants a year, concentrated in a few parts of the country, of which New York City is one, has had an enormous cumulative impact. "Between 1965 and 1978. . .17 percent of legal immigrants, some 954,000 persons, established their initial residence in New York City," Emanuel Tobier tells us. New York City, with a mere 3 percent (and dropping) of the population of the United States, and suffering in the mid-1970s from a severe financial and economic crisis, lost no fewer than 1,162,000 people from net out-migration in the 1970s. Without foreign immigration, the city's population could well have declined by 20 per cent instead of the 11 percent shown by the census.

The immigrant flow into New York seemed unaffected, or scarcely affected, by changing economic circumstances, by the phenomenal decline in manufacturing jobs, by the massive destruction of low-cost housing in the great waves of abandonment of the 1970s. Whatever the changes that were affecting New York for the worse in the 1970s, to the immigrant it was still apparently the city of opportunity. And it remains so.

The variable impact of the new immigration streams can be seen in two contrasting *New York Times* articles on two high schools. Erasmus Hall, the oldest high school in the city, located in "an imposing full-block gothic building" in Brooklyn, was cited in 1985 by the state education department as one of the two most "deficient" high schools in the city. Its past prestige is now only a memory among older teachers. Although its student body is 90 percent black and 9 percent Hispanic, its staff views as its most serious problem the one-quarter of the student body that is Haitian. Larry Rohter in the *Times* quoted a teacher who instructs Haitian students in Haitian Creole (one of the bilingual programs in the school): "Many of the recent immigrants are from the lower strata of their home society. . . . Very often they have had very little schooling and are deficient in their own language, not to mention English." The Spanish-speakers could take exams in their own language; the Haitians could not.

In contrast, Jane Perlez reported, in an article titled "Chinese Students Thrive at Seward Park High," that "almost daily, new children from China enroll at Seward Park on the Lower East Side. . . . There are 950 newly arrived, Chinese-speaking students at the school, according to. . . .the principal, who added that the 37

percent Chinese-speaking enrollment was the largest in the city."
Interestingly, the new immigrants are from mainland China:
according to Ms. Perlez, 20,000 mainland Chinese have come to
New York City since 1982, when the mainland Chinese were
separated from the Taiwanese and the Hong Kong Chinese in
immigration statistics. The school has 18 Chinese-speaking teachers
and 17 Chinese aides. Hispanic students make up 56 percent of the
student body, which also includes Pakistanis, Haitians, and Pacific
Islanders. But it is the Chinese students "who are beginning to lend
the school an extra fillip." According to one teacher, "They have a
Chinese work ethic that makes the Protestant work ethic look bad.
They're the backbone of the school."

Is it, then, culture that makes the difference between the Haitians
of Erasmus Hall and the Chinese of Seward Park? Perhaps, but note
the educational background of the Chinese: "One of the simpler
tasks for a student who arrived from Canton two weeks ago will
be to familiarize herself with the Tandy brand of computers. In her
Canton junior high school, she says, she had been learning
programming on an Apple II computer." That does not fit with our
image of developing mainland China. Less surprising is another
student's statement that "The mathematics were more difficult in
China than here." This student "had already started physics when
he left China two years ago . . . a subject he is yet to get at Seward
Park." The Chinese make up all eight members of the school math
team.

KEEPING COUNT

The visual impact of the new immigration is evident everywhere
in the city. New Yorkers, wrote Elizabeth Bogen, director of the
Office of Immigrant Affairs of the Department of City Planning,
"know that their taxi drivers are likely to be Haitian, Russian, or
Israeli; their newsdealers, Indian; their computer programmers,
Chinese; their fruit- and fish-store owners, Korean." Dominicans
now dominate Washington Heights; Asians and Colombians and
other Latin Americans have settled thickly along the Number 7
subway line in Queens; Koreans and Indians are now prominent in
Flushing. Neighborhood after neighborhood has been changed by
the new immigrants, and some have changed yet again as newer
immigrants flooded into the city. But it is not easy to move from
reporting and ethnography—crucial as they are in telling us what is

happening to the city—to a stable statistical picture of the scale of change.

There are many reasons why this is so. Unfortunately, the United States Census cannot count all the residents of the United States or of New York City. Because blacks and Hispanics are disproportionately undercounted, we may assume that a substantial portion of the new immigrants—a majority of whom are black and Hispanic—are also undercounted. For some years the city has been engaged in a suit to get the census to agree that there were a half-million more people in the city (7 percent more than the reported 7,072,000) in 1980 than it was able to count. The census itself has estimated that it undercounted black males in 1980 by 7.2 percent, and black females by 2.5 percent.

Of course, this undercount is of the native-born as well as the foreign-born. But other factors contribute to our uncertainty over how many new immigrants there are in the city, and how they are divided by race and nationality. Many—how many, we don't know—are illegal or undocumented and therefore may have more than ordinary reasons not to want to be counted. In addition, the census categories for race and ethnicity, which must accommodate a variety of political as well as scientific interests, do not correspond very well with ethnic and racial groups as they are understood in the popular or the scholarly mind. The census for decades recorded the country of birth of the foreign-born and of the parents of native-born of foreign parents, which left open the question of how many third-generation (and beyond) members of any ethnic group there were. In 1980, the census decided to abandon the count of country of birth of parents in favor of a general question on "ancestry," which is hard to interpret. One can get a clearer answer when one asks, "In what country were your parents born?" than when one asks, "What is your ancestry?" So we know who the foreign-born are, but census figures on the second generation of the new immigrants are lacking (although the City Planning Commission can get from the census a count of children in households headed by an immigrant, which helps us to estimate the size of the second generation).

Because the census has always asked about race, we have the number of blacks. And because for many decades it has taken the odd position that each Asian group forms a separate race, we have counts for all Chinese, Japanese, Koreans, Filipinos, and other Asian groups, both foreign-born and native. But questions as to race, nativity, and ancestry, taken together, lead to inconsistent results for many important groups. The most serious problem in interpreting the new "ancestry" question is that in the largest Jewish city in the world, there is no way of getting a count of Jews from the census, which does not record religion and insists that "Jew" or "Jewish" is solely a religious designation. This does not bother the Jews of New York much, since they make their own counts for purposes of social planning; and in any case, Jewish organizations are among the strongest opponents of recording religion on the census. But the fact that the census rigorously closes its eyes to the existence of Jews plays havoc in trying to estimate how many of those who give their ancestry as Russian or Polish, Lithuanian or Ukrainian or German, are really Jews—and the census provides no basis for estimating the size of these *other* ethnic groups.

Nevertheless, the census does give us the basic picture of the changes that have taken place in the city. Thus, we noted in 1980 the first increase in the foreign-born population in the city since 1930, when they numbered 2,359,000—a phenomenal 34 percent of the total. By 1970, the foreign-born had dropped to 1,437,000 or 18 percent of the population. By 1980, the number of foreign-born had risen to 1,675,000, or 23.6 percent of the population. This fairly modest rise was the net result of many deaths among the older foreign-born, move-outs by the latter (and the more prosperous new immigrants) to the suburbs or to other parts of the country, and the entry of 800,000 or so new immigrants. The largest single foreign-born group in the city is still those of the older European immigration, led by 156,000 from Italy. Next, however, comes the Dominican Republic, with 120,600; then China (mainland, Taiwan, and Hong Kong), with 95,000; then Jamaica, with 93,000; in fifth, sixth, and seventh places are the USSR, Poland, and Germany (mostly Jews); in eighth and ninth are Haiti and Cuba; and in tenth, Ireland. Greece, Colombia, Trinidad and Tobago, and Ecuador follow, with about 40,000 each. Some groups that have had a great visual impact on the city, such as Koreans and Indians, are surprisingly far down on the list of foreign-born—Asian Indians in 20th place, with 21,500; Koreans in 24th place, with 18,480. But if we consider immigrants of the years 1975–80 only, 11 of the first 12 countries are Asian, Central and South American, or Caribbean (the exception being the USSR).

These are figures for the foreign-born. Ancestry figures, with all their difficulties, are higher, of course. Italians again come first, with 803,000. Then come the Irish, with 318,000. Russians, Poles, and Germans show 216,000, 196,000 and 182,000, respectively. The

Table 1 Foreign-born in New York City by Country of Birth, 1980 and 1960

Country of Birth	Rank in 1980	Number in 1980	Rank in 1960	Number in 1960	Percent Change, 1960–80
All countries		1,675,160		1,562,281	+7
Italy	1	156,280	1	281,033	−44
Dominican Republic	2	120,600	26	9,223	+1,200
Jamaica	3	93,100	24	11,160	+734
USSR	4	87,360	2	204,821	−57
China[a]	5	85,100	15	19,769	+330
Poland	6	77,160	3	168,960	−54
Germany (West and East)	7	60,760	4	152,502	−60
Haiti	8	50,160	42	3,002	+1,571
Cuba	9	49,720	11	28,567	+74
Ireland/ N. Ireland	10	43,520	5	114,163	−62
Greece	11	41,760	12	28,882	+45
Colombia	12	41,200	34	4,766	+764
Trinidad and Tobago	13	39,160	32	5,495	+613
Ecuador	14	39,000	44	2,796	+1,295
Guyana[b]	15	31,960	**	**	**
Austria	16	26,160	6	84,389	−69
England	17	22,720	8	40,769	−44
Hungary	18	22,660	7	45,602	−50
Yugoslavia	19	22,300	19	12,399	+80
India	20	21,500	54	1,243	+1,630
Philippines	21	21,260	39	3,977	+434
Panama	22	20,840	33	677	+267
Korea (North and South)	23	20,380	59	562	+3,526
Barbados[b]	24	19,680	**	**	**
Rumania	25	17,560	14	24,784	−29
Total 1–25		1,231,900		1,249,541	−1
All other countries		331,620		305,835	+8
Not reported		111,640		7,102	+1,472

[a] Includes Hong Kong and Taiwan.
[b] Figures are not available for 1960, because Guyana and Barbados were included in the total for the British West Indies.
Source: 1980 U.S. Census Public Use Microdata and 1960 U.S. Census, prepared by New York City Department of City Planning, from a forthcoming book on New York City immigration by Elizabeth Bogen.

Dominicans are swallowed up in a huge number of undifferentiated "other Hispanics" (462,000). There are 115,000 Chinese, 106,000 Jamaicans, 61,000 Cubans, 43,000 Haitians, 36,000 Asian Indians, and 21,000 Koreans. These are all figures for "single ancestry." Many individuals report two, three, or more ancestries. Some of these figures can only lead to head-scratching. How can there be 18,480 Korean foreign-born, but only 21,000 Koreans by ancestry, when there has been a growing Korean community for 20 years and the Koreans are a family-centered population in which there are many native-born? How can there be 50,000 foreign-born Haitians, but only 43,000 by ancestry?

Results such as these make demographers doubtful about the new ancestry category. People apparently are confused by the ancestry question, which seems to lead to serious undercounts of the size of many groups. But if the census undercounts, the ethnic organizations undoubtedly overcount. Thus, the Haitian Centers Council in Brooklyn and other sources estimate 300,000 to a half-million Haitians for the metropolitan area. The Korean Association of New York estimates 150,000 in the metropolitan area; another estimate is 200,000. According to one estimate, there were more than 250,000 Colombians in New York in the mid-1970s, even though the 1980 census counted only 41,000 Colombian-born in the city. A 1985 newspaper estimate of 160,000 Asian Indians in the metropolitan area contrasts with the census count for the city alone of 21,500 Indian-born.

A key difficulty in getting the figures right is the rapid movement to the suburbs of upwardly mobile immigrant groups, particularly Asians. The Asian population of suburban counties around New York showed very sharp increases in the 1970s, albeit from very small bases. It is clear that Koreans, Chinese, Asian Indian, and other groups are moving rapidly to the suburbs—a shift made possible by the high numbers in these groups of professionals and business people whose income permits such a move, combined with their great concern for schooling. To ethnic organizations, the distinction between city and suburbs is not very meaningful. To these organizations the metropolitan area is the effective community, whether from the point of view of patronizing ethnic specialty stores, of attending movies, or of organizing for political action.

Great attention has been focused on the illegal immigrants who swell the numbers for many groups. But how many are there? Estimates have ranged from the wildly exaggerated to the very moderate. Some time ago, a regional Immigration and Naturalization

Table 2 Foreign-Born in New York City, 1980, Who Entered Between 1975 and 1980

Birthplace	Number
All countries	353,900
1. Dominican Republic	35,860
2. USSR	29,020
3. China[a]	25,520
4. Jamaica	23,660
5. Guyana	15,720
6. Haiti	13,840
7. Korea	11,660
8. Colombia	11,420
9. Trinidad/Tobago	10,640
10. India	10,500
11. Ecuador	9,820
12. Philippines	7,060
13. Greece	6,680
14. Italy	6,560
15. Barbados	5,480
16. Japan	5,440
17. Israel	4,660
18. England	4,640
19. Panama	4,540
20. Poland	4,220
21. Iran	3,560
22. Vietnam	3,280
23. Peru	3,080
24. El Salvador	3,000
25. Rumania	2,860
Total 1–25	262,720
All other countries	68,480
Not reported	22,700

[a] Includes Hong Kong and Taiwan.

Source: 1980 U.S. Census Microdata File. Prepared by New York City Department of City Planning.

Service director estimated 1.5 million illegal immigrants for the region and 1 million for the New York metropolitan area. At a time when the national figure may be as low as 2 million according to a National Academy of Sciences estimate, this figure seems impossible. But in a well-regarded analysis of the 1980 census, Jeffrey S. Passel and Karen A. Woodrow showed clearly that some 200,000 illegal aliens were actually counted in the city by the 1980 census. It would seem safe to double that figure, to reach the estimate of the Immigration and Naturalization Service.

THE EBB AND FLOW

While the change in the city's ethnic composition over the past 20 years appears to be the most striking visible change in the city's demographic profile, it has taken place within a context of changes of longer standing, which have steadily transformed the city and which provide a larger demographic context for the ethnic change we have described. Between 1940 and 1970, New York's population remained almost stable at near 8 million, sustained, in this most mobile of all societies, by a combination of huge outflows and huge inflows. But the balance between outflow and inflow was radically upset in the 1970s, and the city's population fell 10 percent. From the overall figures, it appears that whites flowed out while blacks and Hispanics continued to flow in; that the well-to-do flowed out while the poor remained. The more highly educated and those in professional jobs, or those starting families and sending children to school, regardless of race or ethnicity, showed a strong propensity to move out. But there were many more whites and Asians among the prosperous and the family-forming than there were blacks and Puerto Ricans.

Evelyn Mann and Joseph Salvo have estimated that, overall, 15 percent of the New York population of 1975 had emigrated by 1980, which indicates how much in-migration, from abroad or the rest of the United States, was necessary to limit the loss of population in the 1970s to 10 percent. Most mobile were the Asians, an estimated 22 percent of whom moved out of the city between 1975 and 1980, followed by the whites (17 per cent). Only 10 percent of blacks, in contrast, were out-migrants during this five-year period. Puerto Ricans, despite a generally low level of education and high rate of poverty, also moved out at a substantial rate (17 percent)—but unlike Asians and whites, who moved to the suburbs, Puerto Ricans moved back to Puerto Rico. Similarly, most of the blacks who moved went back to the South. It appears that making it in New York leads to moving to the suburbs, and not making it leads to moving back to one's origins.

The end result of these migratory trends was that the black and

Puerto Rican component of New York City showed very modest absolute increases: 7 percent in the black population, 5 percent in the Puerto Ricans—and the black increase could be accounted for by the black migration from the Caribbean. Because of the huge white movement to the suburbs, the *percentage* of blacks and Puerto Ricans in New York City's population grew substantially, but the actual absolute increase was small.

While all these trends continued in the 1980s, the patterns changed, so that we have seen a turnaround in the decline of the city's population. Projected declines in population made quite recently must already be corrected. Between 1980 and 1985, Katherine Trent and Richard D. Alba have estimated, the city's population grew by 183,000, or 2.6 percent.

OTHER DEMOGRAPHIC TRENDS

Two other long-established trends continue to change New York City. First is the decline in average household size: in 1980, this was down to 2.49, and undoubtedly this trend has continued. As a result, the number of households remains stable even as the population declines, and it increases substantially when population increases slowly. The city's households declined only 2 percent in the 1970s, while its population dropped 10 percent. This trend not only contributes to the permanent tight housing market, but must also limit the number of immigrants who might otherwise select New York City as a destination. Concentrated in family-formation ages, immigrants are under great pressure to move to where family housing is more available—and that increasingly means New Jersey, in which since 1982 more than half of all new housing units in the metropolitan area have been built.

The other major trend contributing to the increase in the number of households is the aging of New York's population—among the white population, but increasingly among blacks as well. The percentage of the population over 65 has increased steadily: 10.5 in 1960, 12.0 in 1970, 13.5 in 1980. And the numbers of the very aged have increased more rapidly. According to the Department for the Aging, the number of city residents aged 85 years and older increased 37 percent between 1970 and 1980, and another 32 percent between 1980 and 1985. Although accounting for only half the population of the city, whites make up more than three-quarters of the aged. Various forces affect the number of the aged: increased longevity of the white and black populations, differential emigration of the retired, the relatively small percentage of the aged among new immigrants to the city.

Does the city continue to attract young, upwardly mobile whites from the rest of the country, despite the overall trends of emigration and aging? Of course. It has always shown a surplus of young adults moving into the city, and it still does. Indeed, one of the great fears that New York has to deal with is that it is these energetic new migrants from the rest of the country who, along with the immigrants, take the jobs the city's reviving economy provides, leaving native-born blacks and Puerto Ricans in huge numbers unemployed and in poverty.

WHO MAKES UP THE MAJORITY?

The overall change in the city is clear, as it has been for 40 years: the number and percentage of whites drops, the numbers and percentages of blacks and Hispanics rise. But these three broad categories are increasingly inadequate to describe the reality of demographic change in the city. We find now a rising number of "others"—principally Asians, once too few in number to be considered a major population component. Also, within the black population is a growing group of new immigrants from the Caribbean, including Jamaicans and others from English-speaking lands, a growing number of French-Creole-speaking Haitians, and many Spanish-speaking blacks. And within the Hispanic population, at one time almost entirely Puerto Rican, is a rapidly growing segment of new immigrants from many countries. Thus, there are important divisions within the two great minority groups that we dub in too sweeping a fashion as simply "black" or "Hispanic."

We have long made this tripartite division of the city into three categories of "white," "black," and "Hispanic," in part because of law and politics. Affirmative action regulations, which have played havoc with civil service tests for the police in the city, use the same categories, as do counts of children in the school, whether for purposes of tracking the degree of segregation or assessing the seriousness of educational problems. And so it seems to make sense when a demographer announces that the city now has a "majority of minorities." But what sense—socially, politically, or economically—does it really make to say that the majority of the city is now "minority"? Should we equate the Asians with the blacks? Or the new Caribbean immigrants with the Puerto Ricans? Should we lump all against the "whites," themselves divided among so many groups and socioeconomic levels? The differences among Asians, Hispanics, and blacks, and between newer immigrants and older native groups in each racial-ethnic category, are sharp enough to throw the significance of such overarching categories into question. One reason why these three great divisions mean less is that we have seen the immigrants, of all races and backgrounds, pulling ahead of, and differentiating themselves from, the black and Puerto Rican streams of the 1950s and 1960s.

IS NEW YORK STILL THE LAND OF OPPORTUNITY?

The new immigration has two significant implications. The first is that the City of New York still, perhaps surprisingly, provides the setting—primarily economic, but also social and political—for new groups of very different ethnic and racial origins and different educational and economic backgrounds to find a satisfying life, or at least to take the first steps toward such a life. In view of the enormous changes in New York that would seem to have reduced its capacity to serve this function, this is surprising and gratifying. New York has suffered a massive decline in jobs in manufacturing; grave weakness in its educational system, certainly in comparison with its reputation when it was educating the children of the great waves of European immigration in the 1920s and 1930s; an enormous destruction of low-cost housing; and the creation of a permanent crime problem of massive magnitude. Yet immigration, legal and illegal, continues.

The second implication of the new immigration is that New York may be in for serious racial and ethnic conflict in the future, as new immigrants pull ahead of older low-income populations that seem unable to connect with the city's opportunities.

In the 1950s and 1960s, it was reasonable to project that the newest entrants into New York's complex ethnic mix, blacks and Puerto Ricans, would in time rise in the city's economic structure and become only modestly differentiated, in economic position and political power, from those who had preceded them—just as the Jews and Italians before them rose, in the economic and political spheres, to the level of the Irish and Germans who had preceded them. This was the expectation voiced by Oscar Handlin in *The*

Newcomers, and it was my expectation in *Beyond the Melting Pot*. But it hasn't happened.

The clearest demonstration that it has not happened can be found in a Department of City Planning study by Evelyn S. Mann and Joseph J. Salvo comparing the new Hispanic immigrants with the old—that is, the Puerto Ricans. Until 1965, Hispanics in New York were primarily Puerto Rican. Immigration from Central and South America and the Spanish-speaking Caribbean has increased since 1970, and by 1980, only 61 percent of the city's 1,406,000 Hispanics were Puerto Rican. The non-Puerto Ricans included 61,000 Cubans; 23,000 Mexicans; and 462,000 undifferentiated "other Hispanics," the largest group among which were Dominicans.

The Mann–Salvo analysis compares Puerto Ricans with all other Hispanics, and shows that these newer arrivals are already doing better than the Puerto Ricans, whose major period of immigration came in the 20 years after World War II. Puerto Ricans had a lower percentage of families headed by married couples (51.3 percent compared with 61.5 percent for other Hispanics), and almost half the Puerto Rican families with children were female-headed (49.8 percent), compared with 39.4 percent for other Hispanics. Puerto Rican women also were bearing more children than other Hispanics and had had less education, despite the presumed opportunity given them by long exposure to a free educational system (something believed to be one reason for the immigration of other Hispanics). Puerto Rican men had a median of 10.3 years of education, as against 11.6 for other Hispanics; Puerto Rican women 9.7 years, as against 10.3 years for other Hispanics. Median household income was $8,181 for Puerto Ricans, $11,698 for other Hispanics. Both for married-couple families and family households with no spouse present, the gap was substantial—$13,712 against $15,477 for the first, $5,111 versus $7,271 for the second. The percentages of Puerto Ricans in the labor force are far smaller than those of other Hispanics: 34 percent of Puerto Rican males are not in the labor force, compared with 23 percent of other Hispanic males; 66 percent of Puerto Rican females are not in the labor force, compared with 48.5 percent of other Hispanic females. Much greater percentages of Puerto Rican households draw public assistance: 38.9 percent, as against 19.6 percent of other Hispanics.

The story is a similar story for the black immigrants to New York, compared with native blacks. Immigration from the English-speaking West Indies continued after the drastic reduction of immigration from Europe in the early 1920s, because people in colonies of European countries could come in under the European quotas, and the quotas for the United Kingdom were large and far from filled. Under the McCarran–Walter Act of 1952, however, this loophole was closed, and colonial possessions were limited to token quotas of 100. But with the passage of the immigration act of 1965, West Indians, who had established immigrant communities in New York City relatively recently, were able to make use of the preferences for family relations in the act. Immigration from the English-speaking West Indies (as well as Haiti and the Dominican Republic) zoomed.

The new immigrant blacks are doing better than the blacks of native origin. The 1980 census showed the median family income of non-Hispanic West Indian headed families to be $15,645—not far short of native-headed family income of $17,631 and considerably above the median family income of blacks generally, $12,680. A remarkably low 6.7 percent received welfare, as against 14.7 percent for native-headed families. Female-headed families do (comparatively) well: their median income was $10,791 in 1980, against $7,625 for native-born female-headed family heads, who are dominantly black and Puerto Rican. One reason for this disparity was that more than 30 percent of employed West Indian women were working as nursing aides, registered nurses, or licensed practical nurses—relatively stable and better-paying jobs, compared with those generally available to black and Puerto Rican female family heads.

The third major component of the new immigration, the Asian, has also demonstrated a remarkable economic and educational validity. Asians make up an estimated 11 percent of the enrollment in the various senior and community colleges of the City University of New York, although even with recent increases, they probably do not make up more than 6 percent of the city's population. They also are making an impact on other, private, colleges and universities. One sees their economic enterprise in the Korean takeover of the fruit-and-vegetable markets and expansion into the important convenience grocery business, and in the Indian impact on newsstands and their expansion into stores selling magazines, newspapers, and notions. Although they are immediately visible to New Yorkers, these communities may have declined somewhat in socioeconomic profile in recent years. The first immigrant waves contained a large proportion of professionals who came under occupational preferences, but now relatives who may not have professional qualifications are coming in under family-relations preferences. Nevertheless, it is hard to believe that these groups will ever make up any large part of the underclass.

Indeed, one of the most striking figures in a recent Department of City Planning analysis of the census numbers on New York City Asians is that only 12.8 percent of Asian families with incomes below the poverty line received public assistance, compared with the 52 percent of non-Asian families in poverty. The failure to seek public assistance suggests that these families view themselves as low-income workers expecting to rise, rather than as failures in achieving economic independence.

This emphasis on educational and economic adaptation and success should not be taken to mean there is not substantial hardship among the immigrants. Many family members are required to work to make up a minimally adequate family income, in view of the low wages in the service industries; many work incredibly long hours in retail businesses; and thousands of Chinese women toil in the sweatshops of the rapidly expanding Chinatown. The educated of all immigrant groups suffer substantial downward mobility in occupation and social status, and all the hardships of the city afflict even the prosperous. Despite the highly visible impact of new immigrants on the small and independent business sector, immigrants are concentrated—except for the Asians, with their high levels of education—in private-sector wage employment and in manual occupations. Although manufacturing employment in New York has been radically reduced overall, immigrants continue to flow into this declining sector and today make up a disproportionate share of the workers within it. A study by Adriana Marshall reports that while the foreign-born totaled only 21 percent of all workers in the city, they made up 44 percent of workers in manufacturing employment in 1980. The immigrant inflow has held down the increase in manufacturing wages in New York, compared with other cities, and maintained a number of industries (apparel, plastics, footwear, leather goods, and the like) that without immigrant labor would very likely have declined further in the face of foreign competition.

One effect of immigrant inflow, then, is that it is maintaining low-paid industry in New York. Jobs are available, even if they are only poor jobs. People educated to middle-class status in their home countries will take jobs in manufacturing or services in the United States. As one Dominican woman put it, "In the United States, people are poor because they are lazy or want the government to take care of them. No one needs to be poor in the United States if they work hard." This seems, according to Patricia Pessar, a characteristic view—and the Dominicans, we should recall, are the least successful among the non-Puerto Rican Hispanic immigrants.

The striking and sobering fact is that the new immigrants are avoiding dependency, entering the work force, taking advantage of the city's educational opportunities.

This raises some difficult questions for the future. The success of these groups, it seems clear, will become more marked with time. They have taken the kind of immigrant path that was projected for blacks and Puerto Ricans 20 and 30 years ago, but which for some reason they have failed to follow. The old "tenement trail" that Samuel Lubell described 30 years ago in the *Future of American Politics* did not materialize for native blacks and Puerto Ricans. Despite the enormous changes in the American economy, which have been resorted to by many analysts to explain the failure of blacks and Puerto Ricans to take the trail in the numbers expected, it seems the trail is still open—on the basis of education (and not only the advanced education that we have been told is essential to get jobs in today's economy), on the basis of effort, and on the basis of family cooperation. Indeed, sheer hard work and the avoidance of the destructive mechanisms that ensure failure seem sufficient for socioeconomic mobility even in a changed New York.

How do we explain this startling superiority of the immigrants to native minority populations that have had the benefit of exposure to the city environment, with its educational and economic opportunities, for a longer period of time? Is it that there is no benefit to long-term exposure to the city, with its well-developed welfare institutions and underclass culture—which grew so markedly in the 1970s and on which we have made no impact at all despite 20 years of substantial effort?

We have to ponder this contrast, and try to understand it. But we also have to worry about what it will mean for the city as the native black and Puerto Rican population sees new immigrants—Hispanic, black, and Asian—passing them, and establishing the stable life and the platform for future advancement that still eludes them.

Chapter 4

GETTING AROUND NEW YORK

Jose A. Gomez-Ibañez

New York City and its suburbs face serious transportation problems in the next few decades. The suburbs, which need to accommodate rapid traffic growth, are likely to accept as solutions to their transportation problems more road construction and, to the extent that road construction is too costly or politically sensitive, more development of outlying areas. In downtown Manhattan, the core of the metropolitan area, the problems are far less tractable, for they involve moving millions of people from points all over the region to a few square miles at the lower end of a small island.

More cars and rising public-transit fares threaten to make travel to Manhattan an increasingly frustrating and costly experience in the coming years. The best hope for maintaining accessibility lies in a combination of policies that would allocate scarce and congested highway space more sensibly and encourage more forms of lower-cost, more-flexible public transportation. Such policies would force motorists to pay their way, increase competition, and permit market mechanisms to adjust the various factors of supply, demand, location, price, and quality.

AUTO USE AND TRAFFIC CONGESTION

The ever-increasing transportation congestion in Manhattan has little to do with growth in total travel volume. Manhattan employment has actually remained relatively stable at around 2 million for several decades, and although jobs do appear to be increasingly concentrated below 60th Street, the overall number of commuters has not increased. Rather, it appears clear that the automobile is capturing an increasing share of Manhattan-bound workers. This may seem somewhat surprising, since the vast majority of Manhattan-bound travelers use public transit and transit receives the most attention from transportation planners. Nevertheless, auto's share of Manhattan-bound commuting trips has grown steadily, from 10.4 percent in 1960 to 15.8 percent in 1980, and although a 15.8 percent share may still seem rather small, it reflects a 52 percent increase in the number of persons trying to commute to Manhattan by automobile.

It should be noted that total rush-hour auto traffic to Manhattan has not grown quite as fast as commuting traffic, probably because commuters have, to some extent, displaced noncommuting motorists during rush hours. Thus, while the census reports a 52 percent increase in auto commuters between 1960 and 1980, traffic counts indicate that total auto traffic to the Manhattan Central Business District (CBD) increased by only 35 percent between 1956 and 1984.

Manhattan's ability to accommodate further auto traffic is very limited. The key constraint is that Manhattan is an island reachable only by bridges or tunnels, and these river crossings were already operating at 92 percent capacity during rush hours in 1983. When volumes on highways, tunnels, and bridges exceed 85 percent of their capacity, stop-and-go traffic develops and delays increase exponentially with additional vehicles. The largest and most convenient facilities for entering Manhattan, such as the Lincoln and Holland tunnels or the Brooklyn and Queensboro bridges, are at 100 percent capacity, which means that traffic volumes exceed capacity during the rush hour and long queues form that are only dissipated in the late morning.

While past traffic growth was accommodated through major expansion in the Manhattan river crossing capacity, the era of new bridges and tunnels appears to be over. The number of traffic lanes crossing the Hudson River increased from 16 to 24 between the early 1950s and the present, with the opening of additional tubes in the Lincoln Tunnel in 1957 and the completion of the second deck of the George Washington Bridge in 1962. But high costs and political controversy now make the construction of such new facilities impossible. Even if a new tunnel the size of the Lincoln Tunnel were built, it would increase Manhattan river crossing capacity by less than 10 percent, or less than a decade's traffic growth at past rates.

Whether auto traffic will continue to grow depends in part on whether its underlying causes are short- or long-term ones. A comparison of Manhattan cordon counts and employment data suggests that employment changes do not account for much of the increase in auto use. Thus, auto use may continue to grow even if Manhattan job levels stagnate. For the past 30 years, the number of people entering Manhattan on a typical weekday has fluctuated around 3 million—the exact number depending closely on the level of downtown employment, which increased by 12 percent between 1960 and 1969, fell by 9 percent between 1969 and 1977, and has been rising since 1977. But the auto's share of person-trips to Manhattan has increased steadily, even while employment was declining, and the number of persons entering the Manhattan CBD by car over the long term has also risen steadily despite employment fluctuations.

The real culprit behind increased auto use is rising household incomes. More income increases people's ability and willingness to pay for the amenities associated with automobile commuting: most notably, door-to-door service, privacy, seating, and often reduced travel time. Median household income in the New York metropolitan region increased by 18 percent in real terms (i.e. net of inflation) between 1960 and 1970, although it declined slightly between 1970 and 1980. It is unclear whether income will continue to grow as rapidly as in the 1960s, but any income growth will add to auto's share of commuting trips.

Another, less significant development that has encouraged car use has been the move by many Manhattan workers to homes in the outer boroughs and suburbs. With rising incomes, households tend to upgrade the quality of their housing and to seek features more readily available in the suburbs. Because newly developed suburban areas have low densities and are hard to serve by conventional public transit, the automobile becomes a relatively more attractive mode of transportation.

Finally, deterioration in the quality of public transport service has encouraged the growing use of cars. Contrary to popular impressions, public transportation has not gotten significantly more expensive or crowded. With the exception of a brief period in the late 1960s, when fares rose abruptly, transit fare increases have only barely outpaced inflation, so that over the long haul transit rides have not become much more expensive relative to other goods and services. Today's $1 fare is the equivalent of 22 cents in 1950, when the actual fare was 15 cents. The degree of rush-hour crowding on subway trains approaching the Manhatten CBD is also similar now

Table 1 Trends in Employment in and Travel to the Manhattan Central Business District on a Typical Fall Weekday, 1950–84[a]

	Employment (000)	Persons Entering by All Modes (000)		Persons Entering By Auto, Taxi, and Truck (000)		Percent of Persons by Auto, Taxi, and Truck (000)		Vehicles Entering All Day (000)
		All day	7–10 AM	All day	7–10 AM[b]	All day	7–10 AM[b]	
1950	2,230	n.a.	n.a.	n.a.	n.a.	n.a.	n.a.	n.a.
1956	2,140	3,313	1,555	828	190	24.9	12.1	519
1960	2,005	3,349	1,627	954	220	28.4	13.5	590
1969	2,255	n.a.	n.a.	n.a	n.a.	n.a.	n.a.	n.a.
1971	2,120	3,167	1,574	926	233	29.1	14.8	646
1977	1,825	2,862	1,395	924	211	32.2	15.1	645
1980	1,945	3,013	1,497	930	214	30.8	14.6	648
1984	2,030	3,274	1,551	1,112	256	33.9	16.5	734
Percentage change								
1956–71	−0.9%	−4.4%	+1.3%	+11.8%	+23.1%			+24.5%
1971–77	−13.9%	−9.6%	−11.4%	−0.2%	−9.3%			−0.2%
1977–84	+11.2%	+14.4%	+11.1%	+20.3%	+21.4%			+13.8%

[a]Employment data from Regional Plan Association, "MTA Ridership: Trends and Prospects," paper no. 1 of Transit on Track, a joint project of the Regional Plan Association and New York Metropolitan Transportation Council, *Hub-Bound Travel 1984*, December 1985.
[b]Calculated by the author from data in New York Metropolitan Transportation Council, *Hub-Bound Travel 1984*.
[c]Preliminary estimate: New York Metropolitan Transportation Council, 1987.

to what it was in the 1950s and 1960s. Moreover, transit service has actually improved in certain important respects, such as the availability of air conditioning and smoother and quieter rides for some trips. On the other hand, the subways are less reliable, clean, and secure than they were in the past, and breakdowns on the average subway car increased from an average of one per year in the 1960s to six per year in 1981, although the rate is now declining due to new equipment and renewed maintenance. Also of importance is the fact that crime on the transit system has increased dramatically, although transit crime is part of a larger social problem and represents only a small fraction of all crime in New York.

PROSPECTS FOR CONTROLLING AUTO GROWTH

If declining transit service were more important in encouraging driving than were increasing incomes or suburbanization, the restoration of satisfactory transit service might offer some real hope of reducing auto use. However, evidence strongly suggests the contrary. Not all public transit has lost ground to the auto over the past three decades. The subway's share of Manhattan-bound commuters fell much more than the auto's share grew, while the commuter railroads, the Port Authority Trans-Hudson (PATH) subway, buses, and rail lines that connect Manhattan with suburban areas of Long Island, New Jersey, upstate New York, and Connecticut increased their shares slightly. All the bus growth was on express lines, many of which serve suburban areas beyond the subway's reach—a further confirmation of the importance of suburbanization. However, even on express bus routes that parallel subway lines, patronage increased because rising incomes and declining subway security and reliability increased commuters' ability and willingness to pay the premium fares.

These findings have important implications for efforts to slow the rate of auto traffic growth. In the first place, public transportation services to Manhattan must be made more competitive, both by improving service on existing subways and buses and by encouraging innovative new services, such as express buses or van pools. Moreover, the improvements must be made both within the city and in the suburbs. Usually the suburbs are assumed to be the culprit, and planners focus on the possibility of extending rail and bus lines into low-density areas to intercept motorists. But in fact, most of the increase in auto use has come from within the city itself, both

Table 2 Percentage of Persons Entering the Manhattan Central Business District by Different Travel Modes, 1956–84[a]

	All Day			8:00 to 9:00 AM		
	1956	1984	Difference	1956	1984	Difference
Autos, taxis and trucks	25.2	33.9	+8.7	9.3	11.9	+2.6
NYCTA subway	58.1	46.6	−11.5	69.3	61.3	−8.0
Bus[b]	7.5	9.0	+2.5	5.4	9.8	+4.4
Commuter railroad and PATH subway	8.1	9.5	+1.4	14.6	16.0	+1.4
Ferry	1.1	1.0	−0.1	1.3	0.9	−0.4

[a]The 1956 data from Region Plan Association, "MTA Transit Ridership: Trends and Prospects," paper no. 1 of Transit on Track, a joint project of the Regional Plan Association and New York Citizens for Balanced Transportation, March 1985, pp. 39–40. The 1984 figures are from New York Metropolitan Transportation Council, Hub-Bound Travel, 1984, December 1985, pp. 30, 44, and 47.
[b]Bus figure includes trolley service in 1956 and the Roosevelt Island tramway in 1984. Both the trolley and the tram account for less than 0.1 percent of all persons in 1956 and 1984, respectively.

from outlying areas that have more in common with the suburbs than the city, and from neighborhoods that are, by conventional standards, relatively well served by public transport.

This analysis also implies, however, that we cannot stem the tide of growing auto traffic with public transportation improvements alone. As real incomes continue to rise, public transportation services will have to improve simply to keep the auto's share of commuters constant. A subway system restored to the service standards of the 1950s, even with modern conveniences such as air conditioning, would not recapture the same share of commuters living near its stations as it enjoyed 30 years ago. Either public transportation services must improve well beyond the standards of 30 or 40 years ago and keep on improving, or some direct and sharp disincentives against the use of automobiles, such as higher highway tolls, will be needed as well.

PUBLIC TRANSIT COSTS AND DEFICITS

Because New York's highway space is so limited and congested, public transportation dominates New York travel to a degree unequalled in any other North American city. In 1980, public transport was the principal means of commuting for 44 percent of all metropolitan New York workers. By contrast, only 8 percent of all U.S. metropolitan workers use public transport to commute to work. As a consequence, metropolitan New York accounts for about one-third of all the public transport riders in the country, even though it accounts for less than one-20th of the nation's population.

Despite the advantage of a nearly captive market, New York's public transportation agencies face growing financial difficulties that cast doubt on their ability to retain their current ridership, let alone improve service enough to stem the rise in auto use. These problems are most readily illustrated for the New York City Transit Authority (NYCTA), whose subways and buses carry about three-quarters of all public transport commuters to the Manhattan CBD. Similar problems exist on the commuter railroads, which are operated by NYCTA's parent agency, the Metropolitan Transportation Authority, and on PATH.

Thirty years ago the NYCTA's operating expenses were financed entirely out of passenger fare receipts and concession rentals. Beginning in 1957, the NYCTA has operated at a deficit, and in recent years user revenues have covered only about half of operating expenses, with the balance made up by subsidies from local, state, and federal governments.

Transit deficits grew because transit costs increased faster than fares. Although ridership declined between 1956 and 1984, fare receipts actually increased during this period faster than inflation, growing 31 percent in real terms as a result of a 55 percent real increase in the fare that was imposed largely in the space of a few years during the late 1960s.

The 31 percent increase in real user revenues, however, was swamped by a 157 percent increase in real expenses, including operating expenses plus debt service but excluding current capital outlays. Since ridership declined by 16 percent during that period, the real cost per passenger increased by an astonishing 201 percent, or nearly four times faster than average fares. Virtually all of the increase was operating expenses; debt service has been a relatively minor portion of NYCTA's budget, because most capital expenditures have been financed by grants from state and federal governments that do not appear on current expense accounts.

The Regional Plan Association has suggested that over half of the cost increase from 1960 to 1984 was attributable to rising labor costs. It points out that the real operating cost per passenger increased from about 50 cents per rider to over $1.50 per rider measured in 1985 dollars. Labor costs accounted for 53 to 58 cents per rider of the increase: 35 to 38 cents because wage rates increased faster than inflation, and 15 to 23 cents because of declines in productivity. Wage increases were rapid in the 1960s but slowed during the fiscal crisis of the late 1970s, when some wage and benefit increases were actually lower than inflation. However, the wage savings of the late 1970s were offset by accelerated declines in labor productivity, probably caused in large part by ham-fisted work-force reductions borne disproportionately by the maintenance departments that eventually contributed to car failures, derailments, track fires, and other problems. Many of the maintenance workers were hired back in the 1980s, and labor contracts negotiated since 1980 again call for wage increases that outstrip inflation.

Changes in ridership patterns have been almost as important as labor in increasing costs, adding 27 cents per rider to subway costs and 39 cents per rider to bus costs in 1985 dollars. Falling ridership has lowered the average number of riders per vehicle, and longer journeys to the suburbs have increased the length of routes. NYCTA management was partly to blame for failing to cut frequencies or adjust services promptly in response to changing ridership levels. In fairness, however, managers often faced strong pressures against service changes from riders and their elected representatives.

Nonlabor costs have accounted for relatively little of the operating-cost increases. Rising energy prices have added only 2 to 4 cents per passenger, both because energy has never been a very large portion of the transit operating budget and because the NYCTA negotiated access to some low-cost hydroelectric power between 1975 and 1984. Other increased real outlays of 13–15 cents per passenger were due to expedited purchasing of materials and parts to deal with deferred maintenance, and to higher payments for public liability.

If operating expenses continue to increase at recent rates, by the year 2000 the cost per passenger will rise to $3.50 or more in constant dollars. Unless present government subsidies are tripled, such an increase would require either drastic service reductions or a tripling of real token prices, to $3 per ride. Even if operating expenses increase only at the slower rates of the 1975–80 period, real costs per passenger will increase to almost $2.50, requiring roughly a doubling in either government aid or token prices.

CAPITAL COSTS AND THE NEW CAPITAL PROGRAM

For the past two decades capital costs have been a relatively minor financial burden for New York's transit agencies, because grants from federal or state governments funded most capital spending. Federal transit capital grants paid 66 to 80 percent of the costs of new subway expansions and buses and subway cars purchased since 1965. But relying on federal and state capital grants had become an increasingly untenable strategy by the early 1980s, not only because of cutbacks in federal grants under the Reagan Administration, but also because the near collapse of the transit system in the late 1970s made it obvious that the pace of capital spending had to be accelerated. The capital programs of the 1960s and 1970s had focused largely on visible, politically attractive projects, such as construction of new lines and vehicle replacement, and relatively little on refurbishing of existing track, signals, power distribution systems, and structures.

In 1982 the Metropolitan Transportation Authority announced a $12 billion, ten-year capital spending program, half to be financed by grants from city and state agencies and half by bonds secured by passenger revenues. These revenue bonds were the first major transit revenue bond issues to be offered in the United States for many decades. The underwriter's prospectus stated that the bonds could be repaid, if all government aid were stopped, only by raising fares to four or five times current levels.

Costs per passenger would probably increase rapidly without the capital program, as worn-out facilities and equipment caused more and more operating problems. But the capital program is unlikely to reduce costs per passenger below current levels—and in fact, is more likely to raise them. By increasing NYCTA debt service to about $225 million per year, the first phase (1982–86) of the capital program will probably require a 20-cent increase in the present $1 token. The planned second phase (1987–89) will add another $466 million to debt sevice, potentially pushing up the token by another 40 cents. The 60-cents-per-passenger added debt service may be partially offset if restoration of the aging physical plant generates operating-cost savings.

Savings of 60 cents per rider, however, would mean a rollback of more than half the real operating-cost increases accumulated over the past 25 years, most of which were caused by factors largely unrelated to the decline of the capital stock, such as higher wages. In a sense, the NYCTA was living on borrowed money during the 1960s and the 1970s: NYCTA's cost and deficits for those decades were understated because the budgets of the transit agencies excluded charges for depreciation. The transit authorities are now finally being forced to pay for depreciation that they already incurred. The capital program cannot substitute for increased efforts to control transit operating costs and wages and, indeed, may make such efforts more important.

USING HIGHWAY FACILITIES MORE EFFICIENTLY

The trends of rising traffic congestion and escalating transit deficits are so strong that longer term and politically difficult counter-measures will be needed to ensure that New York's core remains accessible through the year 2000. Among the most important measures to avoid gridlock are policies aimed at using New York's scarce street and highway capacity more efficiently, particularly by discouraging private automobiles in favor of buses, commuter vans, car pools, and other high-occupancy vehicles that require less street space per passenger carried than do private automobiles. Two ways to encourage the use of high-occupancy vehicles are to create exclusive lanes for buses and other high-occupancy vehicles and to impose substantial tolls on critical bridge and tunnel connections to the Manhattan CBD.

During the 8:00–9.00 AM rush hour, buses carry almost as many people into the Manhattan CBD as do automobiles, taxis, and trucks. The buses carry an average load of 47 passengers versus the auto's 1.6. Using the traffic engineer's rule of thumb that a bus takes up about as much street space as 2 or 3 cars (allowing for the buses' size, poorer maneuverability, acceleration, and braking), in 1984 the buses carried 45 percent of the persons entering Manhattan on streets but used only 5–7 percent of the street space.

New York was among the first U.S. cities to adopt exclusive lanes and other measures to give high-occupancy vehicles priority in traffic. The approaches to several of the bridges and tunnels leading to Manhattan have exclusive bus lanes; the Port Authority's bus lane entering the Lincoln Tunnel is perhaps one of the most heavily used and best-known bus lanes in the world. Curbside lanes for buses are reserved along several important avenues in Manhattan, at the cost of increased congestion on the remaining traffic lanes and an aggressive ticketing-and-fine program. An expansion of New York's reserved-lane system, to protect efficient vehicles from congestion, offers one of the best chances for holding or increasing public transportation ridership in the future.

If the private market provided highway access to Manhattan, tolls would be higher, since higher prices are the market mechanism that keeps demand and supply in balance when demand is growing but supply cannot readily be increased. Higher tolls would not only reduce total vehicular traffic, but would also encourage car pools and other higher-occupancy vehicles as well, since the toll per passenger declines as the number of passengers per vehicle increases.

New York has been slow to take advantage of tolls to encourage more-efficient street use. The half of the roadway capacity across the rivers that is controlled by the city has never been tolled, and the Triborough Bridge and Tunnel Authority (TBTA) has been raising tolls on the bridges and tunnels it controls only at about the rate of inflation. The Port Authority of New York and New Jersey (PANYNJ) has not even raised tolls as fast as inflation on the Hudson River crossings; its 1988 roundtrip toll of $3 was the equivalent in 1960 dollars of less than 28 cents, although the 1960 toll rate was $1. PANYNJ, moreover, sells a multiple-ticket commuter book at a 30 percent discount, or 52 cents for the round trip in 1960 dollars.

Many of the usual objections to auto tolls are less compelling in Manhattan than in other cities. The administrative cost and motorist inconvenience is small, because Manhattan is an island with a limited number of entry points, most of which are already tolled. Also, higher tolls are probably also less of a financial burden on Manhattan motorists, who tend to be relatively well-off and have comparatively good public-transit alternatives.

Potentially more troubling is the objection that Manhattan auto commuters are such a special breed that tolls might well have relatively little effect on their behavior. Commuters who drive to Manhattan are alleged to be so wealthy that they are relatively insensitive to increases; tolls represent a small fraction of their total costs, compared with parking fees, ownership and operating costs, and the high value they place on time and convenience. Similarly, trucks making deliveries to Manhattan might be unaffected by toll increases because of the lack of alternatives.

Some simulations do show, however, that highway traffic could be reduced by 5–10 percent by raising the tolls on the untolled and PANYNJ bridges to the levels charged on TBTA facilities. The imposition of tolls on the free bridges across the Harlem and East rivers would generate most of the benefits. Because motorists who use them can save a roundtrip toll of $4.00, those facilities carry roughly 80 percent of the traffic from the east and the north, even though they represent far less than 80 percent of the capacity. Studies in the mid-1970s estimated that charging users of the untolled facilities the same amount as users of tolled crossings would reduce the number of autos crossing into Manhattan over the East and Harlem rivers by 5–13 percent and might cause a 3 percent reduction in crossings on the Hudson River as well. The PANYNJ estimated in 1978 that doubling the tolls during the peak hours only and eliminating the commuter discount would reduce traffic on Hudson River crossings by 3.5 percent.

Traffic reductions in the range of 4–13 percent won't solve New York's traffic problems, but they would offset 5–10 years of normal growth and would significantly improve traffic flow as well, since congestion increases exponentially with traffic volume and the variations in toll rates encourage some motorists to go out of their way to use untolled or undertolled options. PANYNJ's 1978 toll study estimated that a 3.5 percent reduction on Hudson River crossings due to elimination of commuter ticket books and doubling of peak tolls would reduce traffic delays by 23 percent, or nearly 1800 vehicle-hours every workday. The projected saving in delay time would be twice as large, moreover, if the PANYNJ retained the ticket books, which decrease the average transaction time at the toll booth and significantly reduce delays.

From the economist's perspective, rush-hour motorists fail to "pay their way" by not recognizing the delays that their use of the road imposes on other motorists. When an automobile enters traffic, its presence delays the rest of the vehicles using the road, bridge, or tunnel. These delays are relatively trivial when the facility is lightly used, but they can become enormous as traffic volumes approach the facility's maximum capacity and traffic jams or queues start to develop. The logic of a highway toll is to make motorists pay for the real costs they impose on others, thereby bringing congestion down to more socially desirable levels.

ENCOURAGING PRIVATE MASS TRANSPORTATION: EXPRESS BUSES AND VANS

Attractive alternatives to the automobile are the fast-growing private express-bus and van services that provide mass transportation, largely without the help of government subsidies and often in areas poorly served by conventional subway or commuter rail lines. Unfortunately, New York's public transit authorities have been slow to recognize the potential advantages of private mass transit and have actually placed unnecessary impediments in its path.

Express buses were started in 1968 as private mass-transportation services. The NYCTA initially feared the competition with its subways but began to offer its own express buses once their popularity was demonstrated. NYCTA now provides about half of all the express-bus service offered in the city; ten different private companies provide the balance. Together, private and public express buses now carry over 6 percent of daily and 8 percent of morning rush-hour travelers to the CBD. Forty percent of the riders come from the boroughs of New York City, almost none from the northern suburbs.

Private commuter van services, which are not yet as important as private express buses, made their first appearance only in 1980, during a transit strike, and still face relatively strong harassment and ticketing from public agencies. Van operations tend to be of two types: express services to the CBD and feeder services connecting residential areas with subway stops. As of 1985, CBD-bound express vans carried 8,000 riders, or about 0.5 percent of the persons entering the CBD in the peak periods. Thirty percent of these riders travel from New Jersey, 25 percent from Staten Island, and 19 percent from Queens. Feeder van service to subway stops carried over 2,500 passengers during the morning rush hours in 1985, mostly in Queens, Brooklyn, and the Bronx.

Express buses and vans attract riders by eliminating transfers and offering the assurance of a seat, schedule reliability, and physical security. These amenities are so important to riders that some express-bus lines compete in neighborhoods with subway service despite the fact that their fare is triple the subway fare. In some cases, where physical security is the dominant concern, express buses serve as a mechanism for maintaining racial and economic segregation—the most obvious example being the express buses from the north Bronx, which enable riders to avoid the subway stations in the south Bronx and Harlem on their way to Manhattan. In other neighborhoods, however, physical security is only one of several amenities for which riders are willing to pay a premium fare.

Of the important public benefits flowing from the private express and van services, the foremost is the financial advantage. Beyond the use of public streets, the vans receive no government funding, and the private bus companies receive city subsidies only for their unprofitable local routes, not for their express services. Public bus services cost more to operate than private buses do, and new subway extensions to outlying areas where residential populations are growing would cost $100 to $200 million per mile to build. Secondly, by offering premium service to these areas, private express buses and vans may discourage riders from shifting to the automobile even as their household incomes rise.

The principal objection to the expansion of private bus and van services is that they increase public-transit deficits because they draw most of their riders from public transit rather than from cars. Only 6–9 percent of express-bus riders are former auto users, whereas roughly 50 percent used public transit before. A slightly smaller proportion of van riders are former auto users. But the charge that private bus and van services increase public transit deficits by skimming off the "cream" of profitable services generally ignores the cost saving to the NYCTA from not having to carry the passengers diverted.

The only serious study of the cream-skimming issue in New York examined private vans connecting Staten Island and Manhattan, which by 1982 had reduced ridership on competing NYCTA express-bus lines by as much as 17 percent. The study found, however, that

NYCTA was losing an average of 85 cents per passenger on its express buses from Staten Island, despite premium fares of $2.50. So on Staten Island at least, commuter van competition could actually reduce the transit deficit as long as NYCTA cut back its schedules as replacement private van and bus services appeared.

The competition between private buses and vans and NYCTA subway lines, which has been most troubling and controversial, probably does not involve cream-skimming either. In 1984, when the subway fare was 90 cents, subway operating costs averaged $1.54 per passenger, excluding outlays for transit police, capital engineering, and debt service. Critics of private buses contend that subway service may be profitable even at a 90-cent token, because the marginal or incremental cost savings from not carrying a passenger are far below the average cost, and below even the 90 cent fare. Marginal costs are low, they argue, because the NYCTA expenses for station attendants, cleaning, signals, and other costly activities are not affected by passenger volume. This argument overlooks the fact that most of the riders lost to private buses are rush-hour commuters, and extra rush-hour trains and crews are particularly expensive to provide because they are often underutilized during the rest of the day. Peak-hour subway riders also tend to take longer trips than do off-peak riders, which further adds to the cost of serving them. In addition, the marginal cost figures should include a charge for depreciation or debt service, since lower rush-hour ridership reduces vehicle and other capital equipment needs. A detailed cost accounting would probably show that the marginal cost of serving a rush-hour subway rider is well above the 90-cent fare and that private bus and van competition reduces rather than increases the NYCTA deficit.

Another objection to public express buses and vans is that they add to traffic congestion. Buses and vans often block downtown streets, especially when picking up or discharging passengers, and residents along several key Manhattan arterials complain that heavy bus traffic creates noise, pollution, and safety problems. The charge that express buses and vans increase traffic congestion is probably unfounded, however. In the first place, the argument overlooks riders who would eventually shift from the subway to autos if express buses were not available. Moreover, buses are so efficient in their use of street space that they reduce congestion as long as only 10 percent or more of the bus passengers are former or would-be auto users. Vans in feeder service almost surely reduce traffic congestion, since they usually compete with poorly loaded local buses, and express vans reduce traffic congestion if only 10 to 15 percent of their riders would otherwise switch to auto. Space for layovers and for picking up and dropping off passengers may pose a problem, but dedication of scarce street space for loading and unloading zones is justified by the potential reduction in auto growth.

Despite the benefits that private buses and vans offer, many government agencies tender them only grudging tolerance rather than encouragement and promotion. Some government regulation is clearly needed to assure adequate insurance, safety, and minimal disruption of traffic flow. But the city has been extremely short-sighted in designing regulations that prevent private companies from competing with public agencies, that restrict their use of key streets, and that place the burden of proof on them to demonstrate that extra service is needed. It would make more sense to limit the number of cars using certain avenues rather than the number of buses. And since private bus and van services are more likely to reduce than to increase public transit deficits, the burden of proof should be placed on the public transit agencies to show that their services are making a profit. Placing the burden on the private applicants risks stifling the initiative that developed these services when no public agency saw the need.

Since subsidies only reduce the incentives to control costs and find new markets, the present city policy of not subsidizing private express buses seems appropriate, although it would be more so if auto tolls were raised to make motorists more nearly pay their way. If entry and exit in the private bus and van industry were made easier, the city might go even further by deregulating fares, allowing them to float at competitive levels. Liberalized entry and exit coupled with deregulated fares would offer private bus and van operators tremendous incentives and flexibility to keep their costs low and to search out markets where services are needed.

STRENGTHENING PUBLIC MASS TRANSIT: GOVERNANCE

The way that public transit is governed and funded must be radically changed if the system is ever to address its fundamental problems. The basic problems of cost increases, escalating wage rates, declining transit productivity, and unresponsive services remain unresolved, not because they are not well-known, but rather because the solutions require politically difficult decisions. Well-organized and influential transit unions regard wage increases in excess of inflation, with few productivity increases to support the wage gains, as their right. Local community groups and elected officials resist service cutbacks, no matter how poorly used the lines, while constituencies for new services that might be needed remain poorly mobilized.

Public subsidies make problems worse by weakening the incentives of transit managers to make the tough choices necessary. In New York, as in most cities, rapid growth in public subsidies, particularly after 1965, coincided with the beginning of escalating real wages, deteriorating labor productivity, and underutilized services. While cause and effect cannot be fully separated, most observers suspect that the availability of subsidies leads to increased dependence on them.

Diffused responsibility for funding mass-transit deficits also contributes to an inability to make tough choices. When the New York City Transit Authority was formed in 1953, it was supposed to support its operations out of the fare box, with the city contributing only capital outlays. This position slowly eroded as first the city, and later the federal government and the state, assumed major financial responsibilities for funding capital and operating deficits.

Since each contributor pays only a portion of the costs, however, none feels fully responsible or accountable for the system's performance. Transit management can blame state and local government for freezing fares and service without providing enough resources, while the state and local politicians can blame management for being incompetent and each other for not contributing a fair share. In spite of the cost, moreover, the mayor, City Council, governor, and state legislature like transit subsidies, which give them influence over one of the most important public services in the region. Everyone wants to be involved, but so many are that no one is accountable.

The best form of governance for the transit system would be one that gives the directors stronger incentives to control costs and the power and responsibility to do so. One obvious possibility would be to "privatize" the system and require that it be operated for a profit. Since transit ridership is relatively insensitive to fare increases—a 100 percent fare increase, about what would be needed to cover operating costs, would cause only a 10–20 percent loss in ridership—the system could be self-supporting with only a modest loss in ridership. Ridership losses would be even lower if motorists were also forced to pay their way as was suggested earlier, and if privatization brought cost and productivity improvements. Encouragement of private bus and van lines would also reduce the chance that this new private corporation would have an effective monopoly on transit services.

The key potential drawback of the private solution would lie in its impact on traffic congestion approaching Manhattan. A 10 or 20 percent reduction in transit ridership might easily translate into a much larger percentage increase in autos commuting to Manhattan, since auto commuters are a much smaller share of the present base. New York can only cope with transit fare hikes if auto tolls are increased to more realistic levels, and if private and public express buses and vans, protected from congestion by more exclusive lanes, are also available as an alternative.

Conventional wisdom to the contrary, higher fares probably would not be a serious burden on New York's poor. A 50 percent increase would cost the commuter at most an additional $250 per year—and probably much less, given that some of the burden of the fare increase is likely to be shifted to employers in the form of higher wages. Those transit riders who are poor tend to use off-peak and shorter-distance services that cost less to provide, and ought to be subject to the smallest fare hikes. Indeed, on many transit systems, high-income riders appear to be more heavily subsidized than low-income travelers.

An alternative to the private solution might be a new transit and commuter rail authority, still accountable to the public and subsidized but given strictly limited access to subsidies. The availability of subsidies would reduce the potential problems of traffic congestion and hardships for low-income riders. But subsidies would be strictly limited (say, to certain bridge and tunnel toll receipts or to a set percentage tax on gasoline), so that managers would still have incentives to make hard choices about costs, services, and fares. State and city officials would appoint the authority's board of directors, since public funds would be involved, but the responsibility for solving problems and the resources to do so would rest entirely with the board.

The obvious problem with the authority alternative is how to limit access to increasing subsidies. Subsidies for the original NYCTA of 1953 were supposed to be restricted to capital expenses, but that principle was eroded as the city first picked up the costs of the transit police and then gradually made payments for more and more expenses. Any limit on subsidies is bound to be inherently arbitrary and, therefore, hard to maintain. Even if the limit is credible when initially established, changes such as metropolitan population or employment shifts will always provide excuses for altering subsidy arrangements.

A CONGESTED FUTURE

As bad as traffic congestion and transit deficits are now, they may have to get far worse before the majority of New Yorkers feel the need to take fairly drastic measures. It is clear that traffic congestion is going to get worse, perhaps by a great deal, and that transit costs per rider will also be substantially higher—perhaps twice their current levels in constant dollars. To some extent, greater congestion itself will eventually slow the shift to autos. The net result will be to increase the cost in both travel time and money of commuting to and from downtown.

Whether such an increase in commuting costs will reduce the level of economic activity in the CBD is a crucial concern. All other things being equal, any increase in commuting costs will clearly make the CBD a less attractive location for business. Downtown employers will have to pay their workers higher wages to compensate them for the greater costs of commuting, and this will put downtown firms at a disadvantage in competing with businesses located in the suburbs or in other metropolitan areas.

This concern with downtown employment levels is probably a little exaggerated, however. In the first place, higher commuting costs increase the incentives of workers to live closer in, so as to save on commuting time and expense. So, even if the number of Manhattan jobs declines, some increase in the residential population may occur to help keep the city lively. Whether Manhattan's residential population would increase or not would depend upon whether the incentive for downtown workers to move closer in was enough to offset the decline in the number of people holding downtown jobs who need to live within commuting range. Any increase in the close-in population would also mean more pressure on housing rents and prices and the construction of new housing in Manhattan and adjacent boroughs.

Moreover, the potential loss in Manhattan jobs (and the gain in Manhattan residents) is likely to be small even if commuting costs increase substantially, because many factors besides commuting costs and wage rates influence the location of households and business. A 1986 study by the Urban Research Center at New York University,

91

for example, revealed that employees of a Manhattan corporate headquarters had an *average* commute of 67 minutes each way (70 minutes for executives and managers), whereas those in suburban campus-style headquarters spent an average of only 33 minutes commuting (32 minutes for executives). Clearly, powerful attractions hold businesses in Manhattan despite the enormous commuting costs. And the desire for a backyard for children to play in, better public schools, safety, and other concerns will keep workers from moving into the city even if commuting costs increase significantly.

It is unclear whether a slightly altered distribution of jobs and residences would be good or bad for the city or the region. A decline in Manhattan's employment levels would not be all bad for the city, since the loss in tax base would be partly offset by reduced demands for city services and the gain in residential population that might accompany a job loss would offer some compensating advantages.

The real cost of a more congested future is less likely to be the shifts in jobs and population than the enormous and unnecessary increase in the social and economic resources used in commuting. Wasted resources are partly reflected in higher government budgets. If transit costs increase rapidly, for example, the metropolitan area will spend hundreds of millions of dollars more per year than necessary to provide transportation. Similarly, if auto growth remains unchecked, the pressure to expand an unnecessarily large road network will grow enormous. Given the pressing social problems in New York, the waste of public resources cannot be taken lightly. But perhaps more important than the government outlays would be the increased frustration and inconvenience in the everyday life of New Yorkers. The added hours they will have to waste commuting is time that might otherwise be spent with their families, at productive work, or on pleasurable leisure. Increased congestion and commuting costs would represent an enormous and unnecessary reduction in the quality of life in New York.

Chapter 5

CLEARING THE REGULATORY CLUTTER

Harold M. Hochman

Persistently and pervasively, through licensing requirements, development regulations, and price controls, government in New York City has displayed an uncommon gift for interfering with private behavior and turning good intentions into harmful results.

While few of its specific practices are distinctive, New York's regulations are unmatched in breadth and, in some instances, stringency. The city requires licenses and permits to protect consumers from risk (putatively), and producers from competition (inadvertently), for 600–700 different activities. The administrative code and municipal ordinances restrict development through building codes and bulk requirements (which specify conditions of construction and occupancy) and zoning rules (which limit what can be done at particular locations). Moreover, New York City controls prices in 16 areas. Some of these such as apartment rents or taxi fares, are much discussed, but others are obscure. In addition, the state imposes controls, such as the minimum markups in retail liquor sales that were recently invalidated by the courts, in many more. Indeed, for a business to locate in New York as matters now stand, the advantages must be overwhelming.

Basic economic changes and unsound fiscal practices, not regulation, precipitated the extensive deterioration in New York's economic fortunes during the 1960s and 1970s. But the panoply of regulatory practices in which New York indulged, ostensibly to "protect" its residents, its labor force, and its visitors from predatory activities, had systemically weakened New York's economy, both by raising the private costs of everyday activities and by making the city a more troublesome and expensive place in which to conduct

93

business. Indeed, in their existing form, some regulations seemed to serve no practical public purpose, but rather to promote the private goals of the regulated interests themselves by protecting them from competition.

Admittedly, only a small minority of the regulations seemed totally unnecessary. Usually, the problem lay in their administration, in their intensity, and in the interaction among ostensibly sensible rules that made the cure worse than the disease. Whereas regulation, properly administered, should function like laser surgery, New York often appeared to be wielding a butcher knife, carving more deeply into the substance of market transactions than public objectives warranted, and ignoring the implicit epidemiology of its actions. There seemed to be little or no understanding that tinkering with the self-correcting properties of the market process to enhance the good of each ultimately operates to the detriment of all.

Beginning in the 1970s, there have been some changes in New York's regulatory practices, initiated primarily by officials charged with making the city more attractive to business. These include some changes in licensing, in occasional opportunities for "one-stop-service" to reduce the difficulties of coping with multiple licensing requirements, and in inspections. Such cosmetics notwithstanding, New York remains an overregulated city.

LOOKING FOR A RATIONALE

It is a bit disconcerting that public policy in New York seems more readily explained by social philosophy, well-intentioned though naive, than by dispassionate analysis. In its *Consumer Affairs Information Guide* the Department for Consumer Affairs asserts, with manifest pride, that "the New York City Consumer Protection Law Regulations constitute the most effective, comprehensive set of remedies against abuses in the market place available to any jurisdiction in the country." Though this objective, enunciated by the agency most prominent in administering licenses and permits, sounds admirable, it reflects without subtlety a fundamental and unqualified distrust of markets that is symptomatic of the syndrome of overregulation. It presumes that consumers cannot or will not protect themselves from abuse by refraining from repeated transactions with sellers who fail to offer fair value, *and* that it is worth incurring the *full* costs of statutory protection—including its intrusiveness, active and latent—even if abuses are isolated and few in number. Each time an abuse is uncovered, the city's instinct seems to demand a new regulation, regardless of whether the contingency is one against which it is really worth insuring. If the benefits of regulation were free, this position might withstand scrutiny. Unfortunately to those who enact and administer regulations, the benefits do seem unambiguous, for they provide gainful employment and agency revenue, while the cost is borne by the community-at-large.

The fact that regulation interferes with market allocation is not, in itself, damning. After all, its purpose is to provide for the correction of market failure. Indeed, in this sense regulation is singularly attractive, because it absorbs minimal fiscal resources. If, however, a specific regulation is to be justified, the market failures it is correcting must entail social costs that exceed the negative side effects of intervention. Political determination of whether a particular statute meets these criteria is complicated, however, by the fact that the allocative or deadweight costs of regulation attributable to distortion of choice are diffused and ill-understood, whereas the effects of the market abuses at which regulation is directed are concentrated and readily discernible.

One way to try to evaluate regulations would be to distinguish between those that improve markets by reducing risks against which self-insurance is impractical or collective insurance is less expensive, and those that hinder markets. But contingencies or risks vary, ranging from the risk of purchasing shoddy merchandise to the risk of a rent increase attributable to broad shifts in the housing market. In addition, the fact that the availability of private insurance varies with the degree of risk and the income of the insurer raises the question of fairness.

Instead, regulations might be evaluated in terms of whether the stakes are large or small, whether the victims are average citizens or people who lack adequate means of self-protection, or whether the alleged market failure is actually a rationalization, enshrined in the fabric of law, of vested interest. Though such distinctions are invariably ambiguous, common sense usually suffices.

Based on considerations such as these, when intervention through regulation still seems justified, it is important to determine whether it is too stringent and whether its administration is expeditious or cumbersome. This is what most observers, including many city officials, believe true in New York.

HAROLD M. HOCHMAN

A THEORETICAL JUSTIFICATION

The economic analysis of much local regulation involves a shifting of risk from the individual to the general public, or from buyers to seller. For example, consumer regulations reduce uncertainty for buyers about the quality of the goods and services offered. As a result of such uncertainty, bid-prices are lower than sellers are willing to accept, causing a progressive decline in the quality of the goods available in the market, a phenomenon economists call adverse selection. An example can be found in the used-car market. Because consumers cannot distinguish between good cars and "lemons," used-car prices, to a large extent, appear to be independent of quality. Good cars are held off the market, and the quality of the used cars that are for sale is understandably suspect.

In theory, governments impose consumer regulations, through licensing and other standards, to circumvent the unfortunate result of quality uncertainty. The solution, however, can produce new and even more severe problems. To compensate for the direct costs in money and time and the indirect costs in inconvenience and intrusiveness that regulation entails, sellers raise their effective prices. This transfers wealth to three groups: to the most risk-averse of prospective buyers, to those with a bureaucratic or political stake in intervention, and to sellers who obtain monopolistic protection as a consequence of measures such as occupational licensing. Such groups gain at the expense of the average buyer, who would prefer lower prices and more risk. Moreover, because regulation inherently alters prices, especially if it engenders monopoly, it distorts consumer choices and the composition of economic activity, and thus reduces the average consumer's welfare. Accordingly, regulations that are unwarranted, too stringent, or improperly structured, given the underlying justification, can easily result, even in the short run, in a net social loss.

In general, the losses individuals can suffer in isolated transactions are small. Competition and the flow of information, given the breadth of the markets in question, usually provide consumers with adequate protection. Ironically, regulatory intervention often reduces the scope of competition. It is unclear whether regulations reduce the costs of search, and compliance costs can be quite high. For many activities, then, simple registration combined with more-vigorous enforcement of the statutes against fraud might turn out

96

to be just as effective as regulation in protecting buyers from consumer abuse.

The fact that, within a large perspective, the direct effects of regulation on city revenues may seem inconsequential does nothing to vitiate these conceptual arguments. While administrative agencies are not permitted to make a profit and the direct costs of inspection do not dominate agency budgets, revenue considerations do motivate agencies, because both their prestige and their budgets are correlated with the range of their activities. Thus, agencies pay less attention than they should to real compliance costs in money, time, and inconvenience, even when the type of regulation in question is warranted, because the agencies do not bear them. In New York, these compliance costs are graphically illustrated by the existence of a corps of specialists known as expediters, who have the connections and skills required to "walk" multiple applications for licenses through the bureaucratic maze.

WHY NEW YORK LOVES REGULATION

While it seems obvious that a distrust of the market process is particularly pervasive in New York, other factors that underlie the impulse to overregulate are more elusive. In the large, this bias does not seem to be a response to the political demands of minorities or the poor, but the unintended product of a dialogue among elites, reflecting (absent understanding of economic principles) their vision of a well-ordered world. Even those New Yorkers who should understand the pitfalls of endemic regulation seem to place more trust in conscious actions of government than in the self-corrective properties of markets. Millionaires participating in New York politics seem to behave philosophically like socialists, calling for enactment of protection from risks of all sorts without due regard for cost. Though never admitted, and rarely understood, there seems to be a prevalent belief, reinforced by the media, that public and vested interests coincide, that perceived problems can be cured without undue side effects simply by promulgating or perpetuating rules.

There is no entirely satisfactory explanation for why the entrepreneurial spirit for which New Yorkers are acclaimed has thus been tempered in public affairs by paternalism. Sociologically, it may be derived from an intellectual identification with the socialist tradition, which treats as given a divergence of interest between active investors and a large, changing, immigrant-and-minority population that is limited in its ability to protect itself from predatory business practices. Or perhaps it is simply that political interests, inherently short-sighted, find it useful to define *predatory* broadly, thus capitalizing on the empathy of those who feel obliged to do something active about conditions they perceive as unfair.

The argument might also be made more generally in terms of a "public choice" interpretation of political behavior. Drawing on Mancur Olson's book *The Rise and Decline of Nations* (New Haven: York University Press, 1982), this argument attributes the antimarket ethos to the city's political age. Through overregulation, mature and entrenched bureaucracies act out their own political interests, particularly if civil service protection and public service unions insulate them from competitive forces. Rigidities inherent in the political activities of special interests cumulate. Such reinforcement is greatest in older and larger urban areas with well-developed and self-sustaining systems of patronage, such as New York. It is intensified if regulation infringes on the liberties of people who, being less active politically, seem anonymous, such as the recent immigrants who operate many small retail businesses.

At the political level—in the Board of Estimate, the City Council, and the Borough Halls—regulations, cloaked in the pious garb of community well-being, often reflect trades among interest groups or between consumers and the media, at the expense of those with less political clout, especially small businesses.

Another reason for the pervasiveness of regulation in New York may be the unremitting coverage of crime by the city's assiduous reporters and media. While no isolated instance of crime elicits a political response, even from activist politicians, repeated abuses assuredly will, even if their frequency is no greater, relative to the total number of transactions, than in smaller cities. The larger a city, and the larger its legislative body, the more media coverage there will be and the more frequently remedial legislation will be written.

If, however, the general perception is that a statute is too stringent or too inconvenient, it will be weakly enforced—a pattern that breeds disrespect for justified and unjustified regulations alike. As an alleged abuse is absorbed in the fabric of the local economy, like the omnipresent street peddlers, it draws decreasing attention. While legislation may ensue, it is ignored if it flies in the face of accepted characteristics of city life. If everyone in a society violates a law, it is unlikely to be enforced at all.

LICENSES AND PERMITS

Licensing illustrates most of the problems created by overregulation. Inherently, licensing places the right to participate in a market activity in the hands of the government and, in so doing, shifts the burden of proof to the individual consumer or producer. It is this factor (not the license fees, which invariably are small potatoes) that accounts for licensing's intrusiveness and, where it is unwarranted, its distortive effects. Even at its worst, licensing is not a powerful destructive force like rent control, but a nuisance, resembling insect bites rather than cancer. Yet we all know that a vacation resort in which the mosquitoes are ubiquitous is less likely to prosper.

Government construes a license as a revocable privilege, valid for a specified time period, usually a year, so long as the license-holder satisfies certain restrictions or side conditions—such as cleanliness, safety standards, or "good moral character"—that it deems in the public interest. Permits are similar, but apply to one-time events. Fees are a minimum cost of entry. Unless a licensee is willing to proceed illegally, licensing power can determine his economic life. In practice, violation is not uncommon, especially when multiple licenses, each requiring a different inspection, must be obtained from different agencies and the costs of delays in forgone revenues, inconvenience, and time exceed the expected penalties for noncompliance.

Table 1 categorizes the various licensing requirements in New York City in terms of appropriateness and justification. Only where public health and safety are at issue—the best example is bulk storage of flammable materials—do the stakes seem high enough to make the case for regulation incontrovertible. Obviously, fires spread more readily in densely populated areas, and risks are higher for people less likely to take self-protective measures, such as residents of low-income areas. Although death or injury can never be prevented entirely, random third-party effects, as well as abhorrence of preventable tragedy when even a single life is at stake, dictate intervention when density and clearly perceived hazards are involved.

Similarly, the licensing of places of public assembly, such as theaters, is necessary because given the large number a mishap might affect, no single individual can make a reasonable assessment of risk. Thus, individual protection is costly relative to public action, and the classic "public good" argument for intervention

Table 1 Categories of Licensing in New York City: Validity of Rationale

Category	Rank
Use and storage of flammable materials Places of public assembly Protection of children Cleanliness Use of public streets and sidewalks	Significant rationale
Temporary business Health services Tourist-oriented business Transfer of possession of personal property Bingo and Las Vegas nights Employment agencies Crime-oriented businesses Fences for stolen merchandise The protection of public morals Final disposition of the deceased	Debatable rationale

Source: Hochman, *op. cit.*, p. 205.

applies—provided, that is, that the good is equally available to all at no increase in cost.

But the same is hardly true of some other licensing categories, particularly in the consumer affairs area. With the licensing of auctioneers, for example, the risk is monetary rather than mortal, the amounts involved are relatively small, transactions are independent, and proper incentives are in place. Although information is imperfect, dishonesty will drive away trade, albeit with delay. Statutes against fraud would seem sufficient to protect the public. Similarly, regulating church bingo nights because gambling is infiltrated by criminal elements (or, in these days of public lotteries, because bingo competes with government) seems to stretch logic. Even organized crime, one might expect, would shrink at skimming the profits of a local parish fund-raiser.

Licensing to protect public health poses similar issues. Restaurant inspection, if efficient, honest, and tolerant of trivial oversight, seems a reasonable way around limited consumer information. However, as recently revealed scandals prove, restaurant inspection seems to invite corruption. Other licenses are especially perverse. Reason is not well served by the fact that barbers and beauticians, who earn incomes that vary with individual competence and do only trivial damage if they are incompetent, require occupational licenses, whereas "mohels," who perform ritual circumcisions, do not, because their market is "self-regulating." Behind the rhetoric, ostensible objectives often prove spurious, with licensing actually serving to control entry and protect vested interests. Why else would the plumber's examination include essay questions? Do writing or a command of English bear any relationship to a plumber's competence?

On the other hand, there is a valid rationale for licensing use of the public streets and sidewalks. Fees, if set properly, are appropriate charges for use of a common property resource, just as property taxes are, in effect, user charges for other government services, such as police protection and trash collection. Sidewalk cafes pay significant fees, which may reflect both site rent and public service charges. Sidewalk vendors also use both sidewalks and public services, but they pay no property tax and collect little or no sales tax—the one sense in which they represent unfair competition. Moreover, since license fees do not vary with location, peddlers and pushcarts tend to congregate in well-trafficked commercial areas where site values are high. Basic economics suggests that rules and fees for mid-Manhattan ought to be more stringent than are those for other areas.

In most cases, the rationale for licensing requirements is debatable. Frequently, common law, private interest, and simple registration to supply information would suffice without inspection. Examples include businesses such as the few remaining pawnbroker shops in the city, which, it is feared, might be used to "fence" stolen merchandise; bowling alleys, which are thought to be criminal hangouts; and, stretching reason, coin laundries, which house "slot machines." The first two examples ignore the fact that the target activities can readily shift venue. The third, though patently ridiculous, was used, in a classic example of the regulatory mentality, as a rationale for a proposal to extend consumer affairs licensing to coin dry-cleaning establishments.

The economic effects of licensing are in large part a function of the administrative procedures applied to implement them, particularly when there are multiple restrictions. To open a new luncheonette or restaurant for example, requires fully 11 procedures that take some two to three months to complete and must often be helped along by an "expediter." But for every potential establishment, whether it is to be operated by experienced restaurateurs or by novices, by native Americans or by those who speak mainly Chinese or Greek, having to send a representative to a Health Department training course for a two-week series of one-hour sessions seems of dubious value. The question is not whether such a program has benefits, but whether the benefits exceed the costs. Furthermore, since compliance costs seem more-or-less independent of scale, there appears to be a bias against smaller firms.

Perhaps the most troubling aspect of licensing is its ambiguity. Agencies possess a variety of discretionary powers and tend to be enforcement-minded and prosaic. They control entry by requiring examinations and by screening for "good moral character"; they investigate and inspect to enforce rules; and they adjudicate disputes, imposing sanctions such as fines, suspensions, and revocations. A licensee must satisfy them from start to finish, for allegations of violation, even if untrue, are costly to contest or disprove, and the loss is not compensated.

DEVELOPMENT REGULATIONS

Development regulations differ from licensing in subtle but important ways. Like occupational licensing, some standard development regulations, such as zoning, confer monopoly power, because locations are distinctive and not interchangeable. Deviation from permitted uses and building sizes is only possible if the applicant, on whom the burden of proof resides, obtains a variance. Implicitly, the operative property right is the city's, not the agent's.

In an important way, however, building regulations and land-use controls are more critical to the well-being of the urban economy than is licensing. While the implications of licensing may loom large for the business environment in the aggregate, their first-order effects usually impinge on activities for which reasonable alternatives exist. Licensing makes the urban economy run like a five-year-old automobile with its original spark plugs, like Leningrad or Mexico City rather than Hong Kong. Though embarrassing, this can hardly be fatal.

Excessive or inappropriate intervention in development and land use, on the other hand, can prove crippling, because it impinges directly on location, the engine of the urban economy. If development regulation is improper, what results is more like a systemic infection than a bruise. Since a long-lasting stock is at issue, current effects may be impossible to reverse. Once land rents and the cost of space are driven up and businesses shift from Manhattan to Stamford or Englewood Cliffs, it may be near-impossible to entice them to return, even with costly tax abatements or other distortive subsidies. This is true also for the residential choices of upper- and middle-income families who move to the suburbs because they find taxes too high and city services inadequate.

Particularly troubling is the city's tendency to change the rules of the game in midstream, especially to the extent that it adds to investor uncertainty. A good example of midstream rule changes is the moratorium on conversion or replacement of single-room occupancy (SRO) rooming houses and hotels, which inhibits the filtering of such properties to higher-valued uses. To the extent it reflects a concern with gentrification, the regulation demonstrates a blindness to fiscal realities, which are ill-served by redistributive measures that create perverse demographic and developmental incentives.

Another example of midstream rule changes is the "loft law." When, a decade or so ago, New York suffered a major decline in manufacturing, many lofts were converted to residential use through leases with specified expiration dates and conditions of occupancy. Subsequently, as the economy recovered and residential leases expired, owners found it preferable to restore such properties to commercial use. However, they found that in the interim, residential tenants had gained the protection of housing regulations that, in effect, converted their leases to grants of tenure. Again, the implications are clear.

Building regulations are substantively more rigorous in New York than in other cities. Whether such rigorousness is warranted by differential third-party effects of uncontrolled private actions depends on such variables as the age and height of structures, population density, and demographic, economic, and racial factors. It is harder to argue against, for example, a requirement that fail-safe electrical wiring be used in New York's high rises, stacked one against another and occupied by thousands, than it would be to argue against similar regulations in Arizona. But it is also inappropriate to apply the same standards to a duplex in Staten Island as to an apartment block in Brooklyn or an office building in Manhattan. Although little more can be said on this subject without careful study, general caution is in order. Regulations are designed and enforced by specialists with a bureaucratic and professional incentive to overvalue the benefits and understate the costs of stringent standards. It is difficult for a layman to argue with the Fire Department over methods of fire prevention. But some external audit of standards, with the participation of private firms affected by the rules, would assure balance.

The city not only has adopted many special zoning districts to preserve or encourage significant residential or commercial neighborhood characteristics, but also carries on an active landmarking program to protect buildings and neighborhoods with architectural or historical significance. Landmarks cannot be altered without a complicated authorization process. While such land-use restrictions involve some of the same issues as the more mundane licensing regulations, they also share some of the more important characteristics of takings under the power of eminent domain. The difference is that in landmarking cases, the owner has no right to monetary compensation, even though the restrictions imposed can significantly damage the market value of his property. Thus, balancing preservation of the urban heritage against efficient land use inevitably raises broad problems of fairness. Given the ease with which "causes" are politicized in New York, ostensibly sensible landmarking and rezoning programs add to investor uncertainty about property values and inhibit development.

Interestingly, building developers and owners do not see the stringency of the development codes as their most onerous problem. Typically, systemic effects tend to be ill-understood, while particular features or aspects of the regulations are magnified. Among professionals, the major source of dissatisfaction is over the way the codes are administered—over the transactions costs rather than the allocative distortion. Zoning is administered by the City Planning Department, by local community boards, and by the Board of Standards and Appeals. Decentralization, even within agencies, delays in inspection and enforcement, the monetary and time costs of complying with multiple licensing, the Uniform Land Use Review Procedures (ULURP), and the need to "expedite" arouse virtually universal criticism. The main issue is whether "one-stop service" could be implemented on an interagency basis, reinforced by incentives forceful enough to stem resistance, by a strong mandate from the Mayor's office or through reorganization. But it is the essence of tautology that the byways of an established bureaucracy are easier to criticize than to change.

All in all, the best policy for New York might be a "nonpolicy" of not trying to fix what isn't broken—doing as little as possible to inhibit the flow of locational resources to their highest-valued uses. It would be eminently more sensible to build in checks and balances and refrain from measures that only make the city locationally unattractive, than to impose well-intentioned constraints, mostly in response to distributional politics, and after the fact, attempting to remedy their damaging effects through expensive economic development programs and selective dispensations.

PRICE CONTROLS

Price controls, like other regulatory instruments, are uncommonly prevalent in New York. Of the services subject to price regulation in New York City, only five were controlled by 50 percent or more of the cities that responded, approximately a decade ago, to a questionnaire on this subject. The explanation lies in the impulse in New York, discussed above, to regulate not just serious abuses, but typical market risks, without acknowledging that compliance can create new and even worse problems.

No price regulation has had an impact as pervasive as rent control, which produces nonprice rationing, discourages investment, and invites corruption. Because it was thought that free-market rents would be unfair to some tenants, those tenants fortunate enough to occupy rent-controlled or rent-stabilized apartments, by virtue of tenure, family ties, or "key money," enjoy large subsidies from landlords. Others, as a consequence of implicit redistribution and the welfare loss associated with distortion, pay more than they would if the market were free.

Consumer protection against potential monopoly is the standard rationale for administrative price ceilings. But the local monopolies to which price controls apply result, as often as not, from licensing itself. Regulation of private-bus fares reduces the quality of service in the outer boroughs so that public transit will not suffer "unfair" competition. Public park concessionaires, along with taxis, also enjoy publicly protected monopolies. Though the number of taxi medallions has lagged demand by decades, taxi operators recently sought to protect their valuable monopoly by organizing protests against the Taxi and Limousine Commission's proposal to issue new medallions, even at a rate modest enough to cushion windfall losses; and jitneys, a potential source of competition for medallion taxis, are altogether prohibited.

This is not to say that price oversight is invariably improper from

105

a public-interest perspective. Market outcomes may seem patently unfair to consumers confronted by "temporal" monopolies, as in roadside automobile emergencies. Such monopolies are often present, as well, when specific services are minor complements of something else, such as with wardrobe checking in public buildings.

To some—particularly short-term visitors with neither the time nor the background to learn the byways of navigating by bus or subway—taxi fares reflect such a monopoly. Uniform posted prices negotiated by the government as agent for consumers may be justified because the latter cannot identify suppliers in advance of purchasing their services. But however valid this argument, pervasive controls are a *non sequitur*. In general, the elimination of most entry restrictions would lead to improved service and more competitive fares. The case for liberalizing taxi regulations is supported by evidence from cities such as Washington, D.C., where entry is essentially free, subject to driver certification, and shared rides are permitted, despite the fact that crime is no less prevalent. Ironically, however, New York has moved in the opposite direction by extending regulation to gypsy cabs, even though they may make service less available in low-income areas. If nothing else, this fact surely raises doubts that the political drive for regulation has weakened.

Another instance of the ambiguous welfare effects of price ceilings is found in the regulation of interest rates. People who borrow from pawnbrokers typically do so because they lack an alternative. But interest ceilings that ignore the inherent riskiness of such loans have led to a severe contraction of this trade, making loans less available to high-risk borrowers.

There is no good reason to regulate cable television tariffs. Cable is not a natural monopoly, and the service is neither a public good nor a necessity. To be sure, over-the-air competition is regulated; but cable regulation simply compounds the wrong. Access to public utility rights-of-way could readily be negotiated competitively. New York created a monopoly where none need have emerged when it divided Manhattan into service territories, rejecting a proposal by the FCC that would have franchised a third firm and then taxed the "monopoly surplus" through franchise fees and a requirement that cable companies provide free or low-cost channels for public use. As a consequence, cable companies suffered consistent losses, and thanks to the scandal-tainted system of public franchising, most residents of the outer four boroughs are, to this day, without cable service.

CONCLUSION

In the parable of "the prisoner's dilemma," two prisoners fail to achieve gains that are possible if both accept the risks of trust and cooperation; seeking safety through distrust, both suffer losses. Regulation provides the comfort of good intentions; its full consequences are ill-understood. The gains to individuals for whom the issue is salient dominate, even though they fall short of the loss to the full community, which is well diffused.

In New York, regulation has created a cluttered landscape, which design by deletion could surely improve. New York, in a sense, seems characterized by an impulse to regulate. It is difficult to put one's finger on the total costs of its regulation, but they are clearly higher than most people realize. Like the public welfare effects of an extortionate tax, the relationship between regulatory excess and its side effects is exponential, nor proportional. The compulsion to act, out of fear of the impersonal forces that drive markets, betrays a failure to understand that trying to achieve an urban utopia through social engineering winds up serving vested interests while harming the economy as a whole.

Overregulation in New York will not be corrected by changing the puzzle piecemeal, because the obstacle is its overall design. Naively, one might wish for a restructuring of urban political incentive, producing a change of heart and a new faith in markets. But it is fantasy to expect overregulation to disappear overnight, or in the next year or the next decade. Political ideas are not concepts but habits, which are self-perpetuating—all the more so when one political party remains dominant, without significant competition, for generations. Progress can at best be incremental, reflecting changes in the cast of characters and the prevailing ethos.

Nonetheless, it remains useful to think through ways of altering the intellectual and political ambience so that regulation can facilitate, not stifle. A first step would be to place the burden of proof on the regulator, not the individual or firm at which regulations are directed. This would mean that government, rather than automatically stepping in to set things right at each perceived injustice or quasi-catastrophe, would bear the burden of proof, especially when proposed regulations are broader and more stringent than the national norm. At a minimum, each measure would be backed by benefit-cost calculations that take side effects into account, and such studies—the more cynical the better—would see the full light of day.

Something close to unanimous public approval, rather than the minority support of those with intense interests, should be required to put new regulations in place. Existing statutes should be subject to periodic reexamination and to sunset provisions. Where feasible, registration should replace licensing, and each specific requirement should be tailored to its essential dimensions. Just as the city managed to strip away problems of compliance to encourage the movie industry, it should remove impediments to other industries that can contribute to its economic base.

If New York does nothing about its propensity to regulate, it will not slip away into the Hudson, but it will slowly be crippled by what was called, a decade ago, the British disease—an economic lethargy that derives from the dulling of incentives. In the long run even the vested interests who benefit from overregulation will be worse off for their indulgence, and other cities will set the urban standard for the country.

Chapter 6

CONSIDERING PRIVATIZATION

E. S. Savas

New York is a paradox. It is exciting and vibrant, a mecca for immigrants seeking the American dream and an incubator of innovative entrepreneurs. At the same time, the quality of life for most New Yorkers is undeniably mediocre. Schools are failing, crime is commonplace, streets are filthy, transportation is a test of endurance, drug addiction is a curse, teenage pregnancy is rampant, public incivility and foul language are the norm, ugliness assails the senses, housing is in short supply, and derelicts line the streets.

Millions of New Yorkers have moved out over the past 20 years because their intuitive calculus revealed that they could get a higher quality of life and better schooling for their children, at a lower cost, in the suburbs. Further, by this act they could escape a debt burden that amounted to about $10,000 per family of four in 1984.

Why doesn't city government seem to work in New York? Why does its performance seem so inept, regardless of who is mayor? City government always seems to promise too much and achieve too little; in trying to placate every pressure group, it undertakes a wide array of functions almost regardless of cost or feasibility. It maintains a costly municipal hospital system that is a tribute to noble intentions but only succeeds in serving the poor inadequately. It promises cheap housing but creates a "temporary" housing shortage that has lasted for 40 years and driven up the cost of what little housing has been built. It promises safe streets but turns

Note: This chapter is based in part on the author's *Privatization: The Key to Better Government* (Chatham, N.J.: Chatham House, 1987).

hardened criminals loose even before the arresting officer completes all the paperwork and gets back on patrol.

In media-rich New York, politicians have learned that credit accrues for detecting problems, pointing to alleged culprits, posturing in public, and making costly but symbolic gestures to demonstrate the depth of their commitment to newly discovered causes of yet more interest groups.

Capital construction has particular political appeal, and sometimes funds are spent on highly visible projects, even when there is no money to operate or maintain them; Woodhull hospital in Brooklyn is a sad case in point, built at great expense but mothballed for years before it opened. The bias toward capital spending and against maintenance expenditures is understandable, considering the high visibility of the former and the near invisibility of the latter. A ground-breaking or ribbon-cutting for a new structure is an opportunity for crowds, speeches, photographs, media coverage, and wine-and-cheese receptions where the flesh of potential campaign contributors can be pressed. Thus, capital budgets create political capital and cement political ties. In contrast, what kind of ceremony can one organize to celebrate the prompt repair of a leaky sewer? Moreover, capital projects cost the incumbent only three cents on the dollar, assuming 30-year bonds are used to pay for construction; his successors will foot the bill for the remaining 97 cents.

That myriad and ever-changing special-interest groups tempt democratically elected public officials to overextend themselves is not unique to New York. Governments in many places and at all levels have suffered from a loss of public confidence, even as they have grown and prospered and even as people seem to accept the implicit claim that government is omnipotent, capable of solving all their problems. In fact, government is severely limited in what it can do. Fortunately, however, society has other institutions besides government that address people's needs. It is time to sort out the relative roles of government and these other institutions. What is it that the city government can and should be responsible for? What is it that it can't do, and shouldn't pretend it can? What can society handle through other means? How can city government take advantage of other, private-sector institutions?

The private institutions available to address society's needs include, first and foremost, the family, which is the original department of health, education, welfare, housing, and human services. In addition, there are churches, businesses, unions, the marketplace, neighborhood associations, and nonprofit voluntary associations of all kinds, many unique to the United States, as Alexis de Tocqueville noted with

110

wonder 150 years ago. These institutions can be summoned—or allowed—once again to play a greater role and relieve city government of some of its insupportable burden, enabling it to do well those things that only government can do.

How can New York better utilize its private sector? Privatization is the key. Misunderstood, maligned, and feared—and certainly a clumsy neologism—"privatization" means relying more on private institutions and less on government to satisfy people's needs. Joining neighborhood safety patrols instead of clamoring for more police officers is an example of New Yorkers practicing privatization. Leasing Bryant Park to a franchisee who will keep it clean, attractive, and free of muggers, addicts, and pushers is a form of privatization, as is allowing free-market vans to serve commuters' transportation needs. Prudent contracting with private firms to operate municipal hospitals, repair police cars, and sweep the streets, and contracting with not-for-profit churches to deliver "meals-on-wheels" to elderly shut-ins or to operate halfway houses, are ways to privatize. Food stamps and housing vouchers for the poor are other instances of privatization far better than government-run farms and grocery stores, or more public-housing ghettos. *The New York Times* opts for privatization when it chooses a home-delivery service instead of the U.S. Postal Service to deliver the morning paper. Strengthening and relying more on the family, religious institutions, and aroused local groups to help tackle the problems of teenage pregnancy and drug addiction are other illustrations of privatization. These are not abdications by government, but rather realistic acknowledgements that democratic government can go only so far in dealing with certain problems; the private sector can often be more effective and more efficient.

The mechanisms that government can use to bring the strengths of the private sector to bear on city problems include the free market, franchises, voluntary actions, vouchers, and contracts for services. The following sections explore how each of these mechanisms can be applied in New York.

ENLISTING THE MARKETPLACE

Most economic wants are satisfied by someone who identifies the need and acts to fill it. The marketplace implements this process through two main features, *prices* and *competition*. Prices reflect the cost of providing goods and services and tend to allocate society's limited resources efficiently. Competition brings forth new and better ways to provide goods and services. These two elements enable well-functioning markets to serve people's needs successfully.

Market principles can be applied to New York's problem-plagued surface transportation system. As Jose Gomez-Ibañez points out in Chapter 4, private buses, jitneys and deregulated taxicabs can be allowed to compete with the Metropolitan Transportation Authority (MTA). Entrepreneurs should be encouraged to supply superior services, such as express service, and amenities such as newspapers, coffee, headphones, and television, particularly during rush hours, thereby reducing the need for money-losing public bus runs. Chartered subscription services and van pools can also serve commuters with vouchers issued to school children, the elderly, and the poor. Contracts awarded by competitive bidding to private bus, jitney, and taxi firms to serve lightly traveled routes and off-peak periods could enable the MTA to take advantage of the freedom and flexibility private operators enjoy to use more-appropriate vehicles and part-time drivers.

Opponents argue that if private firms were allowed to compete with the MTA, they would "skim the cream" of the profitable routes and leave the MTA with only the money-losing ones. But as Gomez-Ibañez indicates, the MTA's biggest losses occur because it has to have enough buses and drivers to handle peak demands during rush hours. By contracting with private firms to handle part of the peak load, the MTA would actually save money. Government should gradually get out of the business of owning, operating, or franchising bus monopolies and restricted-entry taxi systems. It should remove entry barriers and relinquish its role as a producer of transport services. Instead, it should become a facilitator, coordinator, and purchaser of contractual and market-supplied services, and an inspector and enforcer of vehicle and driver safety. This competitive, economically deregulated climate can offer better and more responsive transportation service to riders, lower costs to the public, and reduced government expenditures.

FRANCHISING

Another means by which the city government can utilize the capabilities of the private sector is through franchising. Some municipally owned golf courses and tennis courts have already been turned over to franchisees, who pay the city, charge the users, and operate the facilities far better than the city can. The same approach could be used for pools and beaches, as in Europe, where sections of public beachfront are franchised to private organizations that provide chairs, umbrellas, food, and drinks, and keep the beaches clean and orderly.

Municipal hospitals, a perennial problem, can also be operated by franchises. While retaining ownership to minimize costs, the city could permit private organizations to take over any of its hospitals that they find attractive. Experience in other cities has shown that private operators are more diligent and effective in obtaining Medicaid and Medicare reimbursement for patients, more conscious of cost containment, and generally better at hospital management. The city already contracts out clinical services in most of its hospitals to nearby medical schools; this proposal would logically extend the process. For those indigent patients whose medical costs are not fully covered by existing programs, the city and state could purchase supplemental health insurance.

VOLUNTARY ACTION

Voluntary organizations at the neighborhood level have long been at work in New York. These include block and neighborhood associations that organize safety patrols and park cleanups, volunteer fire and ambulance units, business improvement districts, and full-blown minigovernments such as those in Breezy Point, Sea Gate, Fieldston, and Forest Hills Gardens. Breezy Point, a 500-acre, predominantly middle-class area in the Rockaways, is owned cooperatively by the residents, who assess themselves to provide a range of basic services usually provided by city government. Although the residents also pay all city taxes, they pay this assessment because it gives them greater control over the quality and mix of local services—something denied to most other New Yorkers. For example, the co-op operates fire and ambulance services staffed entirely by volunteers, and co-op employees collect refuse from individual homes and bring it to a transfer station at the edge of the neighborhood for the city to remove. Security guards hired by the co-op provide added protection against crime. The co-op purchases water at its property line and distributes it on a metered basis through a network of pipes, which it owns and maintains, to individual households. Almost all roads, parking areas, walkways, and the beach are owned and maintained by the co-op. The co-op also runs recreation programs and a shuttle-bus service that uses minibuses and station wagons. This kind of neighborhood voluntary arrangement can be

113

fostered by giving residents a proportional rebate of their property taxes for the services that they pay for themselves. Houston and Kansas City follow such a policy.

There is fertile ground for this sort of development among the co-ops and condominiums that have emerged in the past two or three decades. These constitute nothing less than a new level of government, smaller than a community district and often smaller than a block, but larger than a family. As they deal with common problems, they are reacquiring citizenship skills that have atrophied from disuse in New York. These organizations should be encouraged to expand their focus of concern and assume formal responsibility for their building's surroundings as well as their interiors. In St. Louis, local streets have been turned over to residential cooperatives, with salutary results.

Business Improvement Districts offer similar potential. Recent legislation at the state level makes it possible for property owners in a neighborhood to levy compulsory special taxes, to be used for local improvements. In many cities, mechanisms have been created whereby private organizations take over the maintenance of public parks. New York should exploit all these techniques to the fullest and empower neighborhood groups to plan and provide more of their municipal services.

VOUCHER SYSTEMS

In a well-functioning marketplace, the consumer can choose among competitive suppliers on the basis of price and quality. Sellers compete for consumers by offering the best combination of price and quality they can. When it comes to "worthy goods"—that is, goods that everyone should have, such as shelter and education—government typically subsidizes the producer in order to make the goods available for all at an affordable price. But this violates the principle of consumer sovereignty, for the consumer has no choice and the producer has no incentive. Voucher systems, however, uphold the principle of consumer sovereignty, yet achieve the same worthy goal of delivering needed public goods.

Under a voucher system, government subsidies go to the consumers, not the producers, of a service. For instance, food for poor people *could* be provided through government farms, canneries, and grocery stores. But it is far better to give poor people vouchers—that is, food stamps—to augment their purchasing power so that they can obtain food the same way everyone else does. Similarly, government can subsidize construction of housing for low-income households or build and operate public housing, or it can give housing vouchers (of a carefully calculated value) to eligible recipients, who can then choose their own housing. This approach is more efficient, and it gives poor people greater dignity as well. They can exercise greater freedom of choice in the private housing market and select the housing they prefer that is within their voucher-expanded means. The public still pays taxes to provide housing for poor people, but it does not force them to live in housing labeled, in effect, "for the poor only."

Education

This simple principle, of subsidizing the consumer instead of the producer, and thereby expanding the consumer's choice instead of leaving him at the mercy of a single supplier, has enormous potential for improving one of the most unsatisfactory of all city services—education.

New York's public school system is as impressive in size as it is unimpressive in performance. It has 940,000 pupils, 1,100 schools, and 80,000 employees, but a stunning 42 percent of its students fail to graduate from high school. Numerous reforms have been urged, but the most promising reform is greater parental choice in selecting schools for their children. This is the essential lever for improving education. The National Governors' Association endorsed this approach in 1986, and teachers' union head Albert Shanker noted that "attendance is much higher and dropout rates are much lower in those public schools—vocational and optional academic high schools—that students themselves have chosen."

It is highly revealing that in many American cities a higher percentage of public-school teachers send their children to private schools than do families in general. In Chicago, for example, 46 percent of public-school teachers who live in the city send their children to private schools, compared with a citywide average of 23 percent. In New York, where 25 percent of schoolchildren are enrolled in private schools, the corresponding figure showing the extent to which public-school teachers avoid sending their children to the public schools is not available. One would guess, however, that far more than 25 percent choose private schools, and many more have chosen suburban schools.

"Choice, not assignment," is the theme. The growing chorus for

115

parental choice accounts for the mushrooming interest in vouchers and in tax credits for tuition paid to private schools, as both of these approaches help parents afford nonpublic schools.

There are numerous ways to introduce competition and choice both from the "buyer's side" (the parents) and the "seller's side" (the school). Parents can be allowed to send their children to any public school in the city, or even to a private school, and funds from their home school district can be transferred accordingly, including any state aid to which the district is entitled. When restricted to public schools, this approach is simply an open-enrollment program, but it has drastic consequences for schools that cannot attract enough pupils to stay in business, for they could no longer compel enrollment of neighborhood children. The few existing intradistrict, open-enrollment programs tend to be feeble. The school that is shunned rarely loses much of its budget (and may even be rewarded with more money, to improve itself), and the school that gains a good reputation is rarely expanded—instead, its waiting list is lengthened. Allowing public funds to accompany the child, or permitting vouchers or tax credits for tuition, would expand educational choice, promote healthy competition, and consequently improve the schools.

From the seller's side, a school can increase its appeal by contracting out the teaching of some courses or the educating of some kinds of students. For example, colleges could be hired to run programs for gifted children, and private firms to run vocational education programs. In a bold proposal several years go, Boston University offered to operate the troubled Boston public school under a contractual arrangement. Perhaps the Board of Education should contract with the City University to run some public schools, building on the long, successful experience of Hunter College.

Another possibility is for entrepreneurial teachers and administrators to form group-teaching practices, analogous to group medical practice. They could then contract with a school district to teach a subject or a grade, or in a more ambitious step, they could assume complete managerial responsibility for an entire school and strive to attract a growing clientele by the excellence of the education offered.

Critics have argued that these approaches would destroy public schools. Several points can be made in rebuttal. Firstly, the essential elements of "public education" are that education be universal and available without a user fee, not that the teacher's employer be public in character. Second, if a school is doing a poor job, it *should* go out of business—the adjective *public* should not grant it immunity to the consequences of incompetence. Third, the competition from private schools may actually *save* the public schools if it succeeds in waking them from their torpor.

To the argument that the best schools would skim off the best students, leaving the remaining schools as a dumping ground, the rejoinder is that a vigorously competitive environment can create schools with specialized "market niches," including schools for children with discipline problems or learning disabilities. It is neither fair nor wise to deprive gifted students of the opportunity to develop their innate abilities to the fullest, instead using them primarily to enrich the environment of others.

Another criticism of this approach is that private schools promote segregation. On the contrary, private schools nationally are less segregated than public ones, because so many suburban public schools are highly segregated. A study in California found that private Catholic schools have a higher population of minority pupils than do public schools. For many inner-city black families, few of whom are Catholic, the Catholic schools offer an affordable alternative to unsatisfactory public schools. (Polls show inner-city blacks to be more dissatisfied with urban public schools than whites.)

Many poor, inner-city black families scrimp and save to enroll their children in neighborhood-based private schools. In Chicago, almost 50 independent schools have emerged in the poorest areas, attended predominantly by black and Hispanic children. The National Center for Neighborhood Enterprise surveyed more than 250 such schools in major cities, most of which are owned and operated by minorities, finding that the children in these schools outperform their public-school counterparts. Parents who have chosen these schools endure significant financial burdens to educate their children; they set aside money from welfare checks, work at multiple jobs, and depend on family and friends to help pay tuition. A survey showed that people making less than $15,000 a year were more than twice as likely as those making more than $25,000 to use a $500 tuition tax credit. Blacks and Hispanics were twice as likely as whites to utilize such a credit, probably because low-income minority groups in large cities are more dependent on monolithic, unsatisfactory public schools than are high-income whites, who can escape to small suburban school districts.

Some critics have argued that if many more children attend independent private schools, we will produce adults who lack a common educational background, and may even lack basic exposure to the nation's history and democratic values. This putative

E. S. SAVAS

shortcoming is easy to avoid, as state education authorities can prescribe certain common curriculum elements and administer common achievement examinations. The results of the examinations would inform parents about their child's progress, affect school accreditation, and help parents assess and choose schools for their children. No doubt private rating services would spring up to provide parents with an analysis of educational institutions—hybrids of *Lovejoy's College Guide* and *Consumer Reports.*

In short, it may not be necessary to privatize in order to introduce competition: the latter could be achieved by allowing parents to choose among public schools, provided that the schools offer the diversity that comes only with sufficient autonomy and independence. It may well be, however, that only competition from private schools, via vouchers and tuition-tax credits, can bring about the necessary diversity.

Parental choice can be viewed in the context of school decentralization, which has proven to be an enormous disappointment. Voter turnout for school-board elections is regularly less than 10 percent, and thus the boards are dominated by neighborhood politicians and the teachers' union—hardly a promising prescription for innovative and excellent education. In a sense, decentralization did not go far enough. Instead of empowering residents to elect neighborhood boards that then select superintendents, principals, and teachers, parents should simply be empowered to select the schools their children will attend. At one stroke this will produce a 100 percent "voter turnout" every year, leaving professional educators to hire school personnel and run the schools, but giving parents the ultimate right to choose among schools that compete for their children.

No responsible individual would argue today against the need for tax-paid education for all, up to some age or level. One can have universal education, however, without relying exclusively on government-run schools, and one can have marketlike competition in education without charging parents a fee for their child's schooling. As long as every child attends school at common expense financed by general taxes, the need would be met. The approach sketched here satisfies these conditions and offers the prospect of a schooling system that will produce educated and productive New Yorkers.

118

CONTRACTING FOR SERVICES

As fiscal pressures intensify, cities seeking greater efficiency in municipal services are turning to private contractors, another form of privatization. A 1982 survey of 59 different municipal services in each of 1,780 local governments in the United States showed that on average, each responding locality contracted out 26 percent of its services in whole or in part. More than 180 different municipal activities were being provided by contract, ranging from adoption services to zoning control. The service most commonly contracted was vehicle towing (80 percent of cities); others were legal services (49 percent), street-light operation (39 percent), residential sold-waste collection (35 percent), day care (35 percent), vehicle maintenance and fleet management (31 percent), and hospital management (30 percent).

A growing body of evidence shows that prudent contracting leads to large cost savings without a loss of service quality. For example, Los Angeles County reviewed its five-year privatization program and concluded that its 434 separate contracts cost only $108 million, whereas if county agencies had done the work directly, the cost would have been $167 million, or 55 percent more. A detailed analysis sponsored by the U.S. Department of Housing and Urban Development found that the cost of street construction by city agencies was 96 percent greater than similar work by contractors, and that municipal costs were greater by 43 percent for street cleaning, by 73 percent for janitorial service, by 56 percent for traffic-signal maintenance, by 35 percent for refuse collection, and by 73 percent for tree pruning. In each case there were no differences in quality.

In support functions such as data processing, food service, and audiovisual services, an analysis of 235 federal-agency contracts awarded from 1980 to 1982 showed that the cost of such work by government had been 38 percent higher than contract work. A similar analysis of 131 contracts awarded from 1983 to 1984 showed that the cost had been 50 percent higher. Early results indicate that the private sector can do better in constructing and operating prisons, waste-water treatment plants, street lighting, and resource-recovery facilities.

Simple pragmatism, not ideology or party politics, is the driving force behind contracting out of municipal services. Officials are learning that they can maintain and even improve services while reducing costs significantly, and today this is important for reelection—at least as important as patronage and swollen public payrolls were in earlier days.

The reason why privatization works so well is not that the people employed by government are somehow inferior to those employed by the private sector; they are not. It works because privatization offers choice, and choice fosters competition, which leads to more cost-effective performance. Contracting out means dissolving unnecessary government monopolies and introducing competition in the delivery of public services. The public can only benefit from this competition, provided that sound bidding, contracting, and performance-monitoring procedures are employed.

Governments are responsible for deciding which services are to be paid for by the public, but they do not have to produce and deliver the services using government employees. In effect, contracting out elevates each government official to the same commanding position as a manufacturer who can decide whether to make or buy a component for the product he is assembling. The efficient manufacturer will maintain a competitive balance among his suppliers—including his own plant—to assure the best possible overall results.

Contracting out is hardly new to New York; the city was contracting for refuse collection as early as 1676. An example of enlightened contracting is found in the city's street-lighting experience. For many years street-light maintenance contracts were habitually given to the same two firms. Service was poor and expensive. In 1980 the system was reformed. The city was divided into eight equal-sized districts, each with about 40,000 lights, and competitive bidding was mandated for each district. No firm can be awarded more than two districts, and contracts are of three years' duration. The city monitors the contractors' performance and maintains effective oversight of the entire operation. The result is that more bidders compete, the quality of service has improved significantly, and the cost has been reduced dramatically. The city created a competitive industry where there had been none.

But New York has also suffered from abysmally corrupt contracting practices, as illustrated by a recent major scandal centered about its Parking Violations Bureau. The combination of bribery and extortion in awarding contracts to process parking tickets, to design hand-held computers, and to tow away scofflaws' cars was rooted in a flawed process: the contracts were not awarded by competitive bidding, but rather by cozy, illicit arrangements whereby corrupt officials gave out contracts in exchange for cash.

Much of the work of the departments of Parks, Highways, Sanitation, and General Services lends itself to privatization by contracting out, as it is relatively easy to define, to write specifications for, and to monitor. In other cities these activities are often performed by contractors, and studies comparing public and private service delivery are available. In addition, because numerous private contracts are already performing similar work, it is highly likely that a competitive climate can be created and sustained.

Each of these activities will be addressed in turn, and the available evidence reviewed. Possible savings in New York are estimated under the assumptions that prudent contracting is carried out and that the results are the same as the average results achieved elsewhere.

Refuse Collection

This is the most-studied privatized service. Nine different major comparisons of public and contract refuse collection have been carried out by academic researchers and by government agencies in the United States, Canada, West Germany, Switzerland, and Japan, with consistent, compelling, and mutually corroborative findings: the cost of municipal collection is 30–40 percent greater than the price of contract collection. Moreover, careful studies show that the quality of service is, if anything, slightly higher when carried out by the private sector. The reasons for this large difference in efficiency lay not in a significant difference in wages, but rather in the use of more-productive equipment, less paid time off, and better supervision.

Actually, the price difference quoted here understates the true difference to the public. About 15 percent of contractors' revenues are paid back to government (federal, state, and city) in the form of fees and taxes. Therefore, taxpayers pay $135 for a municipal service for which a contractor charges only $100 but gets a rebate of $15 in taxes, so that the contract service costs the public only $85. By changing from municipal to contract collection, the public saves 37 percent—the $50 reduction from $135 to $85.

What are the implications of these findings for New Yorkers? The 1986 Sanitation Department direct budget for cleaning and collection amounted to $257 million; when fringe benefits, pension contributions, debt service (mostly for vehicles), and departmental overheads are added, the total cost was approximately $520 million. Given 2.7 million households in the city, the cost was $193 per household, not including the cost of transporting the waste to landfills and disposing of it. If the city were able to contract effectively for this service, and to achieve results comparable to those attained by other cities (35 percent of all cities in the United States contract out all or part of this work), the public would save almost $200 million annually, or $71 per household.

In the 1980s, the sanitation commissioner shrewdly brandished the threat of contracting out and simultaneously blandished the lure of more money to persuade the recalcitrant union to change from 3-man to 2-man trucks. The result was a significant managerial achievement and an annual saving of $20 million. To aim for a $200 million saving, the city should follow the approach used by Montreal, Minneapolis, Newark, Phoenix, and other cities. This would mean choosing perhaps one community district in each borough and putting its refuse collection out for competitive bidding, with carefully drawn specifications, well-planned monitoring of the contractor's work, and penalty clauses backed by performance bonds for poor work and missed collections. Although union opposition can be expected, layoffs can be avoided by gearing the rate of implementation to the sanitation department's normal attrition rate, as the annual number of retirements, resignations, and deaths corresponds to the manning needs of the district.

The cynical New Yorker can point knowingly to a history of noncompetitive and criminal behavior in the private waste-collection industry in the New York area. However, the business is changing rapidly. Several publicly owned firms traded on the New York Stock Exchange, and even international firms now compete for large municipal contracts. A serious effort by the city to contract out a portion of the work would attract highly qualified, reputable firms who will engage in spirited and legitimate competition to gain a foothold in the New York market.

One of the many virtues of this approach is that it will establish a dual yardstick: the contractor's performance can be measured against that of the in-house work, and vice-versa. In Minneapolis, city officials used this technique and rewarded the better performer by expanding his service area and shrinking that of the worse performer. In time, the city agency was forced to adopt the productive practices of the contractor, and it ultimately matched his performance. The residents benefited from this system of permanent competition between the contractor and city forces. Over the long term, in New York, a system of competitive bidding between outside contractors and the sanitation department will institutionalize competition, guard against collusion by contractor, and protect residents from a public monopoly.

Street Sweeping

Street sweeping by private contractors is also a growing phenomenon, and the evidence indicates that it has strong advantages. A careful study of 20 cities found that the cost of municipal street sweeping per curb-mile was 43 percent greater than the cost of contract sweeping for the same frequency and quality of service (the latter as rated by street-cleanliness surveys), and for similar urban conditions. The difference was attributed to greater productivity by contract crews (that is, more miles swept per hour), more paid time off for municipal crews, more chiefs and fewer Indians in the municipal agencies, and better equipment maintenance by the contractors. The costs incurred by the cities to prepare and let contracts, and to monitor the contract work, were properly included in the cost of contract service.

Street Repaving

A comparative study of street repaving in cities that used contractors and cities that did the work in-house found that the latter was 96 percent more costly than the former. Moreover, the quality of the contract work was determined to be slightly better in the former: contractors averaged 4,508 tons of asphalt per full-time worker per year, whereas the municipal agencies averaged only a quarter of that, or 1,180 tons. This enormous difference more than compensated for the higher wages paid by contractors ($29,049 per worker annually versus $18,384) and the higher prices they paid for asphalt ($27.58 per ton, compared with $23.38 per ton paid by municipalities). The underlying factors behind the contractors' high productivity were the use of larger crews on the job site, more-experienced equipment operators, more on-site supervision, more equipment, and better and more-expensive equipment. If comparable results can be attained in New York, the annual expenditures of about $130 million for street repaving would be reduced by 49 percent, or $64 million.

Park Maintenance

A 1986 survey showed that the greatest municipal concern of New York City's 59 community boards was no longer police protection, but rather the condition of public parks. Can contracting out of park maintenance give the city more for less?

A detailed econometric analysis compared public and contract arrangements for mowing, weeding, fertilizing, reseeding, and aerating grassy areas. All costs were considered, including depreciation of equipment and the costs of awarding, letting, and overseeing contracts. The quality of work was rated visually, in terms of color, coverage, extent of weeds height, and edging. After controlling for size of area, quality, and number of activities performed it found that municipal service was 40 percent more expensive than contract work and that the quality of the contract work was better than that of the municipal work, although not significantly so. In Detroit, part of the responsibility for trimming healthy trees and removing dead and diseased ones from city streets was contracted out to private firms after a study showed that they could do the work at one-third the unit cost of the city agency. A comprehensive study comparing public and contract performance of this highly labor-intensive work, in which professional arborists measured the quality of tree care, showed that municipal tree maintenance was 37 percent more costly than was contract service, even though the quality of work was indistinguishable. One-quarter of the cost of contract work, as calculated, was the cost of municipal overheads, contract letting, and performance monitoring.

The reasons for the difference in cost for equivalent work were that municipal workers had somewhat higher wages and fringe benefits: had more paid vacation, holidays, and sick leave days; had more seniority; were less productive per hour worked; and had over them more layers of supervision. Also, municipal supervisors had little flexibility in hiring and firing, municipal agencies were less likely to be responsible for maintaining their own equipment, and municipal work was not scheduled as efficiently as it was by private companies, which took better advantage of the seasonal nature of the work.

The higher wages paid to public employees were partly attributable to the fact that the employees were older and had worked longer in that same function. This finding illustrates one of the inherent defects in the system of tenured civil service. In order to facilitate supposedly objective testing for hiring and promotion, jobs are very narrowly defined. As a result, public employees achieve tenure and often spend their entire working lives mowing grass, or collecting trash, or doing other limited chores. Their wages increase with longevity, but their productivity declines with age and with the increasing boredom of simple, repetitive, manual labor. In the private sector, workers are generally not engaged, or trapped, in these occupations as lifelong careers; such labor is usually viewed as a young man's job—an initial activity that is later outgrown. Quite apart from its efficiency, the latter approach is better for the individual in terms of personal growth and job satisfaction.

If the New York Department of Park and Recreation's annual expenditures for maintenance and operations, estimated at $205 million in 1986, could be reduced by contracting out to the extent indicated by the studies cited above, a saving of $57 million could be realized. Alternatively, some or all of this saving could be used to buy a higher quality of service, satisfying the public's demand for better park maintenance without a budget increase.

SUMMARY

Contracting out refuse collection, street sweeping, street repaving, and park maintenance offers total annual potential savings of $320 million. Applied systematically to all eligible municipal government activities, contracting out could reduce the municipal budget by roughly 25 percent—not only without reducing the level of services, but while actually improving their quality. By gradually applying contracts, vouchers, franchises, voluntary efforts, and free-market approaches to the many areas in which municipal government is failing outright or maintaining an unsatisfactory state of affairs, the city can improve the quality of life and reduce the tax burden. It is difficult to envision a bright future for New York without such increased reliance on the private sector.

City government has long been unable to bring about a truly satisfactory quality of life in New York. By attempting to satisfy every pressure group, it ends up overpromising and underachieving. It has taken on burdens that are too big for government. Private-sector institutions should be allowed to play a greater role in the life of the city. The powerful forces of competition and consumer sovereignty should be harnessed and put to work in the public interest.

"Privatization" is the generic term for a policy that entails less reliance on government. The principal techniques used to privatize are deregulation and devolution (to allow market forces to work), franchises, voluntary action, vouchers, and contracts for services.

Transportation and housing are ripe for economic deregulation, for the marketplace is already supplying mass transit and housing. Franchising of recreation facilities and municipal hospitals can provide better and less costly service than can municipal operation. Voluntary groups at the block, co-op, and neighborhood levels can do a great deal to improve local living conditions, and their efforts should be encouraged by city policies. Vouchers, which subsidize the citizen-consumer of a public service, instead of the monopolistic agency that provides the service, can enhance freedom of choice and foster competition, which is essential for constant improvement. Nowhere is competition more needed than in the city's failing school system. Finally, prudent contracting out has proved to be better than in-house provision of most municipal services, and New York should follow the lead of other cities in using this approach more aggressively and systematically.

Taken together, these five approaches constitute a privatization strategy. Consciously applied, this strategy will enable the city to harness the energy and talent of its people—acting outside the structure of government but within the bounds of society—to make New York a better place.

Chapter 7

SHAPING THE FACE OF NEW YORK

Paul Goldberger

New York is at once the most planned and the most chaotic of cities. Though it is among the most consciously ordered of American places, for most of its history it has grown with an energy that resembles anarchy more than order. In the past, market forces and government controls tended to combine to balance social needs with the needs of commerce. Today, this balance is threatened. While the complexity and number of zoning regulations increase, ever-larger buildings in ever-closer proximity are destroying the sense of order that the city once had, the physical fabric of a once civilized and urbane environment.

THE REGULATORY IMPULSE

There was probably never a stronger assertion of the power of government to determine the physical layout of a community than the Commissioners' Plan for the future growth of Manhattan, adopted in 1811, which ordained the grid pattern of streets above 14th Street. Giving the city map a Cartesian precision, it stands as a symbolic beginning to more than a century-and-a-half of assertive city planning. Central Park, a work of genius by Frederick Law Olmsted and Calvert Vaux in the mid-nineteenth century, was as precisely planned as the grid street layout and represented an expansion of the city's ambitions to embrace what might be called noble civic works as well as decisive planning. Olmsted's great parks and parkways elsewhere in the city continued these ambitions, as did Robert Moses' immense public works in the twentieth century, ranging from highways and bridges to great expanses of artificial beach—all giving further testament to the belief that in New York, civic virtue lay in activist planning.

Most important of all, however, was the commitment to the potential of zoning regulations to guide the physical growth of the city. The first zoning laws in the nation were adopted in New York in 1916, in response to the overwhelming mass of the Equitable Building on lower Broadway, designed by Ernest R. Graham. While this original zoning ordinance regulated building use throughout the city, it is best remembered for its regulations regarding skyscraper mass. The law required that buildings be set back from the street above a certain height, a provision designed to guarantee light and fresh air to the occupants of neighboring buildings as much as to the street itself. It was the intention of the law to assure that behemoths such as the Equitable did not occur again.

That such buildings have been built—and continue to be built to a degree that would shock the advocates of the zoning laws of 1916—makes it clear that other factors come into play in determining the physical form of the city. For today, while the city's planning regulations are as strict as those of any community in the country—not to mention as numerous and as cumbersome—the overall social commitment to planning is, in fact, weaker than it was even a generation ago. Even though a substantially new set of zoning regulations for midtown Manhattan added still more limitations to growth in 1982, development in mid-Manhattan and in prosperous areas elsewhere in the city is taking place at a scale that dwarfs almost everything produced by previous generations. This city of regulation is clearly also the city of seemingly uncontrollable growth. How can this be?

THE ECONOMIC IMPULSE

This situation may seem less paradoxical when one looks at a wider picture of the city's history and considers other factors that have balanced out the regulatory impulse. If the city as a governmental entity has traditionally resisted laissez-faire development in favor of regulation and large-scale, government-sponsored public works, the city's cultural and social traditions have always been much more those of freewheeling capitalism. If public-sector New York leans strongly towards regulation, private-sector New York has been equally committed to economic growth, to the power of private real-estate development, and to the belief that excessive regulation can put a damper on the ability of the private sector to function in an atmosphere of adequate freedom.

This dialectic between regulation and freedom is not at all new to our time, and it is not necessarily a sign of entirely opposing priorities. It is worth remembering here that the Commissioners' Plan, firm example of government regulation that it was, nonetheless took its form because a grid yielded the most easily divisible and saleable lots. There was no belief, as there was in Washington when Pierre L'Enfant's plan was adopted, that a city should be designed on a primarily esthetic basis. Efficiency was the goal in New York; the land was to be divided easily and cheaply into a marketable commodity. If government regulation through a sweeping act of city planning was the easiest means toward that goal, so be it; the end, not the means, was the point.

Obtaining the maximum economic potential from land was, of course, the goal behind the design of the Equitable Building, which merely embodied on a vastly more dramatic scale the impulse of profit maximization that had inspired virtually every builder in New York for the previous half-century, from the makers of dark, dank tenements on the Lower East Side to the architects of the smaller office buildings that preceded the Equitable. And while the outcry over plans for the Equitable led eventually to the creation of the 1916 zoning laws, those laws were conceived as a means of protecting the economic investment of neighboring property owners as much as a way of guarding the public good. Regulation was designed to protect the economic drive as much as to restrain it.

THE IMPERIAL IMPULSE

If one impulse behind the physical form of New York was the tendency toward extensive governmental regulation and planning, and another was the drive to maximize economic potential, a third, which might be called the imperial impulse, was the drive to make the city noble, grand, physically awesome. This is the most difficult impulse of all to discuss in quantitative terms, but it is the one that in its more positive manifestations has done the most to give the city its characteristic look. Indeed, we might think of this impulse as the desire to express a quality of "New York-ness" in the city's architecture—the desire to design buildings with a flamboyance that would distinguish them from their counterparts elsewhere.

129

This imperial impulse developed, logically enough, in the second half of the nineteenth century, by which time the city was sufficiently established in the world economy to have grandiose ambitions for itself. New York had become clearly the nation's preeminent city, and increasingly an international economic center as well. It saw itself as standing above the other cities in this country, in both economic might and cultural sophistication, and as the city's wealth grew, it looked increasingly to Europe. From the middle of the nineteenth century through the middle of the twentieth century, architects of New York relied heavily on the architecture of the past, which held an allure for New York that was little understood in cities such as Chicago, where the blunter, more structurally expressive pragmatism that eventually gave birth to the modern skyscraper held sway.

The imperial impulse would seem, from the vantage point of the 1980s, to have been in obvious conflict with the city's intense commercial drives. Grandiose buildings are not cheap, and they do not offer the easiest way to produce the vast quantities of rentable space that are the developers' essential product in New York. Nonetheless, the imperial impulse was very much in accord with the other aspects of the city's identity. Essential public works such as Central Park, the Brooklyn Bridge and the public works of the Robert Moses era exemplified the city's impulse toward public control as much as they expressed the drive to create an imperial city. So, too, with the great Beaux-Arts buildings of the first decades of the twentieth century, such as Carrere and Hastings' New York Public Library, McKim, Mead, and White's Pennsylvania Station, and Warren and Wetmore's Grand Central Terminal.

Curiously, these Beaux-Arts train stations were particularly characteristic of New York in another way, one that went beyond their sumptuousness—they tended to be squeezed onto modest plots in the tight street grid, as if to suggest a constant tension between their civic monumentality and the commercial city that surrounded them. The grid was amended slightly, but not dramatically, to accommodate them. There was no great square to frame Penn Station, for example; the commercial value of the adjacent property was simply too high to permit giving up any more land than the station itself occupied.

But more notable was the extent to which the drive to express a quality of New York-ness found its way into conventional commercial architecture and the extent to which the commercial architecture of New York came to take on a certain powerful theatricality. The

130

controlling force in New York was theater, not theory; for most of the first half of the twentieth century, the skyline of New York was a dazzling, utterly fanciful array of pinnacles and turrets and crowns, all standing for little but visual pleasure. Cass Gilbert's Woolworth Building, of 1913, was perhaps the most appealing example. A spectacular Gothic skyscraper, its flamboyance was unquestionable; no one could consider this an ordinary enclosure of commercial space. Gilbert's graceful, almost lyrical terra-cotta ornament brought genuine drama to the skyline, at once looking back to Europe and ahead to the power of the American skyscraper.

The Woolworth was at the time of its completion the tallest building in the world, which made it a neat marriage of two of New York's prime impulses—the economic and the imperial. What could be more fitting for New York than to possess the world's tallest building, and that that building should be an office tower erected for the purpose of doing business? When a prominent clergyman referred to the tower as the "Cathedral of Commerce," this was taken as a great compliment; for it seemed right that in New York, a business building should raise its head high and dominate the skyline as the cathedrals did in European cities. Yet how characteristic of New York, too, that this building should be not wholly a banal set of office floors, but a tower of great, theatrical presence.

The Woolworth's qualities did not belong to it alone. Daniel Burnham's Flatiron Building, of 1902, possessed similar theatricality, as did Napolean LeBrun's Metropolitan Life Insurance Company tower of 1909, William Van Alen's Chrysler Building of 1930, and Shreve, Lamb, and Harmon's Empire State Building of 1931, to name but a few. In each case the principles were the same, to develop a site to maximum, or nearly maximum, economic potential, but to do so in a way that made a dramatic, striking statement.

In the two decades following World War II, the economic impulse seemed to grow stronger, and fewer of the even modest compromises with economics that grander and more flamboyant architecture requires seemed to be made. The decline of the city's imperial impulse was abetted by the postwar rise of the International Style in architecture, which made austere, stark boxes of glass and steel esthetically acceptable. By the end of the 1950s, what was cheapest and easiest to produce became a banal architecture utterly at odds with the city's traditions.

The tendency toward regulation during this period began a process of adjustment that made it less a restraint on unfettered development than a handmaiden to it. In 1961 the setback rules that had given

New York towers their characteristic shape were replaced by new regulations written to encourage boxy, International Style skyscrapers that, with a few notable exceptions, were little more than crude and cheap enclosures of space. As the decade went on, other amendments to the 1916 zoning ordinance offered developers the option of building larger structures as a bonus for providing certain public benefits.

THE BONUS SYSTEM

This bonus system is worth looking at briefly in terms of the city's three underlying impulses, for it represents a curious inversion of the city's priorities. In the Broadway theater district, to take the first example to achieve wide use, builders of skyscrapers were permitted to expand their towers by 20 percent in exchange for including a new legitimate theater in the premises. It was an example of the first impulse, the drive toward regulation, being used as means of encouraging at least a small hint of the third impulse, the drive to express New York-ness and make the city a glamorous place—in this case, quite literally a theatrical one.

But the impulse to regulate had become timid. In order to achieve the public amenities it desired, the city felt it had to offer an enormous economic incentive—the right to make buildings one-fifth larger. Real-estate developers who chose to take advantage of this offer had to pay the one-time cost of constructing a theater or some other amenity, such as a plaza, but would receive substantially more rental income for the entire life of their building.

In this sense, the impulse toward regulation essentially became simply a means of making buildings yet larger, and of adding to rather than limiting the economic possibilities on a given piece of land. Given the deeply disappointing nature of many of the so-called "amenities" created under this program—the plazas, arcades, and theaters—the zoning-bonus system was hardly an effective force in stimulating the city's imperial impulse. It only rarely yielded better architecture, and it significantly increased the already serious overcrowding in midtown Manhattan.

By the late 1970s, the zoning-bonus system had become so complex that the zoning code was essentially irrelevant to major Manhattan buildings, whose developers negotiated directly with the city Planning Commission for building size and bulk in exchange for a package of amenities. The economic recession of the early 1970s and the city's fiscal crisis of mid-decade made city officials so eager for large-scale real-estate projects, that few major projects were disapproved. And in many parts of Manhattan, such as on Madison Avenue by the mid-80s, large buildings, constructed cheek-by-jowl, possessed precisely the sort of immense bulk that the original zoning laws of 1916 had been intended to prevent.

If the boxy towers of the 1950s and 1960s testified to the failure of the marketplace, on its own, to create public amenities and achieve a quality of imperial grandeur, the experience of the zoning-bonus system inspired no more faith in the ability of regulation to achieve the ideal city. The zoning-bonus system was presented in the late 1960s as the enlightened planners' best answer to the city's planning problems; in retrospect, there appears to have been no small degree of arrogance in this view, given the poor quality of so many of the amenities and the vastly larger buildings that constitute the bonus system's permanent legacy. And ironically, it is highly likely that the shift in architectural taste in the late 1970s toward buildings that are more dramatic and eccentric in design than the bland boxes of the previous generation would have given enough New York-ness to the skyline in and of itself without city interference.

In photographs taken during the first three decades of the twentieth century, the city seems to represent a certain ideal condition. What made those years, and particularly the period between the World Wars, so remarkable was the sense of balance in the city's physical fabric—balance between the tall towers in mid-Manhattan and the essentially low-rise cityscape of the rest of the city; balance between tall towers and medium-sized buildings around them; a balance between modernism and historicism, as well as a balance between the theatricality of the city's most notable, foreground towers and the more understated background buildings that surrounded them; and a sense that each block represented a balance between the needs of pedestrians to enjoy a lively and distinctive streetscape and the larger urban priority that each block form part of a unified overall streetscape. New York's skyline in those years was a romantic icon, and yet the city was no less a capital of commerce for all the romantic power that it possessed. Its scale seemed at once imperial and intimate. The city was an international capital, and yet it was also a city of neighborhoods.

This delicate balance of large and small, of monumental and intimate, was an accidental result of market and demographic forces, not a consciously created element. But the same forces that once yielded such splended results seem today to threaten as much to

133

destroy this balance as to maintain it. In Manhattan, for example, more and more large-scale construction has upset the overall sense of urban order as the sections of the borough that are developed to maximal or near-maximal potential have expanded dramatically. The office towers of Midtown have moved west across Sixth Avenue and east to Second Avenue, and the high-rise apartment buildings of the Upper East Side have jumped across Lexington Avenue to cover virtually every block to the East River. Four- and five-story brownstones have given way to buildings that are 30, 40, or more stories tall. The sense of varied scale has begun to disappear, replaced by a uniformly large scale that destroys a crucial aspect of the city's identity.

All of these trends cannot be attributed solely to regulation, of course; the energy of the marketplace primarily fueled this growth. But the government bonus system did make possible a 20 percent increase in the size of commercial buildings, and government tax abatements did have the effect of increasing the pace of residential construction. In late 1985, the expiration of the city's 421A tax abatement legislation set off a flood of construction initiated to beat the deadline—an event that was hailed as evidence of the robustness of the free marketplace but was, ironically, actually a potent example of the impact of governmental intervention.

GIGANTISM

By the late 1970s, when construction resumed with a vengeance after the city's fiscal crisis of mid-decade, Manhattan's physical form was less varied and its spirit significantly less spontaneous; many sections of Manhattan seemed to consist almost entirely of very large buildings, and it was not all all uncommon for a 50-story tower to stand next to another building of equal size. By the late 1980s, after a decade of intense large-scale construction, gigantism seemingly had become an accepted value in urban development. Indeed, gigantism seems to have replaced density as the quality most symbolic of urban vitality. In previous generations it was expected that the city would be crowded; only extreme advocates of the garden city, such as Lewis Mumford or, in his own way, Frank Lloyd Wright, disparaged the values of density. It was understood, moreover, that urban density could exist at low-to-medium scales—indeed, that it could often flourish best in such circumstances, as on traditional city blocks of row houses. But now, merely to be densely built up seems not a sufficient badge of urban success, at least for Manhattan; it is necessary that the buildings themselves be immense as well as tightly configured.

The fixation on gigantism has made blocks of brownstones seem like quaint leftovers. Indeed, in many sections of Manhattan, such as Greenwich Village and the Upper East Side, small buildings survive only by dint of the Landmarks Preservation Commission's designation of these sections as historic districts, a use of the landmark's power for what are, admittedly, purposes of planning as much as of historic preservation. In fact, the Landmarks Preservation Commission may have become the most significant planning tool in the city, if only by default of other agencies.

To be fair, the City Planning Commission, to which responsibility for such regulation properly falls, has recently restricted large-scale development in the mid-blocks of the Upper East Side, has limited towers on the Upper West Side, and has enacted modest downzoning for the eastern blocks of Midtown Manhattan. The revised zoning laws for the Upper West Side are particularly striking in that they represent at least a partial return to long-abandoned principles that discourage towers in favor of squatter buildings built out to the street at ground level rather than set back behind plazas. Furthermore, instead of rising straight up—as the sheer towers, encouraged by the last set of zoning regulations, did—the new structures will step back in wedding-cake fashion on their higher floors, as did the earlier "skyscrapers." This is a welcome recognition that in terms of urban design, a city of sheer towers, each disconnected from the next, does not work, and that if New York is to retain even a shred of its traditional look, it is essential that buildings join together to create a "street wall" by being built out to the street-line rather than set back behind plazas.

But these new zoning changes, while yielding a visually pleasing result, suggest that the city continues to go far beyond the original principles on which zoning laws were based: namely, the provision of adequate light and air, in the exercise of broader urban design powers. But while suggesting that the city government is liberal in its interpretation of the zoning mandate, these changes fail to do the one thing that might make a broad use of zoning powers worthwhile—to stem the tide of overbuilding in Manhattan and divert it more evenly across the entire city.

Sometimes the city has attempted to do this, but in such a way as to only compound the problem. In 1982, a revision of Midtown zoning expanded allowable densities on the West Side while reducing it on the East Side, in the belief that the free market needed sticks to restrict it as well as carrots to stimulate it. The result, naturally enough, has been only marginally smaller buildings in the eastern blocks of Midtown but much larger buildings in the western blocks.

Three decades ago, Lewis Mumford warned that the towers of Midtown Manhattan will crowd each other so seriously that "architecture will cease to matter." There is a particular irony to Mumford's prediction, for on a cultural level at least, architecture now matters more than it has since the city's great years between the wars. The indifference and banality of the International Style is now largely a thing of the past; both architects and the general public reacted so strongly against it that the pendulum has been swinging in the other direction for some time, bringing the city such structures as the American Telephone and Telegraph Building, the granite tower with the split-pediment "Chippendale" top on Madison Avenue by Philip Johnson and John Burgee; the same architects' elliptical building on Third Avenue; Cesar Pelli's granite-and-glass towers in stepped-back shapes at the World Financial Center in Battery Park City; Kohn Pederson Fox's granite-and-glass towers with classical detailing; and Helmut Jahn's flashy, futuristic towers of glass and metal. On a purely architectural level, the drive to express a quality of New York-ness is as strong as ever. The architecture of the city's large-scale projects is again full of energy and a determination to make the kind of statement that architects of the 1920s made.

But the private sector works now without the limits that a strong commitment to planning would provide. For all the sheer volume and complexity of zoning regulations, the city's impulse toward regulation and public projects seems particularly weak at this point. City policy is most often directed not toward the larger issues of limits, but toward minutiae and an involvement in the design process, at the expense of the larger issues that directly affect the public welfare. This relative weakness in public planning—the city's first, or regulatory impulse—must be seen against the fact that the city's commercial drive, its second impulse, has been stronger than ever. Indeed, it has been so strong that it has made the renewed vitality of the third drive, the imperial impulse, nearly irrelevant.

The city's present role was shown, sadly but clearly, in the recent decision to sell off the land occupied by the now-obsolete New York Coliseum at Columbus Circle not to the private developer who offered the most reasonable proposal, but to the one who offered the most money. The city, which could have required private developers to conform to strict guidelines, chose to be so interested in short-term financial benefits that it encouraged the creation of a far-too-large structure, designed by Moshe Safdie for Boston Properties, that would have virtually overwhelmed Columbus Circle. The Safdie design has now been abandoned as the result of a substantial public outcry, not only against the architecture but also against the process by which the city, by selling off the land to the highest bidder, became less a regulator than an active participant in the development process. A lawsuit initiated by the Municipal Arts Society, a private group, invalidated the granting of the lease of the Coliseum land to Boston Properties—a judgment that the city is currently appealing. If the city does not win its appeal, it is likely that the entire process of redeveloping the Coliseum site will have to begin anew. But even if the city is successful in upholding its legal position, it has already bowed to public pressure by agreeing, along with the developer, to replace the Safdie design with a smaller building by a different architect. And the planning process the city used here has been significantly tarnished.

There are other examples of gigantism. Times Square Center, a 4-million-square-foot project designed by Philip Johnson and John Burgee, would overwhelm Times Square with four mansard-roofed office towers; and Television City, a project designed by Alexander Cooper and sponsored by Donald Trump that would contain a 135-story tower, are perhaps the city's most conspicuous examples of gigantism yet. Although the Trump project was redesigned after it became clear that neither the city government nor community groups on the Upper West Side would accept the first version, it is clear that the city did not provide clear direction, but rather reacted to plans submitted to it and acted more as a design review board than a planning authority.

THE URBAN FABRIC

What distinguishes the large-scale efforts of today from those of past generations is not only immensity of scale, but also an indifference to the questions of overall urban fabric, of balance. The city's great public and private spaces of past eras, places such as Grand Army Plaza in Brooklyn, the Grand Concourse in the Bronx, Rockefeller Center, Central Park, and the works of Robert Moses, fit into the fabric of the city, enlivened it, intensified it; they did not defy it. To have moved from Rockefeller Center to Television

City in half a century is not, sadly, to have learned very much at all.

There are some encouraging signs, although they are few. The best is Battery Park City, the large commercial and housing complex in lower Manhattan constructed according to a master plan by the architects Cooper/Eckstut Associates under the guidance of the state's Urban Development Corporation and Battery Park City Authority. This important development extends the street pattern of lower Manhattan and contains relatively traditional masonry buildings built along streets and squares in the manner of the traditional city. Its generous esplanade, open to the riverfront, is similar to the fine esplanades of Carl Schurz Park and Brooklyn Heights, and the balance between its public and private spaces is as comfortable as anywhere in Manhattan. Battery Park City is entirely new, and it feels new; yet it is as completely in accord with the spirit of the city as any older neighborhood. Here, and here alone in our time, has that much sought-after intangible New York-ness been achieved.

Whether and how this quality can be encouraged is the real design question the city faces. Battery Park City was the work of a public authority, building on public land, in partnership with private developers; it takes no excessive commitment to the benefits of regulation to believe that strong design guidelines were appropriate under such circumstances. Fully private developments pose a more difficult problem: how to achieve similarly positive results without treating private land as if it were public and hence subject to total regulation. For the commitment to varied scale, to street life, and to the architectural and urbanistic traditions of New York, make sense in all development, private as well as public. Yet the highly specific design prescriptions that governed Battery Park City would not be appropriate in a more private situation.

In fact, in most areas a well-written "as-of-right" zoning ordinance would provide all the prescription that is necessary, while allowing for a more appropriate distance between the city's planners and the private developers who are working under its rules. Zoning would set overall limits to growth and direct large growth patterns, rather than offering highly prescriptive design rules for plazas and arcades. This is not to say that it is never appropriate for the city to deal in specifics, or with what might be called micro-issues. Indeed, it is urgent that zoning laws be fine-tuned to reflect neighborhood character. The regulations requiring that new high-rise construction around Times Square contain illuminated commercial signs, for example, recognize that unregulated expansion of the office district westward would result in the disappearance of the elaborate signs that are Times Square's trademark and, arguably, a cultural amenity worth preserving. Similarly, the new Upper West Side zoning emerges out of an admirable desire to recognize and extend the present architectural context of that neighborhood. The notion is to avoid letting the zoning law be an agent of cataclysmic change.

The most difficult, but perhaps most important, task for the city's planning authorities is to drastically reduce all zoning capacity throughout the high-density areas of Manhattan—to cut it in half, perhaps, across the board. The city's zoning has always allowed too much building, but whereas in the early years of the century the possibility that every site would be developed to its maximum seemed so remote as to be irrelevant, the likelihood that they will all be developed to the maximum is no longer a distant possibility, but a very real threat. All new buildings in a down-zoned district would not, under such a proposal, necessarily be unreasonably small; incentive zoning could provide that they would just not automatically be as big as they are now. Since large buildings are in part a function of high land prices—which in turn arise from the potential to build large buildings—removing the automatic right to build to immense size would inevitably reduce land values, and the cycle would at long last be reversed.

A drastic down-zoning of Manhattan would have the effect of increasing development pressures in the outer boroughs, where efforts to encourage large-scale development have so far moved slowly, in large part because it has been too easy to build in Manhattan. The announcement in midsummer of 1986 that Citicorp would build a 43-story tower in Long Island City in Queens, just across the East River from Midtown Manhattan, was encouraging as a major commitment to development outside of Manhattan's overcrowded core. While the prospect of Manhattanlike office towers sprouting all across the five boroughs is not a pleasing one, neither is it even a remote possibility, and moderate development of large-scale structures in selected and appropriate portions of the outer boroughs can only bode well for the city at large, both as an economic stimulus to their immediate areas and as a way of reducing pressure on the central core.

Manhattan will always remain the city's economic and cultural center. But however potent Manhattan's economic health may be, its existence as a civilizing urban environment is more problematic. There are some encouraging signs—the commitment to a more vital architecture, the gradual improvements in zoning law to bring buildings more into accord with the traditional urbanistic patterns of New York, the lessons provided by Battery Park City. But whether these will be enough to offset the damage to the city's physical fabric caused by the sheer quantity of building, the loss of varied scale, and the concentration on gigantism remains to be seen. New York may well turn out to be a victim of its own success.

Chapter 8

A SOCIAL SERVICE SYSTEM TO END DEPENDENCY

Blanche Bernstein

New York City, the paramount gateway for millions of immigrants, has provided a better life for many but never for all of its new citizens. The poor have always been and remain the object of public and philanthropic concern and assistance in the city. However, after World War II, with prosperity at levels previously undreamed of, the continued presence, and even rising numbers, of the poor in the city has become politically and socially unacceptable. In view of the vast efforts that were made to help the less-advantaged, their numbers are also, to some extent, inexplicable.

New York has historically been in the vanguard in its concern for and care of the poor. The city's standards for cash assistance are among the highest in the country, and the scope of its programs goes beyond the usual specifications of such urban staples as federally assisted Aid to Families with Dependent Children (AFDC) for female-headed families or for two-parent families with unemployed (AFDC-U). Under General Assistance (GA), the city cares for intact families with children and for single individuals with incomes below the welfare standard. Medical care is available free of charge to all of those who receive cash assistance, as well as to others with limited incomes.

A vast array of publicly funded service programs are operated by city agencies or by philanthropic or community organizations. Of the approximately $1.9 billion budgeted for social service programs in 1986–87, $540 million was devoted to services such as home care for the aged and disabled; $200 million to day care for children; and smaller sums for adoption and family planning, programs that can help prevent dependency. More than half of the $1.9 billion

141

goes for foster care, child abuse, shelter for the homeless, and other programs designed to deal with disasters in the lives of children and adults.

But although billions have been spent to mitigate the hardships of poverty, relatively little public effort has gone into helping people escape from it. To understand how the social-services system could function to reduce dependency, it is necessary to examine recent trends in the size and characteristics of the nonaged poor sector of the dependent population.

PROFILE OF THE DEPENDENT POOR

Among the 6.1 million nonaged persons in the city, somewhere between 1.3 and 1.8 million were poor in 1984. In November 1986, about 50–70 percent of the poor were on welfare, representing 20 percent of poor married couples with children but about 80 percent of poor female-headed families with children. Since more precise estimates unfortunately are not available from the Current Population Survey, and since 1980 census data do not accurately reflect the situation in New York, this description of the poor in New York is limited to the dependent poor, based on data from the welfare caseload.

Just over 850,000 persons were on welfare in September 1987—almost 15 percent of the total city population that is neither aged, blind, nor disabled. Among the welfare recipients were about half a million children, of whom 90 percent lived in female-headed families on AFDC. Slightly more than a third of the children were under six years of age, about a third were 6–11, and under a third were 12–18. The bulk of the caseload (80 percent) was represented by the 235,000 female heads of families and their 450,000 children.

Significantly, persons in female-headed families declined from 825,000 in 1976 to 686,000 in September 1987, partly because the number of such families dropped, but mainly because of the decline in the average size of AFDC families. The big increase in the overall welfare caseload has come in the number of single individuals on General Assistance.

The singles caseload increased fivefold between 1963 and 1968, even though these were prosperous years marked by declining unemployment. It jumped again in 1974–77, years of recession in the city, reaching a new peak of almost 90,000; and still again beginning in 1981, to reach a new peak of 125,000 in May 1986.

Toward the fall of 1987, it had declined somewhat, to 106,000, still at a very high level. Many of these individuals are former members of AFDC families, some forced off AFDC by the federal legislative changes embedded in the Overall Budget and Reconciliation Act (OBRA) of 1981, others, having reached 18 years of age, unable to make their way into the labor market because they lack a high school degree and marketable skills. The rise in the singles caseload reflects also the decline in the marriage rate—there are just more singles than there used to be—as well as behavioral problems associated with increased drug use, delinquency, and crime.

The number of intact families on AFDC-U and GA also rose between July 1981 and September 1987; but though the percentage increase was large, the numbers remained small—3,200 families on AFDC-U and about 14,700 on GA, for a total of approximately 61,000 persons, including children. It remains uncommon for the intact family to require assistance from welfare unless unemployment reaches double-digit levels. Further, the need for assistance is generally for relatively short periods of a year or two, or less.

Welfare dependency and poverty reflect in large measure the increasing numbers of female-headed families, a trend evident over the last quarter-century in the city and the nation. This trend is due partially to family breakup through divorce, separation, or desertion, but in larger measure to the nonformation of families by parenting teenagers or the early breakup of such teenage marriages as do take place. The causes of this phenomenon remain a matter of controversy and continued debate. But whatever the causes, these trends have adversely affected the well-being of all ethnic groups in the city, and most heavily and disproportionately the blacks and Hispanics. While only rough estimates are available, it appears that as many as 90 percent of the AFDC caseload consists of blacks or Hispanics, as opposed to 10 percent non-Hispanic whites or others. The small size of the sample on which these data are based may exaggerate the minority ratio, but the figures do not differ much from those obtained in similar studies based on larger samples conducted by the Department of Health, Education, and Welfare before 1979.

For too long, local welfare agencies in New York and other urban areas throughout the country paid little attention to the economic and social consequences of teenage pregnancy. They have also been less than vigorous at best, and delinquent at worst, in placing an obligation to work on welfare clients and consistently promoting training and employment of mothers on welfare. Finally, they have failed to consider that the care and education of children on welfare

143

was their concern as well as that of Boards of Education. This is all understandable, at least in part. The quadrupling of the welfare caseload between 1960 and 1972 and the increasing evidence of high rates of ineligibility and overpayments by the mid-1970s made the task of improving the integrity of the welfare system of paramount importance. It took close to a decade to bring the payment-error rate in public assistance and food stamps down to about the level that has to be anticipated in any complicated system.

Another part of the problem, however, has been ideological and political in nature. Expressions of concern over the deterioration of family structure, rising teenage parenting, and inadequate educational achievement were often considered racist and disparaged by liberals as "blaming the victim." It was not until 1983–84, when black leaders recognized in major publications and public statements that family structure, teenage pregnancy, and inadequate education and training for employment were at the root of the problem of poverty and dependency among blacks, that serious attention and increased resources began to be directed to these fundamental issues. The National Urban League and the National Association for the Advancement of Colored People, along with other major black organizations, then began to give top priority to programs to prevent teenage pregnancy.

Neither the teenage mothers on welfare nor their children do well in school. In 1982–83, among those 20–64 years old in the city's total population, 57.3 percent graduated from high school; in the public assistance population, however, only 24.8 percent were high school graduates. The combination of early child bearing and low educational achievement, frequently accompanied by such social dysfunctioning as juvenile delinquency and drug abuse, severely limits the welfare family's prospects for escaping poverty and dependency.

The litany of social and economic ills arising from early and out-of-wedlock pregnancy is by now exceedingly familiar. Efforts to improve the employability of welfare clients, reduce teenage pregnancy and parenting, and improve the educational achievement levels of the mothers and children on welfare have changed and expanded during the past few years, but a wide gap remains between what exists and what is needed.

EMPLOYMENT OPPORTUNITIES

In October 1985, the city initiated a new Employment Opportunities Program (EO) designed to improve the employability of all employable clients on AFDC. The program provides for an assessment by the regional office of the New York State Department of Labor (DOL). If the client is adjudged job-ready, DOL undertakes to assist the client in finding a job. If not job-ready, the client is referred to HRA's Work Incentive Office (WIN), where after further review and assessment the client may choose a job training program; further education, including training in English; completing high school or obtaining a general equivalency diploma (GED); or going to a community or senior college. A client who chooses none of these alternatives is assigned to the Community Work Experience Program (CWEP)—in other words, workfare. Employable welfare clients are no longer to languish for years in the WIN unassigned pool, as has been common in the past, though a substantial backlog still exists.

As of December 1987, no assessment of the Employment Opportunities program had been made to determine the number of clients who obtained jobs, completed training, or achieved basic English and moved into the labor market. In the first seven months of its operation, however, approximately 30,000 clients were evaluated and assigned, including 11,471 with whom DOL worked in job search; 165 were placed in DOL-subsidized employment; 8,513 were in various training programs, including 4,231 in private schools, 1,524 in high schools or GED, and 1,014 in community or senior colleges, mainly the former. The largest single group, totaling 15,850, were assigned to CWEP. Data on the numbers of clients who fail to cooperate and whose cases should be closed or sanctioned (i.e., the mother removed from the welfare grant) are available only for those who were called but failed to show up for an interview or for assignment to CWEP; during the six months July–December 1986, the figure averaged 24.5 percent; of those, 70 percent were actually closed, 40 percent of which remained closed for three months or more. Thus, about 7 percent of those called for interviews who fail to report were closed and remained closed for three months or more. If it does nothing else, therefore, the imposition of an obligation to work does uncover welfare clients with other sources of income who should not be on welfare.

In 1987, however, in response to revised New York State regulations, a case is no longer closed for failure of the AFDC

145

mother to appear for the interview or the work assignment; only the mother is "sanctioned"—that is, removed from the case and the welfare grant reduced accordingly. The sanction is, of course, less punitive than a case closing, and probably less effective in uncovering fraud. This has to be a matter of concern, since by 1988, according to an HRA official, as many as 75 percent of those being called into the Employment Opportunities program apparently will be directly assigned to the work-experience program. Further, no data are yet available on the outcomes of the various job search and employment training programs. Thus, we do not know how many actually obtain jobs after a job search or completion of training or how many are enabled to manage without welfare assistance.

Accordingly, it is not yet possible to make an appraisal of EO's impact on reducing dependency and poverty. The current and long-overdue emphasis on a work obligation for heads of families on welfare, the provision for job search, skills training, and workfare, will make some difference and must be pursued vigorously. But the program must be recognized as a salvage operation. The welfare mothers are starting late on working careers. Their education is likely to be limited to high school graduation or the equivalent and their earnings are likely to be modest. Some may still require welfare supplementation, and others may have earnings not much above the poverty level.

TEENAGE PREGNANCY

Of all welfare mothers, those most likely to be on welfare and poor for a long time are teenage mothers and their children. New York contributes at least its share to the national problem of teenage pregnancy. Of the nearly 1 million youngsters 10–19 years old in the city, an estimated 150,000 females and 215,000 males are sexually active. In 1985, nearly one of every four sexually active female adolescents became pregnant. Almost 15,000 teenagers of 17 years of age or younger in the city become pregnant each year, and each year 5,000 will give birth, 18 percent are already mothers, and 90 percent are unmarried. An estimated 28,000 teenagers with 34,000 children under the age of six lived in New York City as of early 1986. Among those 15–17 years old, about 5 percent of blacks, 4 percent of Hispanics, and less than 1 percent of whites had a child in 1984.

Recognition of the problem led to the creation of the Adolescent

Pregnancy Inter-Agency Council in the Office of the Mayor in September 1984, to develop policies and programs and coordinate and monitor program initiatives undertaken by city agencies. Twenty city agencies and offices are represented on the Council, including HRA, the various health agencies, the Board of Education, and others. A report issued in August 1986 outlines a broad-scale effort designed to prevent the first pregnancy through family-life and sex education given to parents and children from kindergarten through the 12th grade, and through use of the media; to facilitate teenagers' early access to reproductive health care facilities and a choice of options in regard to pregnancy; and to provide a variety of services, such as assistance in finishing school, job training and employment, and health care and housing, to parenting teens and adolescents at high risk of becoming teenage parents. The proposed plan, which is basically a substantial expansion of existing programs, is indeed comprehensive, and it does give the necessary priority to the prevention of the first pregnancy. But costs and implementation strategies are still unclear.

Obviously, the Council's proposal is going to be expensive, and one cannot be certain of its success, particularly with respect to the already-pregnant or parenting teenagers. A careful evaluation of Project Redirection, designed to assist pregnant and parenting teens on AFDC, begun in June 1980 and carried on over a $3\frac{1}{2}$-year period by the Manpower Research and Development Corporation (MRDC), does not give much ground for hope. The better outcome found among the participants as compared to the control group with respect to education, employment, and a lower rate of subsequent pregnancy apparent after the first program year were mostly transitory. The one slightly hopeful note is that teenage pregnancy rates do not appear to have increased in 1985–86, even though the proportion of sexually active teenagers continued to rise. More seem to be heeding the call to use contraceptives. This is small comfort in a sea of trouble.

EDUCATION

If any one proposition receives universal approbation in this country, it is that education—at least a high school education, and preferably college—provides the pathway to economic and social well-being. By the early 1960s, it was therefore a matter of deep social concern that the large black and Hispanic minorities in New

York, as well as in the nation as a whole, were not achieving the same educational levels as were whites. Efforts to deal with the problem started in the mid-1960s with the establishment at the City University of New York (CUNY) of Seek and College Discovery, programs designed to allow some disadvantaged students with relatively low high-school scores to matriculate in the senior and community colleges. Efforts continued in 1970 with the establishment of open admissions at all the City University colleges of any high school graduate or holder of an equivalency degree. The decision was made, if not without recognition of the problems that would be created by the entry into college of large numbers of poorly prepared students, certainly without adequate preparation to deal with the scale and duration of the problems that the colleges faced. At CUNY's senior colleges, it was found that 60 percent of the entering students required remediation in at least one of the basic skills, and that of these, about half required assistance in three or four. In the community colleges, 85 percent required remediation in at least one basic skill, of whom substantially more than half needed help in three or four.

One result of "open admissions" shown by CUNY figures was a sharp drop in graduation rates between the 1970 and 1971 classes and the 1978 class. For students in the senior colleges, those with high school averages of 80 or more, the graduation rate went from 53 percent to 36 percent five years after entry; for students with averages below 80, it dropped from 32 to 15 percent. Among students in the two-year community colleges with averages of 75 or better, the graduation rate declined from 43 percent to 38 percent five years after entry, and among those with lower averages from 25 percent to 18 percent. This trend reflects not only a decline in the high-school grades of entering students and a decline in the level of academic competence associated with a particular grade, but also an increase in the proportion of older and minority students burdened by family responsibilities, unable to attend college full-time, or even consistently part-time. What comes through clearly is that success in college is closely related to the level of academic achievement in high school. Blacks and Hispanics have been disproportionately fewer among the graduates than among the entrants to the colleges.

As a result of research and experimentation which has taken place since 1975, more-effective retention programs are now available. But remediation at the college level is costly and comes so late in the educational process that even more effective retention programs are likely to achieve only limited success. And remediation substantially prolongs the time needed for both graduation and the attainment of jobs requiring college training.

For the many who do not attend college, high school graduation is essential to obtaining a job at decent wages—or perhaps any job. The limited efforts in the city's secondary schools within the last few years to reduce the student dropout rate have produced only modest results—a drop of a few percentage points, to about 35 percent overall—but the dropout rate for blacks and Hispanics remains almost double that level. The president of the Board of Education, Robert F. Wagner, Jr., announced shortly after he took office in July 1986 that reduction of the dropout rate was his highest priority. But just as remediation at the college level is expensive and difficult, so it proves to be at the high school level, where such efforts also come late. If after eight years of elementary and junior high school, basic values, attitudes, self-discipline, and sense of responsibility have not been established, it is difficult to start teaching them to 14-year-olds.

In short, efforts to reduce dependency, whether through employment programs for welfare clients, programs aimed at teenage pregnancy prevention, or high school retention efforts, are unlikely to achieve more than limited results; they come late, much too late, in the lives of those who need them.

Such a conclusion is particularly distressing in view of the fact that poverty and dependency, teenage pregnancy, and inadequate educational achievement are linked and are, by a large margin, disproportionately concentrated in the black and Hispanic communities. This is not to point a finger in scorn but to underline a crucial problem in the city's societal structure, a problem whose solution requires a new kind of approach. Current efforts must continue, but if we want to diminish substantially the current disparity in the well-being of the major ethnic communities in the city, we must focus on the children on welfare, beginning with the very young.

THE CHILDREN

Among the approximately half-million children on welfare in September 1987, over 200,000 were below the age of six and 173,000 were between six and twelve. Over 90 percent of those children were in female-headed families on AFDC. Some 60–70 percent of the mothers were teenagers then or at the time their first child was born.

Beginning in the 1960s, the philosophy of nonintervention developed in the social welfare community as part of the notion that any and all life-styles are acceptable, and that there is nothing wrong with a welfare family that more money would not cure. Influenced by this philosophy, HRA, except in disaster situations and cases of blatant neglect, has done nothing for, knows nothing about, and does not regard it as its function to worry about whether children on welfare are receiving the care and nurturing that would give them the foundation for developing into responsible adults. It has left this task exclusively to the mothers—often, teenage mothers—completely disregarding their obvious limitations for the task.

Twenty years of experience have made it clear that without some intervention, a welfare family's situation is likely to get worse, not better. The children's physical and emotional health suffer, and they do poorly in school. The girls are more likely than their mothers to become pregnant teenagers, and the boys more likely than their fathers to become teenage fathers.

It would be unrealistic to consider going back to the earlier system, in which an individual case worker visited each family in the worker's caseload at regular intervals. That was expensive and not very efficient. But greater use could be made of the almost 40 welfare centers scattered throughout the city, taking advantage of the fact that the mothers must appear at one of these centers every three months for a face-to-face interview to maintain eligibility for welfare. These occasions could be used to require attendance at group sessions on nutrition, on the health care and nurturing of infants and young children, and on ways to help school-age children and adolescents. It might also be possible, and certainly would be desirable, to require mothers to bring children under six years of age (except those in day care or kindergarten) to the welfare center at least once every six months for a health examination by specially assigned medical personnel, so that nutritional or health problems could be caught early and appropriate referrals made for necessary health services. In cooperation with the school system, other group programs should be directed at preadolescents and adolescents, especially those who have dropped out of school and thus are in grave danger of becoming involved in early sexual activity and other social misbehavior. Experts in these matters can be brought on staff to organize group sessions. Attendance could be compulsory for mothers and adolescents, on pain of reduction in the welfare grant for absence without cause.

Added attention must also be paid to the education of young

150

children. Basic study habits are formed when children are young—from four to 12 years old, when the need to do homework is inculcated and the sense of excitement about learning is established. Children who get little help at home, who are not read to and encouraged, even coerced, into doing their homework, need help from the school system.

The need for early childhood public education, especially for the poor, whether on welfare or not, has been recognized by Mayor Edward Koch and the Board of Education. In 1984–85, kindergarten became available for all five-year-olds whose parents wish them to attend. Further, in a partial response to the recommendations of the Early Childhood Commission, established by Mayor Koch, the city budget for 1986–87 made provision for 3,000 four-year-olds in prekindergarten. Since then, prekindergarten has been expanded in accordance with the Commission recommendation that it be established for 40,000 poor children, phased in over a four-year period and possibly even more rapidly. Proposals are now under consideration for extending prekindergarten to three-year-olds, a necessary next step.

However, we cannot say to the six-year-old child on welfare, "We have given you a headstart, now you are on your own in the educational pool—sink or swim." Too many are too heavily disadvantaged. If the city's educational and welfare system does not continue to help, many will sink. The evidence for this assertion is apparent in six studies, done in various cities, that followed preschool participants up through high school graduation. The preschool participants in these studies did indeed do significantly better than the comparison group; but "significantly better" meant that the dropout rate was reduced from 48 percent to 35 percent. A 35 percent dropout rate is much too high if the goal is to reduce poverty and dependency, especially in the minority communities and among children of recent immigrants. We must allocate additional resources through HRA and the schools to provide tutoring, counseling, and whatever else is needed to promote the values and work habits that will help ensure, to the extent possible, that at age 12 the children are in the appropriate grade in reading, writing, and math and can deal successfully with whatever future academic challenges they face. What the "package" should include to influence values and work habits will require further research and experimentation, but we already have a large of body of knowledge on early child development that can be put to use. The threat of failure means facing not only the heavy costs of remediation in the high schools and public

151

colleges, but also the loss of the potential contribution those children could have made to the city's society.

CONCLUSIONS

Since resources are limited, it would seem more useful to focus efforts with respect to teenage parenting on preventing the first pregnancy, by influencing values and behavior through schools and the mass media, particularly radio and television. One such media effort, mounted by the National Urban League in April 1985, launched a Male Responsibility Campaign aimed at young black males with the message, "Don't Make a Baby if You Can't Be a Father. Be Careful. Be Responsible." This theme, using varying phraseology, has been taken up by other black leaders. A similar message obviously needs to be aimed at young girls. This type of program has the potential for reaching a truly mass audience among all ethnic groups—not only children in school but also those who have dropped out, and their parents—and the further advantage of the lowest per capita cost, and of reaching the same audience now listening to radio programs that send out quite different messages, highly sexy, if not pornographic. The Adolescent Pregnancy Council should give high priority to the expansion of such programs in cooperation with the appropriate voluntary agencies.

It would be foolhardy to underestimate the cost of implementing these recommendations, the difficulties of organization and recruitment, the task of developing detailed programs, or the opposition that may develop to the degree of intervention proposed in the lives of families on welfare. But we ought to try.

If we can improve the nutrition, health, and educational achievement of young children now on welfare, and reduce the rate of pregnancy among preteens and teenagers, we will have a far greater chance than we do now of bringing the poor into the mainstream of the city's economic and social life within a decade or so. We could then look forward to the future with anticipation instead of dread.

Chapter 9

MAKING THE SCHOOLS WORK

Frank J. Macchiarola

It is not the problems of New York's schools that are so troubling, but the problems of its children. Today in New York, as in so many of the large cities of our nation, too many children are being failed educationally by the political system. New York's schools, as the part of the political system most in touch with children, are producing students who cannot read adequately, think clearly, or do basic arithmetic. They are producing students who do not understand what it means to be citizens and to assume the responsibilities of citizenship. They are producing students who cannot prosper in the larger society once their schooling is completed. Even when the schools succeed in retaining students until high school graduation, they confer diplomas without real meaning, and the evidence of that lack of meaning is all around us.

Certainly the problems of New York's children come at us today with tremendous fury. Examine the condition of children in the United States generally. They are growing poorer year by year, and the gap between the economic condition of children and that of adults is greater than at any time in the nation's recent history. Children can depend upon fewer and fewer adults in their home life. The extended family has long been a thing of the past, and as many more families are struggling to make do with one parent, even the conventional two-parent family is becoming a relic. We have coined the term "latchkey child" to describe the youngster who returns from school to home at three o'clock to wait alone for an adult to come home from work.

It is not only physical desertion that makes these youngsters lonely. Parents or surrogate parents are laying out fewer and fewer standards for them to follow so they can grow up to be responsible adults. Our institutions—and most particularly, our schools—offer too little guidance about what is proper behavior; they offer very few role models with roles clear enough, and positive enough, to follow.

The schools, of course, operate within the context of the larger society, and for a long time now that society has not been receptive to the needs of children. Unfortunately, and unnecessarily, this reality has become the basis for excusing the schools from doing the kinds of things that schools are supposed to do. It has become the basis for suggesting that American education is being challenged beyond its capacity. It is an argument that says, in effect, that the schools are better than the students they are asked to serve and must be preserved as they are in the face of huge numbers of students whose needs they cannot meet.

Such a perspective is as pervasive as it is dangerous, and it contradicts the fundamental mission of public education, implicitly dismissing from care and concern millions of American youngsters. This view must be countered directly with a philosophy that stresses not only the universality of access to public education, but also the responsibility of the school system to meet the needs of every child.

This is a difficult task, given the enormity and scope of the public school system in New York, the nation's largest, with more than twice as many youngsters as any other. In its most recent report (1986–87), it reported the enrollment of 939,142 students and a budget of $5.84 billion. Average expenditures per child since 1980 have grown by 70 percent, paralleling similar increases statewide, where education aid has grown over the past five years at three times the inflation rate. The city school system employs 109,144 people, 61,991 of them teachers, and has 1,060 buildings under its jurisdiction.

In addition, New York has the most complicated system of school governance in America, supporting 32 quasi-independent local districts for elementary and middle schooling and a centrally operated High School and Special Education Division, directly under the chancellor. In terms of auxiliary enterprises, the Board of Education transports more than half a million students daily and serves 662,713 meals each school day. This system must be managed—but at the same time, it must be led.

A NEW PHILOSOPHY

I suggest that an alternative philosophy of education in New York be declared, one that affirms the propositions that

(1) All children are equal in the eyes of the school system.
(2) All children can learn.
(3) It is the obligation of the school system to promote that equality and that learning.

The impact of such a philosophy, if it is actually believed and implemented by the school community and shared within that community, can be tremendous. In the first place, it can send a clear signal to the city that the system and its professionals care about schoolchildren and believe that the system's efforts can advance their education. Belief in the equality of children would lead, for example, to an end to school assignment by geographic zoning. Such zoning discriminates among youngsters on the basis of where they happen to live, isolates children within the school setting, places youngsters with handicapping conditions in second-class facilities, and distributes systemwide resources inequitably.

The focus on equality would also make every child's presence and participation in the school a desired objective. No longer would truancy and early dropping out be tolerated as a convenient way to expel the system's most troubled and troublesome pupils. And the system's insistence on the equality of every child should encourage the teacher to accept the proposition that every child in the classroom is as welcome and loved as any other. The faith in equality would require teachers and schools to advance the learning of each and every child with the same sense of urgency and with the same level of enthusiasm. It would make the public school the place of opportunity for all.

Considerable public benefits can flow from a philosophy that sets forth the belief that every child can learn. Such a point of view ensures that the academic program is all-inclusive, and that the rewards of instruction are not limited to the few. It means that all students are expected to achieve, that they can be held to standards of achievement, that when they fall below those standards the school shares in the blame, and most importantly, that the school shares in the task of doing something about it.

Belief in the ability of all students to learn makes the school community focus on the child rather than the subject matter. All too often, schools insist that their primary purpose is to teach, rather than to make sure that the students learn. A philosophical premise based on the students' learning rather than the system's teaching represents a significant departure from the thinking of far too many in the teaching profession.

Finally, a belief in the system's responsibility to promote the equality and the learning of youngsters will raise morale among all participants in the school system—professionals, pupils, and parents. For too many years, educators have looked at the condition of the schoolchildren and shrunk from the responsibility of teaching them because the task has been so formidable. They have resigned from the task before actually undertaking it.

It would be foolish to deny that public education in New York is very difficult. But it would be equally foolish to say that the situation is hopeless. There are many examples of situations in which determination and a strong sense of what is good for children have enabled schools to achieve educational success. There are schools in New York in which effective schooling has already occurred and the "can do" philosophy has resulted in students, teachers, and administrators who are justifiably pleased with the results. Beyond the instances of many individual schools, on a districtwide basis there is the example of District 1 on the Lower East Side, District 4 in East Harlem, and District 13 in Fort Greene–Bedford-Stuyvesant, where Community Superintendents Bernard Mecklowitz, Carlos Medina, and J. Jerome Harris have produced successful results in clusters of schools—proof enough that schools can be successful even with disadvantaged children if there is a sound philosophy of education and a willingness to put that philosophy to work.

Indeed, both the level of student performance and the disparity of that performance among local school districts in New York has to be a matter of tremendous concern and challenge to the chancellor. In the early 1980s, after exceeding reading and mathematics national norms for the first time since those tests were mandated in 1969, the school system's performance on standardized tests has flattened out. In the 1987 report to the chancellor on those tests, the director of the system's Office of Educational Assessment characterized the test results as "decidedly mixed," with a general decline in reading scores. Meanwhile, poorly performing districts continue to be found in poorer neighborhoods and better-performing districts to be found in the middle-class areas of the city. Over time, there have been too few instances in which the gap between the two has been reduced. As a result, districts such as District 6 on Manhattan's Upper

West Side continually show comparatively poor performance on standardized tests whereas others such as District 31 on Staten Island and Districts 25 and 26 in northeast Queens, show highly satisfactory results.

While the New York City Board of Education reports significant success in its efforts to stem the rate of dropping out of school, it shows very modest increases in the graduation rate. It accounts for this disparity by noting that students are taking longer to graduate. Its critics, however, fault the accuracy and honesty of the data collection.

A lack of faith in the ability of children to succeed in school seems widespread in the nation today, above all in our large central cities. And it is this faith in children that must be the foundation for real reform of public education. With a renewed faith in children and their innate capacity will come an understanding that they must be held accountable as well; that they must be given homework, that assignments must have real value, that rigorous curricular challenges can be based on faith in their ability to succeed.

What New York public education needs is a solid dose of commitment, by those inside and outside of the system. With that commitment will come a strong belief that some of the things that are now endemic to the condition of New York's children cannot continue. The schools must confront sexual mores that remove all innocence from children. They must combat directly the distressing reality that one in five of our kindergarteners was born of a mother under 15 years old. The schools must teach youngsters that drugs are destructive. And the schools must do these things not by preaching at youngsters, but by putting forward positive alternatives.

A major impediment to be overcome is peer pressure. Youngsters take their direction from other youngsters because they do not have enough contact with adults who care about them. It is time to do something about the fact that schoolchildren and their culture are too distant from a positive and caring adult culture. Too many children do not know how to behave because no one has taught them how to behave.

In a time of the communications explosion, when children are bombarded with television, movies, and books, they are made more vulnerable to exploitation and threatened more openly with the loss of their innocence. We have sent to children the most destructive and vicious examples of adult behavior—often protected by the First Amendment. And for fear of imposing a sectarian or religious point of view, we have offered no philosophy, no morality, to contradict these influences.

If schools are going to succeed, they need to pursue aggressively an agenda of caring. They are going to have to convince youngsters that they are committed to making certain that the youngsters succeed. They are going to have to show—by attention to the student who is not making the grade in academics, by attention to the youngster who does not seem to be able to cope with the problems of growing up—that they really do care. They will have to open up that extra place in a class that has reached capacity, fill out an additional recommendation for a college applicant, make an extra phone call to find out why the student is absent, ask the extra question that opens up a youngster so that a problem gets heard, ask a student to be a tutor or mentor for another student with a problem, take the time out to notice when a student does something wrong and try to deal with it right on the spot, notice and do something about the student in the lunch room who sits there without friends, notice the student who doesn't join a single club or feel part of a single activity in the school, read the attendance reports to find out who has been cutting classes, form groups of teachers who will spend time discussing problems they seem to notice among students, spend an extra hour in the school to talk to youngsters who are also staying there.

REFORM AT THE TOP

This, and much more, needs to be done. Strictly speaking, such actions are not in the job descriptions and cannot be mandated by school rules. If the school is going to be a place for children to grow and learn and develop into mature and effective adults, however, there will have to be much more encouragement from the leadership of New York's school system. Unless 110 Livingston Street (the administrative headquarters of the city school system) is a place where these values are encouraged and implemented by the central administration itself, the schools will continue to be a failure.

Today and for some time now, 110 Livingston Street has been indifferent at best, and often hostile, to the exhibition and encouragement of the fundamental human qualities that must be at the heart of a successful school system. For example, class advancement policies, which were intended to assure that no student could move to the next grade before he or she had met a minimum standard and that those who fell below the minimum standard would be held back until they completed a program of intensive support, were abandoned—but not openly. Instead, they were allowed to be mismanaged—and then subjected to a critical evaluation that confused the philosophy of the program with the lack of administrative capacity.

Cooperative school/work employment programs were mismanaged so that students who were promised jobs never got them. "Dropout" programs were put together in such haste and with such inattention that they accomplished little in the way of retention. And whenever failures such as these emerged, the central administration sought to escape the blame. Instead, the Board of Education, the chancellor, and the opinion leadership that they influence shifted the blame elsewhere—onto centralized school districts, onto the Board of Examiners, onto the custodians, the pupils, the parents, the budget, the structure of the Board of Education itself—all in the hope that the blame for failure could be located elsewhere.

But the real enemy of effective education in New York is not those who work within the system. The real enemy is the system's leadership in the recent past. Illustrative are a number of decisions that have demonstrated insensitivity and outraged the public. For example, a system of school-based health clinics, located in predominantly minority communities, was set up to dispense contraceptives without prior consultation with parents. A school for homosexual youngsters, the Harvey Milk School, was created; rather than taking the initiative to stop attacks upon youngsters discriminated against for their homosexuality, in other words the system opted for a school that isolates them. The administration is equally insensitive in what it fails to do. Neither the chancellor nor the Board of Education has uttered a word—nor urged any action—to stem the alarming increase of weapons in schools, a trend that has alarmed parents, pupils, and teachers alike.

The administration's attitude of not caring—or more properly, of believing that New York's schools are bound to fail children—has spread into the schools. Schools such as Park West High School were permitted to become places of violence and terror, and were seen as problems for the system only when the media took note. As problem schools remain undealt with, the only strategy employed is to tell the parents with a child in a problem school that the child can be accommodated at another school. That strategy of buying off vocal parents leaves us with schools to which the most vulnerable pupils, the poorest teachers, and the weakest administrators are sent. Sometimes these schools are underfunded. Just as often, they are well-funded, as if dollars were a measure of concern; but they are undercared for, notwithstanding high levels of spending. The tragedy is not that New York is unwilling to spend enough money for public education. The tragedy is that too little attention is paid to the institutions and people that the money is spent on.

If public education in New York is going to succeed, it is going to have to hold its professionals to high standards of accountability for success in educating New York's schoolchildren. This means accountability of both teachers and administrators. Such a concept, let alone a system for implementing it, is far from being in place today.

In terms of implementation, the administration of the school system must set out to do several important things. At this writing, a chancellor-designate, Richard Green, has been named but has yet to take office. Therefore, these suggestions are made at a time when the capacity to effect significant change is at hand.

As the first item on an agenda for reform, the chancellor should appoint several executives and assistants who share his philosophy. An administration in which the chancellor actually has an educational philosophy of some sophistication will represent a significant departure from the experience of the past five years. That there was no candidate for chancellor from the ranks attests to the paucity of leadership available within the school system. The most tangible contribution of the current leadership has been to raise generously their own salaries.

If the chancellor does not appoint a significant number of his own people or if he fails to attract new people of high quality, he will walk naked and vulnerable in one of the toughest bureaucracies in the world. New York public school teachers and administrators are among the most savvy (and self-protective) in the nation. They are able to tell real power and authority from fake, and they have no hesitation about acting accordingly. Long before the last chancellor had his problems with the media, he had serious problems with community superintendents and other leaders in the system. The superintendents actually boycotted the chancellor's meetings, often keeping him cooling his heels as they conducted their own organizational sessions. The chancellor's capacity to lead was impaired by his choice of staff, as well as by the efforts of the president of the Board of Education. The chancellor cannot rely upon staff who are incapable of leading themselves.

A capable staff for the chancellor should also include leaders from within the system. In fact, there are many in the system who would be willing to follow strong and caring leadership. They must, however, be complemented by outsiders who have an understanding of the kinds of educational innovations that have been implemented in other cities in the nation. One of the best recent models for this can be seen in the case of Ronald Edmonds, who was brought to the New York public schools as senior assistant to the chancellor for instruction. Edmonds's background as an education department official in Michigan and as a research scholar and academic at Harvard University enhanced his external credibility as an architect of school reform in New York. With a reputation for commitment to students and excellence as a scholar, he inspired the staff in ways that were extraordinary in a tough city. Edmonds's ability to make the New York schools models for the nation brought tremendous additional credibility to the school improvement effort.

In addition to a systemwide belief in New York's schoolchildren and in their ability to succeed academically, and in addition to having key staff members who share such a vision of success, public education in New York must convince others in the community that it seriously needs and wants their partnership in the process of schooling. The relationship between the schools and the parents is key. For long periods of time in the history of public education in New York, the role for parents in education was to leave their children at the door of the school building and pick them up at three o'clock. Although a great deal has changed—largely through the device of decentralization, which gives parents greater rights of participation in the process of school governance—there is still a serious reluctance on the part of the schools to make the parents feel that they, too, must make an investment in the outcome of their children's education. Plenty of educators bemoan the inattention of parents to the schooling needs of children, but the complaint is empty unless there is a better system for parent involvement.

The school system must also take advantage of the tremendous support recently offered by the larger community. Most significantly, such business–community organizations as the New York City Partnership, the Alliance for the Public Schools, and the "I Have a Dream" Foundation have demonstrated the willingness of the private sector to participate in programs that will help children (most particularly, children with economically and socially disadvantaged backgrounds) succeed in later life. But for such relationships to go beyond rhetorical commitment, they must be implemented by school administrators who welcome the involvement of these new participants.

None of the programs mentioned has had an easy time working with the administration of the New York public schools. Most new participants who have had to come to terms with the bureaucracy describe it in the harshest of terms. They have felt that they needed to expend an extraordinary amount of energy to achieve even modest results. In the recent past, several major corporations withdrew from collaborative efforts with the Board of Education after expressing their exasperation and disgust at the inability of the system to work on behalf of youngsters.

Just a few examples of frustration and failure: problems over the School of Writing with Time, Inc.; a high failure rate of high school graduates on the test for entry-level jobs with the New York Telephone Company; and a failure of several Brooklyn high schools to generate enough graduates to participate in a program sponsored by commercial banks for graduates. Clearly, not only will the school system have to develop better mechanisms for working with outsider organizations who want to help public school youngsters, it will also have to generate higher pupil achievement to encourage the outsiders' continued willingness to lend a hand.

THE NEED FOR LEADERSHIP

The school system's inability to cooperate with outsiders is not restricted to the private sector. For several years now, in the budget process at both the city and state levels, legislators have complained about the way the Board of Education has put together its budget. Specifically, they have objected to how the Board has implemented promises that were made in the budget process. The situation is a "Catch-22." Because the Board of Education cannot be trusted to honor its commitments, legislators insist on putting additional strings on Board appropriations. The Board's negotiators are forced to accept qualifications to funding that require expenditures to be earmarked for special purposes—dropout prevention, reductions in class size, maintenance of school buildings, programs for the talented and gifted. And the list grows from year to year. Unfortunately, the Board has no capacity to ensure that these promises will be met, or even to know whether they have been met or not. As a result, when old budgetary results are examined in the next year's process, promises are found to be unfulfilled, and thus new, more stringent strings are attached for the following year. These are unattended as

162

well. The Board loses its credibility, and its incompetence is mistaken for arrogance.

The chancellor has to restore confidence in the ability of the school system to manage its budget. Only then can the chancellor properly ask to be excused from making last-minute commitments that depart from his own priorities. At present, the Board of Education actually has no budget priorities. By having none—by not deciding what is most important—everything remains unimportant. This creates an open invitation for others to shape priorities.

Anyone who has studied the Board of Education budget closely over the past five years will see the effect of not having a strategy. The Board's budget looks like a decorated Christmas tree. One notices the Brooklyn borough president's sports program, the comptroller's mathematics program, an assembly member's dropout program, the City Council's maintenance program, and so on. Although some of these programs have merit, they fail to reflect priorities set by the leadership of the school system.

Another area calling out for reform concerns the community school boards. Created in 1969 as part of a larger political call for decentralization in New York, the school boards have created both opportunities and problems for central bureaucracy. The advantage has been that the localization of school decisions within communities has made many of those decisions more responsive to local needs. No longer can the bureaucracy at 110 Livingston Street impose an unqualified school principal on a particular school, as was common in the 1960s.

Under decentralization, however, the Board of Education has been incapable of developing appropriate relations with the districts. The Board has been paralyzed by the existence of semi-autonomous school districts that share the power of school governance. The fact that school districts have control over significant parts of the curriculum has meant that the central Board has been unable to monitor that spending in terms of legality or effectiveness. The fact that the districts have the power to appoint community superintendents and principals has discouraged the central Board from examining the process by which these appointments have been made.

None of this needs to be the case. The Board has run away from many of its own responsibilities and has used the lame excuse that its effective power has been removed by decentralization. Nothing could be further from the truth. A strong central administration can, and in fact should, exist side by side with strong community school

163

districts. When the central administration exercises both its leadership and its control, that guidance of the community school boards permits everyone to know the limits of local power and to understand that the central administration will act to ensure that they act appropriately within those limits. The responsibility of the leadership of the New York public school system is to ensure that the Community School Districts perform on behalf of children. And they can meet that responsibility under the law as it presently exists.

The same holds true for the exercise of leadership in the face of special interests that all too often attempt to exercise extraordinary control. None of these interests is more powerful than the teachers' union.

There are indisputable benefits that arise from a strong teachers' union. The union can unite behind an agenda of school reform, it can galvanize support for public education through its extensive political network, it can control dissidents within the organization, and it can assist in the implementation of school system objectives. Many people within the union movement are committed to the improvement of instruction. Problems arise, however, because the central administration has been weak and has given in to union pressure, even when inappropriate. There has to be a healthy tension between strong central leadership and strong union leadership. Recent demonstrations of union power have been extraordinary. It is no secret that the union has been able to block appointments within the administration of late—even appointments to high-level positions. Many other administrative decisions, such as those regarding release time for teachers, transfer policy, training sessions, and the like, have been imposed upon the administration by union pressure.

The power of the union over members of the Board of Education, which became visible for a brief time during the chancellorship selection process, has been evident for more than a decade. The union now holds virtually complete and automatic control over three of seven Board members. This control over the Board, well understood within the bureaucracy, has created paralysis even among the top leaders of the system. The central administration did a disservice to the school system, and one to the children as well, when it concluded a collective bargaining agreement that gave significant additional power to the teachers' union over matters of transfer, assignment of staff, grievance procedures, and mandated time out of the classroom. It did so, moreover, without consulting community school-board representatives, who historically have participated in the collective bargaining process. Among those who watch power closely (and the bureaucracy at the Board is considerably talented in this regard), it is clear that while the Board of Education has expressed its concern at its lack of power over significant parts of the system (such as community school boards, school custodians, and school principals), it has surrendered to the teachers' union, both in policy and in practice, many management prerogatives. The new chancellor will have to reclaim these prerogatives, but not in ways that divide the system. He will have to devise ways of increasing productivity—and instilling the quality of caring—in such a fashion that the teachers will feel a certain ownership of the result.

It will also have to be made clear to the bureaucracy that its members cannot make end-runs around the chancellor. The chancellor's junior administrative colleagues are often the beneficiaries—the knowing beneficiaries—of policies and practices that can be his undoing. Any new chancellor recruited from outside the system starts out with a depressing historical record before him: only two chancellors (or superintendents of schools, as they used to be called) were brought in from outside the system in modern times, and within 18 months both were rendered ineffective. Superintendent Calvin Gross was actually out of a job in that brief space of time, and Chancellor Harvey Scribner virtually gave up his control over the system to the political appointees named to the central Board of Education. There is no reason to believe that today's circumstances will offer any less of a challenge to the new chancellor. And there are no assurances that he will be warmly received by the bureaucracy that has managed over time to chew up almost every person to hold the position of chancellor or superintendent of schools.

Other internal disputes confronting the system must be resolved, or at least brought under control. The old arguments about merit and fitness have resurfaced, with attempts being made in Albany to eliminate the Board of Examiners. This institution has truly outlived its usefulness, and yet it seems to garner support every time it appears close to being abolished. It is the most inefficient operation at the Board of Education, responsible for delays in testing, inappropriate testing practices, and indifference to the teachers and administrators who must inquire into the status of their licenses. It is also patronage-laden, and perhaps worst of all, it seems determined to promote the least-capable and least-committed staff. In the name of merit testing, it has managed to devise tests that actually penalize satisfactory performances in the schools.

In another dispute, the school system has declared war on the custodians and their union. While it is true that the custodians have exercised extraordinary and unwarranted control over the school buildings, levels of maintenance, and after-hours use, the blame for this state of affairs is by no means one-sided. It has been within the prerogatives of the school system to determine the conditions under which the custodians perform their functions. The current custodian mess got worse when unionized supervisors elected to join the custodians' union in the early 1970s after the Board of Education was unable to negotiate a labor contract acceptable to them. The custodians' frustration resulted in an appeal to the state Public Employees Relations Board that permitted them to join the same union as the workers they rated and supervised. The Board of Education appealed this arrangement, but such labor practices are tolerated more extensively than might be imagined. For example, assistant principals are in the same union as the principals who supervise and rate them.

Another battleground in the school system pits the administration against the Council of Supervisors and Administrators, the union that represents school principals and other supervisory personnel. At issue is tenure, which the Board of Education is trying to abolish through state legislation. Tenure was taken away from the supervisors at the time decentralization was implemented, then restored when Governor Hugh Carey was preparing to run for a second term. Tenure for principals is a relatively rare phenomenon in public education, and New York is virtually alone in granting a principal tenure in an assigned school rather than within the district. Thus, the argument goes, the chancellor's power to reassign or fire incompetent principals is severely circumscribed. The argument is specious: tenure may be a powerful protection—and perhaps an inappropriate one—but it cannot withstand the power of a chancellor determined to remove a principal.

The system does not really suffer from a lack of legal capacity, as the chancellor is free to discipline and reassign school administrators. The system suffers from the failure of a succession of chancellors to exercise the power that is already at their disposal. For example, countless probationary supervisors under the direct authority of the central Board—that is, in the Division of High Schools and the Division of Special Education—have acquired tenure without any scrutiny. In addition, the powers to evaluate and remove principals or administrative personnel for failure to perform has only rarely been invoked by the chancellor.

REFORMING THE BOARD

At the heart of many of the problems besetting the school system is the Board of Education itself. In the past, when the Board was subject to criticism and recommendations for reform, it managed to survive unchanged upon the appointment of a new chancellor. After an appointment, all of the attention has focused on the new chancellor, not on the conduct of the Board. This should not happen again. Three of the seven Board members, including its president, have publicly called for major changes in its composition and have called for their own removal. If the matter is not addressed by the political leadership of the city and state this time, the latter will bear the full responsibility for the continued failure of the system. The new chancellor cannot survive, let alone innovate and reform, unless the Board's powers are substantially curtailed.

The grievances against the Board are legion. Analysts of sound management practices might focus on the failure to differentiate between policy and administration. They might point to the hundreds of instances in which day-to-day meddling of Board members and the intervention on the behalf of special interests has resulted in poor decisionmaking. But the deficiencies are not only those that inhabit textbooks on good government—they can also be found in the qualifications of the Board appointees, who with few exceptions, are totally undistinguished. In fact, only the actions of the current president of the Board, in a display of true genius, kept other Board members out of the process of selecting the chancellor until the final week. As a result, they were not able to derail the six-month-plus search, nor to prevent its happy resolution. In that brief one week that the Board did involve itself in the search, the public saw a willingness on the part of some members to represent the agenda of the teachers' union, a willingness to upset the rules of selection that they themselves had agreed to, and above all a willingness to pretend that aside from the moment they cast their vote, they were consequential players in the process.

New York's Board of Education has day-to-day custody of the education of almost 1 million New Yorkers. However, just as they do not know how to behave when it comes to choosing a chancellor, they have no idea of how to behave toward their 1 million charges, or how to serve the 7 million citizens of New York, few of whom have faith in their capacity to lead the school system. If the selection of Chancellor Richard Green proved that the Board might not always

167

be wrong, it gave no reassurance that they might regularly be right. The present Board must be replaced with a new one designed to maximize accountability, preferably by allowing the mayor to select all Board members with the advice of a screening committee. In addition, as is the case with the Metropolitan Transportation Authority, the chancellor should also be chairman of the Board of Education. That would make the chancellor the chief executive officer of the system.

One must also address the contention that additional resources are a prerequisite to reform. All too often those in charge of programs claim that more could have been done if only they had better funding. The causal connection between levels of funding and degree of program success in New York City, or any school system, is tenuous at best. In public education, success or failure relates more to how funds are spent than to the amount of funding available. Obviously, increased support is needed for some things, such as repair of school buildings. But in the absence of real reform, the deployment of additional funds and a better-developed mechanism for spending what is already in place will achieve little and waste a great deal of money.

The school system administration would do better to struggle with the issue of how to allocate scarce resources than to lobby for huge additional sums. In recent years, there has been an infusion of large increments of new money into the system, and there is no evidence that it has been a worthwhile effort. The time has come for New York's school system to take stock of its programs and initiatives and to communicate in simple terms where it intends to put its major efforts, and to demonstrate that it has the capacity to plan and deliver on its plans.

For the past five years now, legislators and the public have been treated at budget time to a beautiful document that outlines the system's needs. It is like the wish list that children are fond of making up at Christmas. Once funding is obtained, however, we are never permitted to see what that wish list has done for the city's schoolchildren. While the Board pleads its case for more funds each year, there are no documents saying "thank you" and reporting on what has been done. It is time to demand such documentation. It is time for the New York taxpayer, like the corporate stockholder, to demand an annual report that gives him bottom-line data that can make him proud, or give him pause. Until the administration reports with credibility and honesty, public support for and confidence in its efforts will be scarce.

SUMMARY

I began this essay by focusing on the needs of children, and by saying that the New York school system can be no better than the regard it has for its pupils, the citizens' children. If they are treated as members of society about whom the schools care deeply, then such an attitude must be reflected in the way the schools work with them. It is all too easy to forget that the schools are for the children, and only the children.

I have suggested a system of care and commitment. A system that holds high expectations for children and a system of accountability that makes those expectations acquire meaning. I have suggested as well that we encourage the leadership of the schools to be advocates on behalf of children and to deal with others on the basis of that responsibility to serve the children well. The Board of Education, the chancellor, and the administration of the schools must be challenged to fulfill the dreams and hopes and aspirations of New York's children. Right now there is too much despair and discouragement within the system to give New Yorkers the confidence that the job can be done. What New Yorkers always have, however, is hope.

Chapter 10

EASING THE HOUSING CRISIS

Roger Starr

In 1987, after more than 40 years of continuous prosperity, New York City faces what many observers describe as a housing crisis. In view of the large amounts of public and private capital that have flowed into housing production—not to mention the public attention given to housing since 1945 and the many state and local laws passed to "improve" the housing situation—the persistence of this crisis deserves at least as much attention as does its seriousness.

When the contrast between the public energy that has been invested in housing and the continuing short supply is brought to public attention by government officials and newspapers, the response on all sides is likely to be that more government activity is needed to produce solutions. The all-too-familiar diagnosis is that government intervention has simply been on too small a scale to matter. Like Christianity, say the advocates of government initiatives in housing, the only thing wrong with their program is that it has not yet been adequately tried.

HISTORICAL BACKGROUND

Public opinion and government policy toward housing has repeatedly changed over the past century and a half. In the 50 years that preceded the Civil War, housing, as such, was simply not important enough to be discussed as a public policy question. Housing made only a minor contribution to the economic growth that was New Yorkers' primary interest in the early 19th century. Building laws were rudimentary and concerned the prevention of fire losses, a natural consequence of the city's devastating conflagrations in 1776 and 1835. Improving the rudimentary water supply, both a fire-prevention and a public-health issue, was the major infrastructure imperative of the pre-Civil War period. There were good reasons for the priority attached to water supply, including the prevention of cholera, a common killer before the completion of the Croton reservoir and aqueduct in 1845.

Subsequently, the city's housing history can be divided into three eras, separated by each of three major wars. The city emerged from the Civil War with the memory of the 1863 Draft Riot terror lively in the consciousness of its elites, who pledged to dissipate fears of social unrest by accommodating the growing population without creating new slums. That objective is not close to achievement over 100 years later; it probably could not have been achieved without stunting the unprecedented expansion of the city's population. Building new housing at better than slum standards would have been so expensive by standards of the time that the ability of the city to accept millions of immigrants would have been seriously impaired. The attachment to growth was still the unchallenged major premise in public opinion and government policy.

Housing regulation that might have prevented the construction of new slums was not enacted until 1901, and it was not until 1929 that the state government made a serious effort to pass laws requiring upgrading of pre-1901 tenements. Even so, retroactive changes were limited to fundamental sanitary measures, notably the ex post facto installation of a water closet for each household (though not necessarily within the householder's apartment). Not until 1955 did the city make heat and hot water a legal requirement in those same buildings.

Legislative reticence was based on an appreciation of the economic consequence of forcing owners to rip apart buildings even when they were dangerously deficient in sanitary facilities. Though reformers pressed for the abolition of slums, the prevailing opinion of the city's leaders between the Civil War and World War I was that without slums into which new arrivals could move, the city's growth would be hampered.

By the turn of the century New York had absorbed its Brooklyn sibling, without wholly eliminating the ancient rivalry between the two once-independent cities, as well as what are now the boroughs of Queens and Staten Island, and the northern Bronx. The empty spaces in these boroughs made growth possible without significantly raising the question of government intervention in housing quality.

Housing policy in the period between the two World Wars generally encouraged private industry simply to build homes on the plentiful open land that was available at low prices. Areas most readily reachable by the new and expanding rapid-transit network, and particularly sites nearest to stations on the transit lines, were developed with six-story, semifireproof, brick wall-bearing apartment houses that met the standards set forth in 1901, plus minor restrictive amendments legislated in Albany in 1929.

Other areas, less in demand, were improved with one-family, or sometimes two- and three-family, homes. Some of these were fully detached, others semiattached; sometimes they were constructed in rows with party walls on both sides of all but the two end houses on the block. Outside the city's fire limits—geographic lines within which it was unlawful to build structures with wooden walls—housing standards were quite liberal, except in the case of three-family houses, which were treated as though they were apartment houses. In practice, zoning bans against three-family homes were not always enforced.

In Manhattan, the materials from which the exterior front walls of characteristic small buildings were built gave them the popular name brownstones, a term that handily distinguished them from similar but smaller and much cheaper houses built later in the other boroughs, usually with brick, stone veneer, wooden shingle, or clapboard siding. Frequently, New Yorker magazine cartoons mocked the indistinguishability of such homes—and inferentially, of their occupants—erected cheek-by-jowl on long stretches of outer Brooklyn, Queens, and the Bronx in the 1920s. In the 1960s, folk singers like Pete Seeger characterized such homes as "ticky-tacky."

To make the finished houses more attractive to potential buyers, real estate tax abatements of up to $1,000 in valuation per room, and $5,000 per apartment, were allowed. The tax abatement statute, which ran from 1921 to 1932, stimulated construction by aiding builders to sell or rent more cheaply. No regulatory controls on quality or rents were required in return for these concessions.

One relatively small, socially-motivated housing program was articulated by Governor Alfred E. Smith in 1926. Called the "permanent housing program" of the State of New York, it was designed to meet the temporary emergency of a postwar housing shortage and housing that met advanced standards for working-class families. Its basis was a limit on the dividends that owners could pay on the equity investment in specially tax-abated housing developments. But only a few projects were actually produced under the program, and even fewer survived, through co-operative ownership, the serious deflation of the Depression. Mostly they were sponsored by and gave ideological support to the labor movement. With one or two exceptions, only institutional "nonprofit" builders, such as the Amalgamated Clothing Workers, found its provisions sufficiently remunerative to be attractive.

The end of World War II saw a radically different spirit in the nation. A depression-weary, doubt-ridden country had stumbled into the war; a confident world power, with reaffirmed faith in the strength of its economic institutions, emerged. The change in perspective opened new horizons. The public asserted new demands on government whenever private industry lagged in accomplishing visionary objectives. State and local governments, especially in the eastern United States, where faith in government ran high, were happy to increase the burden on themselves by promising that new goals would be achieved. Civil servants and politicians foresaw new prestige and new financial rewards for government service.

At the same time, the backlog of unmet housing needs from depression and war was exacerbated by new family formations, and by the revival of in-migration. Some displaced persons arrived from Europe. But far more numerous were the arrivals from the Southern states and the Caribbean islands. These influences stimulated housing production. Simultaneously, segregation of the races became clearly incompatible with the change in attitudes toward invidious discrimination that culminated in the civil rights revolution.

Instead of assuming that new housing would be built on vacant land, national policy, stimulated by rapidly growing fiscal problems in the cities and by public demands, particularly among the elites, that government do more, encouraged building on the site of present slums. That initiative produced debates about the use of public power to abet private enterprise. Public opinion was also split over such new challenges as the relocation of site residents who were disproportionately nonwhite and the attainment of high-quality architectural design. Government involvement seemed to many civic and political leaders to require greater humanity toward relocatees and finer design than the private sector could be expected to provide without subsidy. These attitudes were very understandable, even laudable; they were also costly.

Rent control was another disputatious issue. After World War I, rent control had lasted only about ten years, until the deflation of the great Depression. After World War II, however, long after the federal government had lifted its wartime controls, New York City not only continued them, but extended them to housing built long after the war ended. Keeping rents low was deemed to be as important to the existence of moderate-cost housing as the construction of new, highly subsidized units was to the provision of low-cost housing. At the same time, housing of good-as-new quality was deemed to be so important to the public welfare that lack of ability to pay the economic rental was never to bar occupancy.

Thus the city's housing producers found themselves after World War II subject to a set of demands for the accomplishment of goals other than that of producing housing. In themselves, the social goals had merit; but when entwined with the effort to create housing, they served to restrain the basic economic impulse of traditional housing suppliers. At the same time, quality controls made new housing formidably expensive, discouraging people from vacating older apartments for newer ones and thus making their former homes, usually in legally acceptable condition, available to people of lesser income. Breaking the chain of housing moves by the combination of rent control and higher construction standards probably did more to create the present housing crisis than did any other commonly cited cause.

Rent control not only did not preserve moderate cost housing, it actually starved it fatally by persuading potential developers that the political power of future tenants could imperil their investments. Rent control encouraged what has become an almost instinctive belief among urban tenants that landlords can afford anything—and if they do not provide it, they are simply greedy. The end result has been not only the deterioration of existing housing and the discouragement of new construction, but the passing of the remnants of privately owned housing that might have been available for families of limited income into the hands of really greedy—those determined to avoid adherence not only to excessive standards, but to all standards. Thus, the a priori judgments of legislators came true by social wizardry.

THE WAGNER COMMITTEE ON HOUSING

The shift in outlook after World War II, the revised perception of the role and responsibility of builders, or as they more frequently were termed, developers, was exemplified by the experience and results of the Wagner Committee on Housing. When Fiorello H. LaGuardia was mayor of New York, approximately 15 years after the end of World War I, he articulated goals for housing in one sentence about Harlem tenements that later became the title of a book by Woody Klein, *Let in the Sun*. Ten years after the end of World War II, the committee of citizens convened by Mayor Robert F. Wagner, Jr., to formulate the city's housing policy issued a report that covered more than 100 single-spaced pages and offered 63 suggestions.

The committee believed in the importance of fine architecture and recoiled against the "cookie-cutter" design of mass housing. It believed that new homes should be planned so as to assist in the removal of slums and that slum clearance programs should not only enhance the city's tax base but, in calculating the highest-and-best use of land, should take into account the social benefit to the people living there.

The committee further believed that racial and class integration should be a goal of redevelopment. For some, this meant only a policy of open occupancy, with no discrimination allowed on the grounds of race, religion, or ethnicity. For others, and gradually for the national government as well, the policy came to mean that every building of every assisted project was to be integrated by positive action.

Notwithstanding the goal of planned diversity, the committee espoused neighborhood preservation. Since the word "neighborhood" implies a certain homogeneity among residents, as in a "middle-class neighborhood" or a "Jewish neighborhood," the conflict between the idea of preservation and the integration of hitherto diverse elements threatened further delay and expense for prospective builders, private and public.

The committee, chaired by Henry Bruere, former chairman of the Bowery Savings Bank, brought in its report with only one dissenting voice from among its 102 members. Given the occupations of its members, this was perhaps not surprising. There were 13 architects, 11 so-called community workers, board members of well-established eleemosynary civic institutions, and seven members representing academic and religious bodies. There were also seven real estate consultants, brokers, appraisers, and managing agents; seven bankers; six contractors associated with large structures; five each were drawn from the ranks of professional social workers, lawyers, and public administrators; two were labor union representatives; two were from the publishing business; two were elected officials and one was an appointive official in the housing field.

Missing from the committee to establish city housing policy were people connected with the development, ownership, management, and maintenance of the apartment houses that constituted the backbone of the city's housing supply—the six-story semifireproof apartment houses built to conform with the Tenement House Law adopted by the State Legislature in 1901 and modified and renamed the Multiple Dwelling Law in 1929. Another group totally unrepresented on the committee were builders of one-, two-, and three-family houses, which housed fully 30 percent of New York's population and the construction of which was one of the major achievements of the housing industry in the period between the two World Wars.

The real estate representatives and most lawyers in the committee tended to be most familiar with luxury apartments in central Manhattan, the Forest Hills section of Queens, a few sections of Brooklyn, and Riverdale in the Bronx. Only one of the lawyers on the committee, Samuel Lindenbaum, represented builders of six-story semifireproof buildings or small homes—so-called "speculative builders," a term that sounds somewhat shady but only means that they expect to rent or sell their buildings after completion; they have no advance commitments from tenants or buyers.

With the great benefit of hindsight, it is easy to see that the people on the committee were not concerned with the maintenance of the remaining decent buildings in the city's stockpile. Since the existing post-1901 buildings were in fact still decent, they did not inspire the compassionate interest of the city's civic organizations were concerned with the plight of poor people who lived in old-law tenements. The real estate people were not interested in the economics of operating six-story buildings. Their interests were concentrated in city planning, in the city beautiful, in slum clearance, in improving the city's budgetary stance and enabling it to reduce taxes or increase services. Even the goal of economic development fell victim to the social policies of various segments of the committee.

The architects were interested primarily in ideas, in the discipline of urbanism. They were influenced by LeCorbusier, by Mies Van der Rohe, by the prospect of breaking the confining grid of the street pattern. For them, housing improvement meant new design on a grand scale. For labor members of the committee, improved housing meant an opportunity to solidify union membership by stimulating jobs for construction workers. None of these groups cared about the rehabilitation or maintenance of existing decent buildings. Rehabilitation work and the construction of new small homes was architecturally uninteresting and generally a nonunion affair.

WHY GOOD HOUSING WAS LOST

Building new housing and upgrading the oldest tenement houses were attractive policies to the political leaders of the city seeking to establish themselves as different from and more modern than the politicians of the past. Like their predecessors, elected in opposition to Tammany Hall, they surely did not mind having their leaders' names on signs outside major new housing projects. Such signs conveyed to potential voters the manifold bounties of incumbents who would soon run for reelection. Beyond that, the signs expressed the new social philosophy that the trickle-down theory of economic progress was no longer good enough; saving older buildings that offered satisfactory and cheap housing was too mean-spirited an aspiration for a nation that had emerged victorious from the greatest of all wars. If the wealthy could have new homes, why should the poor be asked to live in the hand-me-downs of an earlier generation? And if new housing were built for the poor, why not also for the middle class—who, incidentally, included most union members and who might be able besides to afford their new housing with somewhat smaller government subsidies?

In 1954 there were 1,205,835 apartments in six-story apartment houses, some built strictly to statutory standards and some to considerably more generous designs, with bigger room sizes, more than one bathroom, wood-burning fireplaces, and so forth. These buildings had provided housing for families whose incomes permitted them to escape from cold water flats in old-law tenements. They were and remain, to the extent they still exist, the basic multiple dwelling in which working-class New Yorkers live.

Also after World War II, the illegal three-family house was a very successful housing type, offering good accommodations to an owning family and two renters with minimal government intervention. The illegality usually consisted of nothing more dangerous to health and safety than inconsistency with the zoning regulations forbidding three-family occupancy in areas restricted to two-family homes. Actually, the illegality seems to have contributed positively to the success of this type of construction. Because the third apartment did not officially exist, the building tended to be assessed by the taxing authorities at a figure well below its market value.

But practical as well as political reasons militated against a commitment to save these types of buildings or to cut builders loose from overly stringent zoning restrictions. Programs benefiting owners were certain to arouse the opposition of tenants. Any proposal to sustain the quality of existing rental housing by public subsidy in middle-income areas would be viewed as a screen behind which landlords would be assisted to undermine rent control. Keeping rents low and safeguarding the lessee's tenure were the two most important housing goals of those who lived in the six-story buildings and who were perceived by political observers to constitute the largest single-issue voting block in the city—1.4 million families, united on the one objective of low rents and permanent tenure.

Builders who did erect new structures resembling those that they had found successful in the past had to compete with low, uneconomic, controlled rents. New high-rise fireproof buildings, markedly different from the six-story stockpile, could be advertised as immensely superior to the older type. Ultimately, government absorbed some of this competitive risk by subsidizing the construction of high-rise middle-income housing with direct loans and tax abatement. As interest and operating costs rose and government sought to raise rents in these assisted middle-income developments, residents simply refused to pay the increase, citing, as one reason, the much more favorable terms enjoyed by tenants living in rent-regulated apartments not financed by the government. The losses sustained by local government through defaults on the mortgages it had financed with money borrowed in the bond market have generally been ignored by everyone. Those losses should offer a stark warning to future advocates of government financing of residential properties who assume that grateful tenants will cheerfully make them self-sustaining.

The long-range problem of housing deterioration as a result of rent regulation might have been dealt with had an adequate annual percentage increase been authorized to reduce the gap between rents in regulated older buildings and those in new, unregulated structures, as the Wagner Committee suggested. Such a change would have reduced the gap between rents in regulated older buildings and those in new unregulated structures in the fully private sector. It also would have removed a major impediment to the production of new rental housing, by new construction as well as by major rehabilitation, and brought supply and demand into better balance. The Committee's sensible suggestion might have helped to stem the loss of post-1901 buildings from the housing stock. The suggestion was, however, preceded by recommendations urging stricter enforcement of rent regulations and more developer responsibility for tenant relocation, both of which effectively discouraged whatever relief might have been offered building owners.

THE PUBLIC HOUSING RESOURCE

New York's policy after World War II was to build as much low-rent public housing as the federal government would subsidize. In the early 1950s, 127,000 public housing units were built, under construction, or being planned with federal commitments in hand. Thirty years later, there were 177,000 units. Cutbacks in federal funding of low-rent public housing were responsible for much of the lag, but not all of it.

Although demand for public housing apartments rises and falls, there has always been a waiting list for vacant apartments, often including as many as 200,000 families, despite the fact that names are automatically removed after two years if they have not been called. Public housing is an even more valuable resource than is apparent from these figures, because at least 20 percent, and perhaps many more, of its apartments are occupied by one or two "unofficial" tenants, people who can find no other place to live.

Unfortunately, the costs of housing operations and capital replacement were grossly underestimated by government at the time the large public-housing developments were built. Market considerations, such as the tendency of people of the same income level to live in the same neighborhood, were overlooked in the pursuit of integration. The city government experienced spasms of conscience—or perhaps self-righteousness—that impelled it to try to place low-rent public housing in middle-income neighborhoods. The resistance of residents and their elected representatives engendered by such proposals slowed the production of the units.

MIDDLE-INCOME PROGRAMS

The construction of middle-income housing in New York after World War II was, in large part, a result of the Limited Profit Housing Company Law passed by the New York legislature. Housing companies that agreed to a limit of 6 percent on their annual return on equity investment could receive partial exemption from real estate taxes and a mortgage from state or city government covering at least 90 percent of the development cost, with interest payable at the local government's own borrowing rate—which generally is well below the general money market rate.

This program, known as Mitchell–Lama after its two legislative sponsors, produced about 100,000 apartments, with the help of special borrowing-and-finance agencies set up by city and state governments. Mitchell–Lama produced good housing on the whole. Some, on urban renewal value-reduced land in or near the city center, rented readily. Developments on less-attractive sites did not rent so easily.

However, many projects were financed with one-year notes by the city and its subsidiaries, and ultimately, these would have to be replaced with long-term bonds bearing higher interest rates. When interest costs rose, it was impossible politically to raise Mitchell–Lama rents to cover the increased costs. The city and its captive Housing Department Corporation incurred debts of more than $2 billion for middle-income housing. When banks refused to buy city obligations during the fiscal crisis of 1975–76, New York found itself paying from its general funds the debt service it owed on the bonds and notes it had sold on the assumption that middle-income tenants would liquidate them in their rental payments. Ultimately the federal government decided to write insurance through the Federal Housing Authority on mortgages held by the city on such middle-income projects. The FHA refused to cover the most delinquent projects, and when it did agree to cover others, the insurance policy was limited to the current market value of the mortgage obligations. It took into account the rents that occupants could reasonably be expected to pay and the current market interest rate on similarly guaranteed obligations. Insurance commitment in hand, the city was able to sell its mortgages, but only for the insured amount. It realized about 40 percent of the face value of the mortgages, losing an unanticipated $1 billion or more on its middle-income housing initiative and being given a bitter economic lesson. The city discovered that in any duel between local economics and local politics, politics wins.

Another strange feature of the Mitchell–Lama program was the fact that many of the people who were middle income when they entered the houses moved up the income ladder faster than median-income families outside the projects. Although tenants were legally required to pay rent surcharges as their income rose, city law made it almost impossible to obtain accurate information about residents' income unless the latter chose, as they usually did not, to cooperate. The law also required residents to leave when their earnings exceed 150 percent of the maximum entering income, but that regulation has seldom been honored. Now, some residents in co-operatively owned developments want to pay the city the money they saved over the years, by virtue of not having paid normal taxes on their property, in return for the right to resell their apartments to people of much higher income and to keep a large part of the capital gain. If that happens, at least some of the middle-income housing projects will become high-rent developments. Despite all the trouble it went to and the losses it sustained in the process, the city will not have produced lasting middle-income homes in those projects.

FHA 608: A ONCE-UPON ALTERNATIVE

A wiser, more prudent alternative to Mitchell–Lama might have been modeled on a former federal program known as FHA 608, which provided federal insurance on to-be-constructed apartment house mortgages. The government insured an unusually high percentage of what it expected the appraised value of the completed development-to-be. Estimates of builders' profits, professional fees, and land costs, among other things, were sufficiently generous so that, in some widely publicized cases, and perhaps many others, builders were able to cover far more than their actual costs when their bank made the permanent federally insured mortgage. The "mortgaging out" feature of the program was treated by the press and by Congress as a national scandal, resulting in a change in the rules that effectively terminated the program. What had produced a lot of standard but not handsome apartment houses under the original ground rules, produced little or nothing thereafter.

Leaving aside the question of whether Congress would have revived the program, or the moral and ethical questions raised, it is highly doubtful that New York would have adopted the 608 process. Whereas the social theory behind FHA 608 was that it would add significantly to the housing stock because it would attract builders, New York's theory was that housing for so-called middle-income families was the pressing need.

The city contended that 130,000 middle-income families were living in substandard housing. But that claim deserves some examination. How substandard was that housing? Was it dangerously

181

substandard by virtue of plumbing or structural defects? Was it grossly or only marginally overcrowded? Was it really necessary to house middle-income families in new housing? If the FHA 608 rents had been higher than those in the Mitchell–Lama housing, would the apartments have been taken by families able to pay them? Would apartments those families left have been available for families earning less than $7,500, making much of the Mitchell–Lama program duplicative?

Nobody knows the answers to these questions. Were the Mitchell–Lama units a net addition of standard apartments to the housing supply? Or was that supply diminished by the deterioration, perhaps to the point of abandonment, of once-standard buildings? What shall one say in a democratic society about the political unacceptability of a housing program that would have accomplished at less apparent cost some of the benefits promised by a more expensive program that, it turns out, failed to accomplish at least some of them?

J51 AND THE OLD–LAW TENEMENTS

The pre-1901 old-law tenements, though deficient in room size, ventilation, sanitary facilities, and heating, housed perhaps 1.5 million people at the end of World War II. They could not be abandoned, as conscientious believers in the significance of housing quality standard hoped. The cost of central heating, the most crucial improvement that old-law tenements required, plus sufficient toilets to meet legal requirements, amounted at that time to $10,000 for an entire five-story old-law structure.

In the late 1970s, experts generally agreed that to rehabilitate much more modern apartments, requiring less fundamental improvements than did the old-law tenements, would cost upward of $60–$65,000 per apartment in vandalized and vacant structures. Interest and amortization required by the $10,000 investment, to say nothing of the then-novel cost of fuel, would have required a doubling of the average rent. So big an increase seemed a formidable obstacle, but at least in part due to the proceedings of the Wagner Committee, the J-51 program combining tax exemption, tax abatement, and moderate rent increases, emerged from the legislature. Heating systems were installed where they had never before existed.

As inflation continued, however, the tax concessions enacted to provide central heat became insufficient to make that improvement affordable by tenants of very low income. To make such improvement costs bearable, the city multiplied and expanded its tax concessions and eventually applied them to better buildings in more affluent neighborhoods. If rents in these buildings had not previously been regulated under the rent control laws, much more modest subsidies might have saved the need for major rehabilitation without displacing those residents who could not afford economic rents.

In the end, despite tax concessions, rentals in the rehabilitated buildings are considerably higher than in rent-controlled structures that may be adjacent to them, and rehabilitated buildings are occupied by a more affluent population (or a population willing to pay more rent) than are the adjacent buildings.

LESSONS FOR TODAY

Following the experience of the past 30 years exerts a certain melancholy fascination. Far more important, however, is the light it casts over discussions now going on. For the history makes clear that today's housing problem is primarily a problem of producing new units, either by rehabilitating unused older units or by constructing new ones. Without massive subsidies from the federal government, such production seems unlikely. It is impossible to build or to rehabilitate a significant number of housing units, at standards required by current law, and at current costs, for very-low-income families.

That leaves the city with the alternative of encouraging housing construction by private industry at whatever price level industry is willing to build at. One time, some builders chose to build for the top of the market, others for the middle market, still others for the low end of the market. But today, builders are only actively building new housing for the top of the market. Presumably they will continue, making it easier for newcomers who can pay the rent to move to New York or allowing new households that might otherwise move away to stay in New York. This process will also permit some city residents to move and release the space they are now living in for someone else to rent. If the builders cannot successfully rent to any of these groups, their products will go into liquidation and foreclosure, and the apartments will be revalued at prices that more people can afford.

There are steps the city can take to encourage private industry to build more new housing. First, the city should terminate rent regulation as quickly as possible, most practically by vacancy decontrol. Ending rent regulation is the only way to convince potential investors in rental residential property that they are not committing commercial hara-kiri by putting their money in an industry whose sales prices are regulated out of deference to the purchaser, wherein the goods and services that must be purchased are not regulated in deference to the vendor.

Second, the city should reduce the real-property-tax penalty assessed against owners who improve their property. Taking a lesson from the tax abatement program of the 1920s, the city should exempt from real property taxes, for 15 years, the first $50,000 cost of improvements per new unit and the first $30,000 per existing unit, adjusted annually in conformity with a recognized index of construction costs. No conditions, no income limits, no geographical steering—just guaranteed immunity from the Finance Department's imposition of arbitrarily high valuations to cover part or all of the abatement incentive.

Third, the city should review all legal obstacles to the construction of two-, three-, and four-family housing and remove unreasonable rules from the multiple-dwelling law, the plumbing and electrical codes, and the zoning resolution. Housing in which residents, without a paid staff, do much of the work of maintenance may be the future hope of the cities.

Fourth, the city should encourage experimentation in new forms of more-than-four-family housing for central sections of the city. If the multiple-dwelling laws, the zoning resolution, and other good-natured attempts to improve the "quality" of construction did not prevent them from doing so, some builders would already have devised a modern substitute for the six-story apartment house.

Fifth, the city should make clear that all housing will be open to all who can afford to pay the rent without discrimination by race, ethnicity, or religion, but that there are to be no efforts to achieve any specific balance or heterogeneity in any particular building. The penalty for racial steering in any new construction would be cancellation of the tax abatement.

Sixth, the city should encourage the federal government to finance low-rent units by providing rent certificates with a 15-year life. If one tenant became ineligible for continued use for whatever reason, the certificate would continue to be payable, for a reasonable period of time, whether or not a new tenant takes over. The certificate could be canceled if the owner unreasonably refused to accept a tenant deemed qualified by the local public agency.

It may be time to advocate a new generation of publicly owned housing, particularly if certificating a large number of tenants causes alarm. In urging such a course, however, advocates should be prepared to answer the question of where such housing should be located to avoid anchoring the nonworking poor where they are least likely to obtain jobs. Advocates must also be prepared to answer questions about a new formula for funding public housing that will provide equitable and adequate subsidies for maintenance and operations and for modernization. It is clear that the 1937 formula, which assumed tenants could pay whatever was needed for those purposes, was grossly in error and that the additional subsidies that have been provided are an unsatisfactory makeshift arrangement.

A new form of low-rent assistance is needed. Federal programs for assisting low-rent housing have depended primarily on income tax shelters and the income tax exemption granted to recipients of interest from local government. Something like the FHA 608, which was far more economical and far more open to public scrutiny than the elaborately camouflaged schemes that followed, should be examined fearlessly.

Local land-use control must be taken away from the vetoes of local planning boards. The Uniform Land Use Review Procedure (ULURP) process takes much too long. Zoning measures enacted since 1945 have only provided amenities for the wealthiest and best-off, while the Landmarks Commission has helped to prevent change in areas where people want to live. Restrictions on bulk and density may be necessary to keep development within the capacity of essential services, but the use of zoning to pay for public improvements, many of questionable value, is a distortion of the original intent of the law.

Quality in housing is only provided at quantity's expense. If quality standards are sufficiently important to make their imposition wise, the public, through taxation, should be required to cover their cost when the occupant cannot afford them. If additions to the housing supply are necessary to achieve social goals, failure to produce the housing will obviously inhibit their realization. If new housing is intrinsic to the establishment of a racially integrated community, standards for racial integration must not be so rigid that no one is willing to build the housing. If the added goals prevent the building of housing, they are useless, indeed destructive.

The more complex government involvement in housing becomes, the less likely are builders to be inspired to produce housing for ordinary incentives. They anticipate, probably correctly, that the added rules and regulations will increase costs by causing delays,

185

interfering with their choice of contractors or architects, and diluting their control. Government often forgets that the incentives it creates to stimulate building are intended to make housing production economically feasible, and that the removal of concessions that were granted so as to achieve noneconomic goals will destroy the motivation that was necessary in the first place. The inevitable reward will be inaction. Housing is a technical as well as an economic and a social activity. Those capable of ingenious solutions for technical problems should not be expected to solve social problems.

Chapter 11

REFORMING THE POLITICAL SYSTEM

Frank J. Macchiarola

The story of New York City politics during the recent past has been a story of political corruption. It started simply and dramatically with the suicide of Queens Borough president Donald Manes, but it has become comprehensive and complicated and has had some effect upon virtually every city department, bringing resignations, indictments, and convictions of high city officials. The unfolding story has interrupted the process of government and has been a topic of headline interest for the city's newspapers. The impact of the corruption and of the news stories has been significant; both have taken their toll on the city administration and its capacity to govern. As a direct result, an endemic paralysis has affected city government. Bureaucrats have slowed down the process of government because they are afraid that their actions will be seen as supportive of corruption. They want second and third opinions. Commissioners can make fewer mistakes when they do fewer things, and so they do fewer things. Officials protect themselves by "double-checking," by reducing risks, and by inaction. And so the price we pay for corrupt government, in addition to the evil of corruption itself, is slow, hesitant, unresponsive, and inefficient government.

Part of the problem of reforming the political system stems from our failure to reform appropriate wrongs. Indeed, reform proposals are often incomplete, and frequently unrealistic. In New York, critics of the processes of local government have almost always focused on the rules of the game. For some reformers the basic evil stems from money, and they have identified the way in which campaign financing practices have created political debts and obligations that lead to corruption. Others have sought to limit the access of political party

187

officials to public office, or to the arenas where political decisions are made. It is clear that once widely practiced political activities such as "rare shows" on government payrolls are being reformed under the press of these reforms.

The shortcoming of these proposals is that they ignore the process of government and the product of government. Instead, they address the issue of how individuals and their relation to government can be made more free of corrupt influences or conflicts of interest. They do not guarantee that governmental actions will be timely, or that the product of government will be improved. In such a circumstance, we are avoiding meaningful reform of the municipal enterprise.

An example of the incomplete recommendations are those of the State-City Commission on Integrity in Government, chaired by the president of Columbia University. In six reports issued in 1986 and 1987, the commission saw the integrity-in-government issue largely in terms of ethical behavior.

As the commission examined campaign financing, it found a "veritable gold rush," and urged (1) a fixed ceiling on campaign contributions, (2) optional public funding of elections, and (3) spending limits on campaigns. The commission also urged a stronger and clearer "conflicts of interest" statute and called for a stronger Commission on Ethics. It urged financial disclosure, and stronger penalties for nondisclosure. The commission urged that political party leaders also be subject to many of the provisions of the ethics law.

In another report the commission urged that protection for whistleblowers be broadened to include private employees who report on public corruption. Contracting and procurement was the subject of a report that concluded with recommendations that the city adopt uniform procedures for all agencies and virtually all contracts. The commission recommended as well that the task of overseeing the design and development of new contract procedures be entrusted to a special body like the Financial Control Board, which includes private-sector as well as government members. In an effort to strengthen enforcement of contract rules the commission urged that the city adopt a permanent Mayoral Contract Review Panel.

The commission's recommendations reflect the traditional "good government" approach to issues of reform. When it strayed beyond definitions of integrity, for instance, the commission embraced such conventional reforms as an appointed judiciary. In an attack upon

New York's judicial selection procedures, it determined that all judges in New York should be appointed following selection by nominating commissions.

EFFICIENCY AND RESPONSIVENESS

As desirable as these structural recommendations may be, given the pervasiveness of the political corruption that has been uncovered, the real reform of New York City's political and governmental system will not be addressed unless the focus of the reform agenda is *efficiency and responsiveness* in government. An unresponsive government is a seedbed for corruption. Those who shelter the homeless, advocate on behalf of handicapped youngsters, care for abused children, or represent clients in judicial proceedings—or even those who need a license to run a sandwich shop—all complain about the fact that government just doesn't seem to respond to them in a timely and orderly, to say nothing of a satisfactory, fashion. Those who want to build an apartment building, rehabilitate a factory, or develop a new office complex face even more obstacles, although their suffering is less severe since they lose only money. With the breakdown of the city's ability to respond to citizen needs, corruption becomes a part of the "rules of the game," a way of getting the system to do its job. It becomes a way of life even for those who do not wish to "corrupt" the system. The "payoff" is a requirement if one is going to avoid unnecessary delays because paper does not move through the system, because inspections do not occur in a timely fashion, or because permits cannot be obtained through normal channels.

The former head of the city's real estate leasing office, who was convicted of receiving kickbacks, was generally regarded as one of the best lease negotiators the city had. In defense of his actions, he said he got the city the very best prices. Many politically well-connected influentials sell their services on the same basis. They offer help in getting things done by a city government otherwise unable to respond satisfactorily. They speed up the paper flow in the agencies, answer the questions of political decision-makers or powerful bureaucrats, introduce the right vendor and supplier to people who seek assurance that the job promised will be well done. All of this happens—and is in some respects even necessary—in a government of multiple decision points, endless paperwork, and inefficiency. This kind of influence—which at first can be innocent

189

enough, but then borders on and becomes corruption—is the direct result of a government that is slow and inefficient.

Ironically, anticorruption measures may actually exacerbate the very behavior which they aim to control. Multiple levels of decision-making—added to insure an "honest" process—can be so time-consuming and costly as to convince bidders or service providers that it is not worth the effort. Many elaborate "safeguards" can have a chilling effect on providers who believe that the system is closed to all but insiders. Instead of opening up the system, these safeguards can actually cause the system to become more closed. They can slow down the processes of government even further by creating additional decision points that render the process less efficient, and thus intensify the tendency toward corruption. The expediter, the person who cuts through red tape—and who may become the corrupter—becomes more necessary in the more complicated process of doing city business when the process of city business is inefficient and unresponsive. Recent growth in the number of lobbyists, in the number of government-affairs specialists working for labor and business, and in the movement of high government officials to firms that do considerable business with government, are all signs of the need for influence within the city bureaucracy. And reforms that address issues of "corruption" in government increase the chances that government will be more inefficient and unresponsive—and hence, more unsatisfactory to citizens.

MAKING GOVERNMENT ACCOUNTABLE

The key to a responsive and efficient city government is one that is accountable. An accountable system is one in which credit and blame can be located within the political system—which basically means one in which the boss is allowed to fire the employee who goofs. For this to work, several things have to be done within government. First, the rules of the game have to be better defined, the right needs to be distinguished from the wrong. Things are often so confusing that people who think they are doing good are accused of doing wrong. Several years ago, when a developer wanted approval from the community for a particular project, he showed his good faith by making local contributions and offering amenities to local groups. Today, a developer can be accused of bribery for attempting to benefit the local community. Nothing can be more confusing to a developer than to learn that what was once considered almost necessary, can now virtually damn his project. Indeed, the rules for development in New York have been under attack from all sides. The discretionary powers of the city's boards and commissions in this area have been used extensively and the decisions have become so particular and unique that charges of influence peddling—even if unfounded—are impossible to refute in a convincing way.

Second, leadership jobs in the complex system must be better defined, teamwork among city employees must be encouraged, and the person who is doing the job must feel the obligation to the city and to the administration to get the job done. For decades we have obscured accountability in city government by reducing the decision-making capacity of city commissioners, circumscribing their power, and hemming them in with mayoral oversight and interference. This tendency has occurred below the level of commissioner, as well. Too often, when the job has not been done effectively by the mandated agency, new agencies or offices have been created to expedite the process. City Hall created a special unit to expedite housing production issues that could not be handled within the Housing Preservation and Development Department, and development itself had to be given to a quasi-independent agency, The Public Development Corporation. This tendency has not been confined to the administration of Mayor Ed Koch; rather, it has been noticeable over the long term. It seems that every time a problem gets mired in bureaucracy, the usual response is to form a special unit. The most recent of such proposals has been the one to solve construction delays within the Board of Education by creating a new agency to build public schools.

The result of "special agencies" for "special problems" can be devastating for those left behind. For this type of solution has meant that for every process lucky enough to be expedited (assuming that the new mechanism works—by no means a certain assumption), the ones left in the old process have been slowed down.

Every special request, every special consideration means many more ordinary ones. Every move in the direction of taking responsibility away from a commissioner diminishes the opportunity for the agency charged with the task to fulfill its own responsibility. Every time the mayor appoints a special official to take matters out of the usual course of events, he admits that the underlying system is failing. The existence of office of Deputy Mayor, with its day-to-day involvement in areas such as social services, hospitals, economic development, education, and capital construction, means that commissioners with line authority have less to say about important matters that rest within their jurisdiction. The result is overload at City Hall, and the inevitable tendency toward crisis management as the city's administrative style.

Continued administrative responsibility at City Hall is not a healthy development for the departments of the government, or for the city. It soon becomes clear that the commissioners' authority is capable of being overridden by decisions made at City Hall. Hence, those who are antagonistic to a commissioner can wait to present their case at City Hall, embarrassing the commissioner and perhaps convincing him that the price of exercising power is its loss.

If real reform is to occur, the commissioners must be given greater power over their agencies. Leadership must be restored to agencies mandated to do the job and to the line commissioners charged with the duty. The city must reduce the number of special assistants and special projects. Special cases must be handled by those who handle ordinary cases, and ordinary cases must be given the attention and consideration now given the special ones. There is no need for the "fixer" or "expediter" in a system that responds to all. This is what democracy at the local level is all about.

Diffused responsibility enables elected political leaders to resist their own accountability. When the seven members of the Board of Education are appointed by six appointing authorities—the five Borough presidents and the mayor—the latter can point at one another to explain why the system has failed. The same can be said of the Metropolitan Transit Authority, comprising appointees of the governor, the mayor, and several county executives. This tendency is not limited to the authorities and commissions. All too frequently the federal government is blamed—as in the case of housing, in which cutbacks in subsidies are condemned routinely notwithstanding the failure of city government to spend funds currently available.

BRINGING IN THE PUBLIC

It is unlikely that the city government will have much incentive to be responsive in an accountable way until the public is brought more fully into the process. This goal, in fact, lay at the core of the reforms creating community governments for schools through the Bundy Commission recommendations and for other forms of service delivery under the Goodman Charter reforms. Since about 1970, New York has slowly been developing stronger forms of local citizen participation as these changes in the structure of city government have taken effect. This process has not been fully developed, as the quality and impact of community government still vary tremendously across the city.

The clearest effects of public participation can be seen in the parts of government dealing with capital construction. Hence, the requirement of local approval has made a considerable difference. The role of the community in other areas of government, such as service delivery, have been less visible. Beyond community leaders, in any event, a great reservoir of personal, individual involvement remains to be tapped. The public has little sense of how well or badly programs have been run or what the cost per unit of service has been; and when it does know, it has no way of acting on that knowledge. Not enough attention is placed on measures that lead to critical evaluation.

This failure to develop a sense of critical judgment about the effectiveness of city government is astounding. After a severe fiscal crisis, we have managed to bring the municipal work force to numbers in excess of what they were before the crisis, and to do so without building measures of effectiveness and accountability into the discourse of public expenditures. We have lost the battle of accountability at the level of the professional, and it is necessary for the public to be brought into the discourse if we are going to hold the natural tendency to spend in check.

In his 1987 State of the State message, Governor Mario Cuomo, celebrating the enormous growth in state spending for education during his administration, claimed that accountability would be a key part of his future education program. If such a focus had been in place before the spending increases had occurred, the city and state would have been far better served. We can assume that such claims are purely rhetorical, because accountability requires not just the celebration of "excellence" but the identification of measures of positive change. An accountability model requires that officials lose their jobs not only if they are corrupt, but also if they are poor performers. And we do not have in place ways in which accountability can be presented for public scrutiny. Save for the election itself, there is minimal public involvement in the political process.

The need for accountability has a parallel in the public's need for more information about the workings of government. Recent laws requiring disclosure of information include open-meetings laws, which require the public's business to be done in public, and disclosure laws, which mandate that public servants and those seeking public office list their assets and declare their business involvements so they can be tested for possible conflicts of interest.

But disclosure requirements are diminished if the media are not attentive to what actually happens. And there are some substantial problems in this area. To begin with, there is the lack of community newspapers in the neighborhoods and boroughs of New York. Such once-significant papers as the *Brooklyn Eagle*, the *Brooklyn Times Union*, the *Long Island (Queens) Press*, the *Long Island (Queens) Star*, the *Bronx Home Reporter* are gone. Only the *Staten Island Advance* remains in the tradition of the local press able to represent, in news and in editorials, the perspective of the community. These papers had a sense of what was going on in the communities and brought a critical perspective that heightened citizen awareness and action.

Even the number of citywide dailies has been reduced with the demise of mighty papers such as the *Herald-Tribune*, the *World-Telegram*, the *Journal-American, The Sun,* and others such as *The Mirror* and *PM*. For the past few years we have been fortunate that *New York Newsday* has been willing to enter the highly competitive New York market. The result has been an infusion of energy in the coverage of local news. But the problem is still one of the ability of the media to do the job of coverage well enough so that the public will be moved to do its part. New York's print media cannot pay adequate attention to New York's government. Reporters cover the mayor and major headline-making stories, but the coverage is not deep. Unless information can be prepackaged—either in a series of connected events, or a set of press releases—it is often not considered newsworthy. Too few reporters know the agencies, or the programs, or what goes on behind the scenes. They are usually not on city assignment long enough to develop an in-depth understanding. We would be better served if the media regarded city government as a long-term beat, and if more reporters were assigned to city affairs, to departments and agencies. But the cost of such commitment would be considerable, and perhaps prohibitive.

The recent corruption crisis has increased the media's interest in city affairs, but as with other crises, the media interest may soon wane. An aggressive press could have long ago discovered the events and processes that led to the corruption scandals. By an examination of the way the Board of Estimate approved contracts, by an analysis of the links between the "influentials" and the deals that were approved that the press was pointed to but ignored, the reporters could have followed up on leads that would have given them a clearer picture of the administrative flaws that invited corruption. Instead, the media only noticed the style and personality of the mayor himself. Even in the 1985 mayoral campaign, the press ignored the criticisms and charges of the mayoral opponents. In races for the borough presidency in Brooklyn and Bronx, the reporters ignored issues of corruption raised by opponents of the incumbents. Even when charges that contributions had come largely from the ranks of developers who were engaged in projects that required the support of the borough presidents were packaged for the press, they were not reported on. Where incumbents did face scrutiny, as in the close election for Bronx borough president, Jose Serrano's ethnicity was given more attention than were questions of the performance of Borough President Stanley Simon, or reports of the connections between his campaign contributors and capital projects in the Bronx.

PUBLIC PARTICIPATION

The concept that the public ought to know, that it can be trusted with facts, that it should be kept up to date with information, has an important corollary. The public should be trusted to participate more in government itself.

It is time to institute classic reform measures such as the recall, the initiative, and the referendum in New York State. These measures have worked in many other localities to cut government spending, and to curb the tendency of government office holders to ignore matters of concern to the public. If the issues get on the ballot and before the public, the political agenda will cease being the province solely of the "enlightened professional" politicians. The public will get the opportunity to be bombarded with information and to be solicited for support. Too many professionals in our political system either fear the people or don't trust their judgment. Such a situation frustrates responsive government. It is time to recognize that we have one-party rule in New York—and that that party has two branches, incumbent Democrats and incumbent Republicans. Incumbents are in effect one-party rulers with virtually permanent tenure. In the elections for the New York State legislature in 1986, for instance, out of 197 races involving incumbents, only *one* was defeated. This situation leads to a closed system—with reform required to come from outside of the political system. To counteract this one-party system of incumbency, in addition to campaign-financing reforms, we need more issues on the ballot, and we need more elections of officials at community and local levels. Indeed, we should even consider whether we want to place a limit on the number of terms that political officeholders may serve.

One solution to the problem of closed political systems includes increased development of community government trends that have been taking place through community boards and community school boards. Even though the presence of these organizations might tend to slow down the processes of government—as in the approval procedures governing land-use decisions—the presence of these organizations has been a positive development in the city.

One certain area of real progress has occurred in the community school districts of the city. Although subject to uneven growth— with some parts of the city not experiencing substantial improvement—there is no question that community school boards in virtually every neighborhood of the city have done a better job in elementary education than the central Board has in special education and in the high schools.

The example of these effective community school boards should be the basis for the reform of school decentralization. Appointment of local boards by the central Board, as some reformers have suggested, would intensify the difficulties, not alleviate them. Eliminating all democratically elected local school boards because some are corrupt would be the wrong thing to do.

The city should strengthen local institutions and encourage community boards and neighborhood development corporations, even if the result is that local interests are able to modify projects in which broader interests are at stake. We must get a participatory system working more effectively in New York, for unless the people have the opportunity to practice democracy at the grass-roots level, they will never develop the broader perspective that is required to exercise intelligently their rights and judgment in a city of this size and complexity. Community school board members are elected, but members of the local community boards are not. They should be. Such an electoral process should act to increase the involvement of citizens at the local level. Another way to devolve greater power to the people is to increase the size of the City Council. Council districts with one representative for every 250,000 people are too large. Reducing their size would increase the number and percentage of minorities, increase the representation of particular neighborhoods, and might even provide for an increase in non-Democratic Party members and hence a more representative city legislature.

The thrust of these recommendations is to remind city legislators that they are their community's representatives. They are not representatives *of* the government, but rather representatives *to* the government. Their job is delivering the people's interests to the government, not delivering the government's interest to the people.

BETTER MANAGEMENT

Increased participation in government will put greater pressure on government officials to be more responsive. But the political system alone cannot translate pressure into effective programs and policy. The bureaucracy also must change. Too often, people who work for government forget that their customers are the citizens and that their responsibilities require that their customers be satisfied. The bureaucracy cannot change, however, without high-caliber leadership. One of the most serious problems facing New York government today is the lack of capable middle managers. With so many opportunities available for good managers in the private sector, the competition for talent leaves government a distant second. Unfortunately, all discussion about recruiting talent stops at the highest levels. Ironically, it is at the top of the bureaucracy that the problem is least severe. Candidates for positions such as commissioner expect a sacrifice in salary and usually accept it willingly. The city's history is replete with outsiders entering government for an assignment of three or four years and doing it well before returning to the private sector. Such an arrangement allows a mayor to choose department chiefs who will be responsive to mayoral direction and not be captured by the bureaucracies they direct.

The real problem occurs at the middle professional levels, where the public–private sector salary differences are significant, and the commitment to public service must be long-term. All too often good people are offered substantial salary increases and lured away to the private sector, in areas such as finance and housing, where the public and private sector employers meet.

The human services agencies face a different middle-management problem. Managers in social service and education, even the good ones, are generally ignored by the private sector. They are stuck in lower-paying city jobs, with little opportunity for advancement or promotion within their agencies, and with virtually no opportunity to go to the private sector. These factors contribute to the lack of morale in the city bureaucracy. Obviously, if we want better services

197

we need better managers. If we want better management, we need changes in personnel practices, recruitment, promotion, and administration.

Finding better managers is not enough, however: there must also be a better system to evaluate their performance. The city's personnel system relies in theory almost exclusively on civil service testing. The Department of Personnel, in practice, goes to great lengths to avoid the limitations of civil service merit testing. City personnel policies need the attention of human resources experts—particularly those from the private sector. The tests have to be modernized to eliminate the racial bias that all too often shows up in the results. Compensation should be related to productivity: the example that was set in negotiations between the sanitation workers' union and the city over the issue of two-man trucks needs to be replicated in other areas. The increase in the municipal work force has reached the point that in 1988, the number of employees exceeded that of pre-fiscal crisis days. It is time to reexamine the job classifications and continue to collapse the number of job categories, permitting management flexibility in assigning workers to their jobs. While these issues are not highly visible, they are important ones in determining the capacity of managers to deploy their workers in an efficient way.

FINDING A ROLE FOR PARTY

The corollary of the city's one-party system is the atrophy of the political process and the decline of the political parties themselves. The political party, which historically acted to counterbalance special interests, has lost much of its power. Twenty years ago political battles occurred within the Democratic Party, as the legendary bosses of Tammany Hall fought the reformers who sought to liberalize the party's rules and bring their version of democracy to the party. Party position was sought after by many who were interested in public service.

Today, things have changed considerably. The Republican Party and minor parties are not taken seriously because they do not elect enough candidates, and time spent in furthering their interests does not result in candidates being elected to public office, particularly at the municipal level. There is virtually no reform movement within the Democratic Party. Interest in party office has waned, and reforms that have been suggested to eliminate political corruption question the involvement of party officials in virtually any part of the political process. Party officials are criticized for doing business with the city; political officeholders are discouraged from becoming party officials.

Intraparty primaries are not deemed worthy places to do battle. Indeed, being a political leader makes one suspect, and the reforms being spoken of today seem to give greater rights to rehabilitated felons than to political party leaders. It is as if the political party is now regarded as the problem rather than as a part of the solution.

While the ongoing passage of the political party as an effective institution in the city is viewed by reformers as a positive development, local-government scholars increasingly are becoming critical of this loss of a once-considerable institution in political affairs. The party, after all, acts as a counterbalance to candidates with personal fortunes, media attractiveness, and/or with limited political experience. Service within the political party structure allows a potential officeholder to be tested for his/her suitability for public office. It allows the citizen's commitment to service to be tested not only with the attractive job, but with the mundane ones as well.

The party's role has substantially been replaced by other institutions that have served to bring constituent groups into contact with the government. Community boards and neighborhood development corporations are relatively new institutions created to articulate the needs of many localities. Through them, unattended needs and special interests find their way into the government. Instead of deploring their work, we should invite these special pleaders into the governmental process. One way of doing so would be to eliminate the party altogether from municipal elections by making city officials run in nonpartisan elections. By eliminating party labels, many more outsiders would become involved. Party primaries, which require candidates to be party members, would not dominate the process, and many registered independents would have a voice in the selection of candidates. Such an open process would invite many good-government groups, community organizations, and individuals into a process from which they have been excluded. It would, in fact, also recognize the trends toward reducing the party's role in municipal affairs.

Reform of the apparatus that has so long supported the political process, the party, should be continued and intensified by bringing more groups and people into important roles so that the work of government will include outsiders as well.

FRANK J. MACCHIAROLA

A LARGER ROLE FOR THE PRIVATE SECTOR

There has been a longstanding tendency to regard government as the repository of all answers to the social problems encountered in American cities. At the same time, as E. S. Savas notes in chapter 6, some trends toward privatization have been emerging in many localities. Developer Donald Trump's completion of the Central Park Skating Rink in less than six months, after the city's Department of Parks had spent an unsuccessful six years on the project, provided reason enough to consider how traditional municipal services could be produced by private parties.

In at least two ways private-sector involvement in the provision of local services could be enhanced. One would be the increased transfer of services of operations that are now performed by public agencies to private-sector organizations. Privatizing services such as sanitation, parks maintenance, and police and fire protection by allowing local community governments to choose municipal services or private-sector alternatives is a logical step in the development of the community government that has been occurring in the city. The other way to boost private-sector involvement would be to privatize entire facilities. Smaller parks, for example, could be supervised and administered by the organizations that actually use them.

The city should actively evaluate its options under privatization by creating a planning office to promote the development of programs that would serve citizens more efficiently and with greater economy. The city administration itself should be committed to finding areas in which local government services could be better performed by the private sector.

BUILDING NEW YORK AS A COMMUNITY

There has been a significant increase in the rhetoric that has described New York City as the modern version of the *Tale of Two Cities*: a city of the rich and a city of the poor; or in terms of government services and benefits, of the citizens who profit in this city and of the ones who suffer. Although it contains many elements of truth, such a view actually ignores a tremendous commonality that affects all New Yorkers. At the same time, it does represent a strong belief that the condition of the poor needs to be a matter of

200

concern for everyone. It is not just a matter for government—it is a matter for all citizens.

Indeed, if the only contact between poor and the affluent in New York City takes place through government, that contact remains a contact of more "income transfers" and of taxes converted into subsidies. Such a role for our citizens denies them the fuller meaning of citizenship. By an expansion of participatory government, through more-active community groups and more-powerful local development corporations, and through strengthened community boards and community school boards, decisions are brought about through direct citizen interaction. The developer must convince community residents that a project will better serve the community itself. And so the rich and powerful must test their wealth and power within arenas that include more than bureaucrats and functionaries.

The inclusion of local citizenry within the structures of government also helps in the process of making the poor believe that their role in our society is not only to suffer the handout and dole, but also to assert their needs and to work to overcome the handicaps of poverty.

In New York City, for too long, elitism has often meant that people who have tried to do good things have found their intentions suspect and their access to government restricted by a defensive attitude on the part of the government that represents them. The tendency toward exclusion, toward trying to tell other citizens what they need and what's good for them, rather than toward listening in a responsive way and engaging citizens in dialogue, is all too pervasive. Such a dialogue is time-consuming and difficult. But in the end it results in programs better able to withstand the crucible of public scrutiny.

Finally, a word on the public good. This essay has had as its major underpinning the belief that the common good requires the participation of most citizens. It has exhorted city leaders to facilitate ways to help more to participate in ways of defining common goals that might better serve New York. Indeed, the development of good governmental practices requires us to remain aware of what the ends of government actually are. The greatest obstacles to achieving the public good are the special interests that dominate the political life of New York City. These interests are not going to disappear—the landlord will not cease acting as such, the municipal unions will not shift their primary allegiance away from their own members, the business community will not focus its concern on social issues. But if the city is to progress as a healthy body politic, the issues of special interest representation must be addressed. Government officials and leaders must go beyond simply balancing interests and presuming that in the end justice will work itself out. The cynical responses that justify poor projects or inappropriate compromises must be scrutinized and rejected. Government officials must resist the tendency to surrender policies to special interests. Special interests must be identified for what they are and forced to submit to the light of scrutiny by an informed electorate, a responsive bureaucracy and strong governmental leadership. The reforms that must occur in New York will require the election of political leaders of understanding, compassion, and vision. Government systems must also be reformed, to include more participants, listen more to what they have to say, and to compromise more as well. Within such a framework, citizens will be both the masters and beneficiaries of their government, not its subjects and supplicants.

Chapter 12

LOOKING BACKWARD—AND FORWARD

Andrew Hacker

Paris and London, Philadelphia and Boston, are historic cities. One can feel and see their pasts simply by strolling down their streets. Not so New York. New York prides itself on being up-to-date, on impatience with traditions, on redefining its character each generation. So it is hardly surprising that New Yorkers know little of their city's past. For most, its chronicle coincides with their own lifespan; those arriving from elsewhere tend to date it from the day they unpacked.

Lacking a sense of history, New York tends to consider every condition a crisis; to see its problems as unique and uncommonly complex. As it happens, many of the dilemmas the city now faces have had parallels in the past. This is not to suggest that history is a textbook with lessons clearly marked. Still, some perspective can be gained by examining a period not wholly dissimilar to our own. I have chosen to focus on 1910, the closing year of a kaleidoscopic decade, which marked the end of an older era and made New York a modern city. For many, it was also a time when the city worked. The streets were safe, public transit ran on time, teachers and policemen were figures of authority. Indeed, a feeling of progress was in the air; even the poor looked forward to a prosperous future.

Yet there was another, more troubling, side to this city. By common agreement, New York in 1910 had the worst slums in the world. "In no other city are the same appalling conditions," one observer wrote. "Nowhere are the evils of modern life so varied." The preceding ten years had seen the greatest growth in the city's history. According to the 1910 census, a superbly detailed document, the population rose from 3,437,202 in 1900 to 4,766,883 in

1910—an increase of about 40 percent, the largest decade of growth before or since. Most of the newcomers were immigrants, largely Eastern European Jews and Italians from Sicily, ignorant of English and unused to urban ways. The city felt inundated, as one official put it, by "vast hordes of people from abroad, alien in language, alien in modes of thought, and alien in tradition."

Most of the new arrivals went directly from Ellis Island to Manhattan's Lower East Side, the city's immigrant enclave. Jammed into 2.3 square miles were 588,496 men, women, and children, of whom only 14,014 could claim American-born parents. One author computed that this district was "the most densely populated spot in the habitable globe." The sheer congestion led a visitor to report that living "conditions in New York are without parallel in the civilized world." A one-and-a-half-acre block bounded by Monroe, Hamilton, Catherine, and Market Streets, today a fair-sized suburban plot, housed 2,280 human beings.

The extent to which bodies were crushed together is difficult to comprehend. A Tenement House Commission survey found a third of all rooms housed two or two-and-a-half occupants (children counted as halves) and that two-thirds had three or more. That often meant more than a dozen people in a flat: "Parents, children, and three to eight adult boarders occupied apartments of two, three, and four rooms." Here is a current description of a single street:

> Stanton Street is a great thoroughfare from the Bowery to the East River. . . . A heavy and evil steam, adhesive, almost palpable and rank with ill smells, hung over it. Here at our feet was garbage, decaying vegetables, and old kitchen refuse, droppings from pushcarts, wisps of hay, remainders of old mattresses, rotten rags, broken bits of old paper boxes, broken bottles, the broken covers of cooking utensils. And children played and rolled in the accretion of diverse horrors.

> A narrow passage lined with planks led rearward to a cramped interior court, wherein were the miserable and decaying wooden sheds that supplied the sanitation for the teeming house in front. Through the passageway and up the stairways, there hung a suffocating stench from the miserable sheds.

> Beyond belief was the clanging din of traffic, mixed with the yelling of pushcart peddlers and the babel of vast throngs that overflowed the sidewalks, a torrent of maddening sound whereat the nerves quivered in lost protest.

Earlier immigrant groups, mainly Germans and Irish, had been settling in the city for over a century. During these years, the Irish had moved up to the West Side, first to Hell's Kitchen tenements between 34th and 54th streets, where the population density was only half that of the Lower East Side, and then into newer apartments further north. Germans were buying their own homes in Brooklyn and Queens, where they began to speak English and to disperse among the population. The outer boroughs, then the city's suburban ring, still had many residents of Anglo-Saxon origin, as had Manhattan's better neighborhoods.

But between 1900 and 1910, the demographic picture changed. Third-generation New Yorkers (native-born of native parents) dropped to less than 20 percent of the total population. Even this figure does not mirror the magnitude of the shift, since most of the immigrants came without children. Despite the photographs of family groups, very few youngsters were taken on the crossings. In 1910, of the 1,927,703 New Yorkers who were foreign-born, fewer than 8 percent were under the age of 15. In fact, almost three-quarters of the persons processed at Ellis Island during 1910 were unaccompanied men. Immigrant couples soon remedied their childless condition, however. Of the 1,075,940 babies born between 1900 and 1910, more than three-quarters were to foreign-born women. By 1910, families headed by foreign-born parents accounted for almost 60 percent of the city's households.

Yet one commentator recalled New York at that time as a place of "civil peace" and "moral order." How did the city manage to absorb so many strangers and still maintain stability and control?

Most of all, the city's economy was expanding, and employment was available for everyone who sought it. Between 1900 and 1910, the job rolls rose by 50 percent, more than matching the influx of immigrants. Of the city's 1,660,236 males aged 15–70, no fewer than 94 percent were gainfully occupied. Women also began work early, accounting for 47 percent of workers under the age of 21. However, women generally gave up their jobs after marriage, since frequent births and domestic chores made housework a full-time occupation. The economy was largely industrial, but most of the factories were small sweatshops, offering less-than-subsistence wages in unhealthy settings. The typical manufacturing establishment averaged 26 employees. According to one report, "Thousands of men and women are murdered annually by permitting them to work in unsanitary factories at starvation wages." Among those doing outdoor work, accidents took a heavy toll.

Manhattan then held 2,331,542 people, 63 percent more than the

1,428,285 counted in 1980. Most were crowded into five-story tenements. Lower Manhattan was also the city's industrial center; a mid-decade survey found 321,488 workers in factories south of 14th Street, compared with 160,368 in the rest of the borough and 102,708 elsewhere in the city. Few factory workers could look for housing further afield. "Most people were dependent on industry situated within walking distance of their home," one study concluded. "So long as wages are low, making carfare such a serious item, conditions of overcrowding will continue." The five-cent subway and streetcar fare was beyond the budget of most working New Yorkers. In fact, the subways were originally built to hurry the "clerical middle classes" to their downtown offices.

One writer cited this fact to refute "the old theory that congestion is due to the congregation of nationalities who desire to live together." Rather, he noted, "in every instance it is the location of the place of work, and not the nationality group, which determines residence." Even in the Lower East Side, many neighborhoods housed a variety of nationalities. A Columbia University dissertation on 200 families in abutting tenements found that 38 were of German origin, 57 Irish, 38 Italian, 62 "Hebrew," and 40 "American"—all living side by side.

But not all analysts agreed. "Foreigners who do not know English feel lost when they are not surrounded by people who understand their own language," a labor official said. "There are many who have never gone out from the district inhabited by their countrymen." Needless to say, there were ethnic enclaves, and old identities stayed strong. Photographs of Rivington and Orchard streets show the store signs with Hebrew lettering, just as Mulberry and Cherry streets were almost exclusively Italian. But a commitment to national origins did not produce residential segregation. Out of the six Lower East Side assembly districts, only one was highly a cluster of Italians; other nationalities were quite dispersed.

The State Conference on Charities and Corrections calculated that an income of $800 a year was "essential to maintain a family of two parents and three children under working age on a reasonable basis." This was 1910's counterpart of our current poverty line. While the census did not gather information on income, a survey conducted in 1904 found factory workers averaged $534 annually—not even two-thirds of the reasonable minimum. Another study of 400 Brooklyn and Manhattan households revealed that at least half earned less than the $800 norm.

Not only family heads were underpaid. Prominent in the labor force were 188,941 girls and women under the age of 21, including 32,615 sewing-machine operators, 27,290 domestic servants, 16,125 stenographers, 11,033 sales clerks, 522 silkweavers, 901 lacemakers, and 1,098 music teachers. These young women were overworked and received less than a living wage, even by the standards of 1910. "The wages paid to women are notably insufficient," one report remarked. "Many department stores pay as low as $5 per week, while the wages of girls in factories run to $3.50."

Perhaps the most graphic portrayal of working and living conditions can be found in a study titled *The Income and Outlay of New York Working Girls*. The authors detailed the human toll taken by wages and hours otherwise cited as statistics. What comes through, in particular, is the fatigue and exhaustion, the erosion of human energy.

> *Alice Anderson.* Employed as a check girl in a 14th Street store, at a wage of $2.62 a week. . . . Her working day was $9\frac{1}{2}$ hours, but before Christmas it was lengthened to $13\frac{1}{2}$ hours, without any extra payment. Alice could not reach home until nearly 11:30 p.m.; and she would rise while it was still dark, at 6:00 a.m., in order to be at her counter at 8:00 a.m.

> *Irena Kovalova.* A girl of 16, supported herself and her mother and her younger brother and sister, on her wage of $9 a week. . . . They paid $207 annual rental, and lived on the remaining $243 through the year.

> *Anna Flodin.* In the evening, she was too tired to leave the tenement for night school or for anything else. In the course of a year, her only pleasure had been a trip to the theater for 35 cents.

> *Sadie Goldstein.* She spent nothing for pleasure. In the course of $2\frac{1}{2}$ years, she had bought one hat for $3 and a suit for $12. For $3 a month, she rented a sleeping space in the kitchen of a squalid tenement. She had to wait until they all left it, before she dragged her bed out and flung it on the floor for her long-desired sleep.

Even before the Triangle Shirtwaist fire of 1911, low wages and inhuman hours spurred women to form unions. In a display of concern during the winter of 1910, Mrs. Oliver Hazard Perry Belmont assembled a group of her friends at Delmonico's to meet leaders in a garment makers' strike. "Mrs. Belmont asked all to promise to wear only union shirtwaists for one year." But one skeptic mused, "I would like to know if either Mrs. Belmont or any other society woman would take such an interest if it happened to be a strike of the female domestics they employ."

An appreciable portion of the population literally perished due to the conditions of life in New York. Only 5 percent of the population reached the age of 60, and a mere 1.5 percent survived past 70. Of the infants born in 1910, one in every five did not live to celebrate a fifth birthday. Indeed, a third of the deaths recorded in the decade were children under five. One commentator found a brighter side to these statistics. "From the standpoint of the efficiency of the city's population," he remarked, "the loss of a thousand infants is not as serious as the loss of the same number of able-bodied men and women."

Children perished from inadequate diets, from playing in filthy streets, and from the crowding, which caused family members to infect one another. One in four households took in lodgers. Among Jewish families in the Lower East Side, nearly 80 percent had outsiders living with them. Sixty percent of the city's apartments had at least one windowless room—usually where several people slept. In Manhattan as a whole, only a quarter of the apartments contained private lavatories; the rest shared one in the public hallway or a shed in a rear court. Less than one in five had separate bathrooms, although some had tubs in the kitchen.

Another cause of premature death was impure milk, which prompted a reform group to point out that "cheap and good milk would cost only 15 cents per quart, which would mean a cost of approximately $1.00 per week for each child." What they did not seem to realize was that given workers' wages, a family with three children would have to earmark almost a third of its earnings simply for milk.

Youngsters also engaged in home labor, often at the expense of sleep. "It is not uncommon for children as young as four years of age to work at home pulling out bastings and doing other confining work," reported one investigation. A probation official testified that "young children were going to school and working until midnight in sweatshop homes." At least 13,000 New Yorkers suffered from tuberculosis, which was usually fatal. A public health official reported that "three-fourths of those now known to have consumption will die." Public and private outlays for what we now call health and social services totaled only $25 million, or about $15 per year for each of the city's families.

In 1910, New York was an orderly city. In earlier generations, there had been areas where even policemen feared to tread. These were largely Irish neighborhoods, where drink and rebellious spirits often led to violence. But by 1910 the Irish became more respectable, while the newer immigrants were remarkably law-abiding and mindful of authority. About the only disruptions of note were a series of strikes, by delivery boys and bakers, and by truck and taxi-cab drivers. However, these were soon settled, and they were in no way violent. The police did not keep data on how many crimes apart from murders were reported or committed. So we must make do with their figures for arrests—admittedly an incomplete index, although in those days the odds were greater that offenders would be caught. In 1910, in a city two-thirds the size of today's, the police made 312 arrests for robberies and 1,179 for actual or attempted burglaries. There were also 234 known murders and cases of non-negligent manslaughter, almost all involving individuals known or related to one another.

Neither newspapers nor politicians found crime a major worry. This is not to say that the police were inactive. Members of the force, which numbered 10,131, were expected to maintain the city's moral tone. To this end, they made 21 arrests for bigamy, 45 for abortions, and two for "concealing the birth of a child." Another 78 persons were charged with illegal prize-fighting, 84 with unlawful voting, 854 for cruelty to animals (mainly horses), and 196 for indecent exposure (usually urinating in alleys). There were also 46 arrests for "seduction," 23 for "sodomy and other crimes against nature," and 734 for "attempted suicide." The largest category of arrests, 29,955, involved "intoxication." The smallest, two, was for persons apprehended with "narcotics in possession."

A further sign that the city was relatively free of crime can be found by scanning the Police Department's Honor Roll. Of the several dozen citations awarded in 1910, typical were those for stopping runaway horses, rescuing children from drowning, and saving lives at fires. Only two cited officers were involved in violent crimes: one for "pursuing and arresting a burglar," the other for "arresting a man with a revolver."

The commissioner said his most perplexing problems were cases of extortion within the Italian community. Prosecutions were all but impossible, since the victims, mainly shopkeepers, were afraid to press charges. He said his men had tried infiltrating the "Black Hand," but the lack of officers conversant with the "Sicilian dialect" limited this operation. "We are trying to handle medieval criminals, men in whose blood runs the spirit of the vendetta," the commissioner explained.

With respect of juveniles, the chief concern was pilferage. By 1910, the barefoot street boys photographed by Jacob Riis had vanished from the scene. "The prevalence of the pushcart on the Lower East Side is a most potent and continual source of crime, by tempting young children to steal," a school official observed. The annual report of the Children's Court made no reference to violence or vandalism, merely remarking that "the most skillful pickpockets in New York City are children." One suggested solution was "adequate provision of parks and playgrounds should be made, where the boys could work off the surplus of animal spirits."

About this time, the Russell Sage Foundation was studying what it perceived as "lawlessness" among youngsters in the Hell's Kitchen district. True, the police frequently found reason to charge local youths. According to the Sage study, these were common offenses: "pitching pennies," "playing ball," "shouting and singing," "selling papers without a badge," "upsetting ashcans," "profanity," and perhaps more serious, "throwing stones and other missiles." On the whole, Hell's Kitchen has had a bad press. Indeed, one young man maligned in a report later sued the researchers and was awarded damages.

If boys were having a good time, the same was less true for the girls. As had been noted, most of the arriving immigrants were unaccompanied men, who boarded with families. While many patronized prostitutes, not all were so circumspect. The Children's Court cited cases of "little children brought to court suffering from syphilis contracted from lodgers." During 1910, a total of 166 foundlings and 288 fetuses were found by or turned over to the police. In one instance cited, "a thirteen-year-old girl had strangled her baby, of which one of the lodgers in the house was father." Apparently the new nickelodeons served as recruiting grounds. "The balconies and aisles are dark," a report pointed out, "and the girls sit besides immoral men, who often inveigle them into immorality."

Still, cases of seduction and intimidation were more exceptions than the rule. Compared with today, there was much less sex before or outside marriage. Indeed, if no records were kept on out-of-wedlock births, it was because illegitimacy rates were extremely low. And this despite the fact that individuals married relatively late.

According to the 1910 Census, among New Yorkers aged 25 to 34, almost 40 percent of the men were still single, as were 28 percent of the women.

Alcohol was 1910's drug problem. The 29,955 arrests for intoxication betokened only the most visible displays of drunkenness, requiring removal from the streets and a night in the stationhouse. A more serious consequence was the unhealthy effect of hard liquor, rendering able-bodied men unable to work. Even worse, the early-mortality figures for New Yorkers of Irish origin were about twice as high as those for Italians and Jews, although the latter tended to be poorer. A report on neglected children in the Hell's Kitchen area noted that almost half lived in families "affected by excessive drinking on the part of one or both parents." Alcoholism was cited as a major reason why many husbands did not bring home regular earnings. Even so, liquor could not counted a cause of crime; there were no indications that drinkers resorted to robbery to pay their bar bills.

A study of 370 working mothers found that despite serious poverty, most of their families had stayed together. In 80 percent of the households, marriages were still intact, even though the husbands were ill or unemployed, or worked only sporadically. Among the remaining 20 percent, the husbands had deserted or the couples were separated; none were divorced. Within the group as a whole, only two of the 370 mothers were unmarried; and in one case the children's father was in residence. Divorces were difficult to obtain, almost impossible for the poor. The 1910 census listed only 8,292 New Yorkers as divorced, compared with 1,805,335 who were married.

Needless to say, there were no welfare allowances for families headed by women. For mothers on their own, or whose husbands were ill or disabled, finding a job was the only option. They worked mainly as domestic servants and office cleaners, or in restaurants and nearby factories. Manufacturing employment averaged almost 60 hours a week; restaurants had 12-hour shifts, with an afternoon break. Office cleaning began at 5:00 PM and ended past midnight, with most of that time spent scrubbing on one's hands and knees, since the women were "not allowed to use long-handled mops." Wages averaged $5.65 per week. Out of this amount, $1.50 to $2.00 had to be set aside for "minders" to look after younger children.

The city's schools, far from being in a state of crisis, seemed well under control. Attendance was required from ages seven through 14. The system was apparently coping well, despite the fact that its enrollments rose from 418,951 to 659,495, or almost 60 percent, between 1900 and 1910. The vast majority of arriving pupils came from immigrant households. However, the superintendent's 1910 report, a tome of some 600 pages, devoted only two lines to pupils' "ignorance of the English language" and the fact that in many neighborhoods "English is not the language of the home." No mentions were made of truancy, or of violent or disruptive students.

Class size in the elementary grades averaged 42 pupils. Over 2,000 classrooms had more than 50 students, and some exceeded 75. This, too, occasioned few complaints. One administrator said she "was quite satisfied to have the registration at 40 pupils, although good work was being done in classes with 45 pupils." Children sat docilely at bolted-down desks, even if they barely understood what was going on—or, indeed, remained awake, considering that so many "young children were working until midnight in sweatshop homes."

No citywide tests were administered, so we do not know how much was learned. What we do know is that 80 percent of the city's children ended their education at their 15th birthday. Virtually all went out to work, many without even a certificate saying they had completed eight grades. High schools had to be applied to, with the caveat that "only those who display conspicuous ability shall be admitted." Since high schools were selective institutions, they enjoyed a ratio of one teacher to every 27 pupils. Moreover, of the 19 high schools in operation in 1910, only five were in Manhattan, by far the most populous borough; and of those, only two were within walking distance of the poorest neighborhoods.

As a rule, Irish and Italian families took their children out of school as early as they could. For many Jews, moves to Brooklyn and the Bronx were spurred by the availability of high schools. Even with this incentive, most of those admitted to high schools did not complete the course. Of the 13,094 pupils who began the ninth grade in 1906, only 2,477, or fewer than one in five, remained to graduate in 1910. And among that elite cadre, 1,514 were girls and 963 were boys. Looked at another way, in 1910 less than 2 percent of the young men in the city possessed a high school diploma.

If New York was still mainly a working-class city, a middle class was beginning to emerge. Between 1900 and 1910, the ratio receiving salaries rose from 10 percent to 15 percent. Symbolic of this shift was the completion in 1909 of the Metropolitan Life Insurance tower on Madison Square. Its 3,184 clerical employees worked only a seven-hour day, which encouraged commuting. One-third resided in Brooklyn or the Bronx, with a considerable group ferrying over from New Jersey—journeys that were possible due to higher white-collar salaries. Since the 1910 census collected no information on income, we can only estimate the range of the city's middle class. Still, a deduction can be drawn from one census statistic, the 139,987 persons who were employed as domestic servants. Given that most housework and laundering had to be done by hand, a 1910 family considered middle-class had at least a daily maid. Others, of course, had sizable staffs. By this reckoning, we might estimate that perhaps one in eight of the city's households could claim middle-class status.

Politics in 1910 were both placid and conventional. There was nothing like the corruption of earlier periods, and the social conditions of day had not become political issues. While muckrakers continued to excoriate corruption and middle-class progressives were exploring urban problems, governmental responses were slow in coming.

New York was very much a two-party city. Of the votes cast in the 1910 contests for state assembly, no fewer than 46 percent went to Republican candidates. Democrats came away with 52 percent, leaving 2 percent for the Socialist slate. The parties were quite similar. Although the Republicans sent patricians such as Charles Dana and Artemas Ward to the Assembly in Albany, they also found room for men named Doherty and Donovan on their ballots. The Democrats may have been the party of the immigrants, but all save one of their assembly candidates were native-born, and half were college graduates. Among the latter were a Levy and a Spielberg, in addition to Foley and a McGrath. Not a single Italian name appeared among the Democratic nominations. Nor was this surprising, as only 8 percent of the city's half-million Italians were citizens. However, a young man named Alfred Smith, who had an Italian-born mother, served in the Assembly for a Lower East Side district.

In the presidential race of 1908, William Howard Taft, a conservative Republican, in fact led the field with 49 percent of the votes. In part, his ideology was overlooked because he came recommended by Theodore Roosevelt, a local luminary and his popular predecessor. Moreover, his opponent, William Jennings Bryan, did not have much appeal among urban Democrats, as testified by his 46 percent showing. However when Taft sought reelection, in 1912, the returns were altogether different. He attracted well under half his previous total, a mere 19 percent of the count. Many of his erstwhile supporters preferred Woodrow Wilson or Theordore Roosevelt, who received 47 percent and 29 percent, respectively.

In 1908, there was also a Socialist presidential candidate, George Hisgen, who ended up with 27,506 citywide votes, or 4.5 percent of the total. In 1912, the Socialist was the far better-known Eugene Victor Debs; even so, his tally came to 33,423, slightly over 5 percent—not substantially better. And in 1910, Socialist candidates ran in all of Manhattan's Assembly Districts, where they received a grand total of 5,979 ballots, or less than 2 percent of the votes. Even in Lower East Side districts, by most accounts the radical center, Socialist support totaled only 1,649 votes, as against 19,711 for Democratic candidates. As it happened, Hisgen and Debs fared better in Queens than they did in Manhattan.

Robert Wood has reminded us of the "sharp limits to the kinds of activity local governments undertook, and their generally weak response to the pressures of the day." He notes that problems of health and housing, and of poverty generally, brought only "puny response from the political system." Indeed, the mayor himself rejected charges that too much power inhered in his office. On the contrary, William Gaynor argued, "the peril to society today is not from too strong government; it is from a government not strong enough." Still, the legend persists that informal aid was common, with precinct captains handing out largesse:

> On each citizen's block there was a Democratic captain—a long-term resident, known and accessible to all. The captain was the agent of the machine, and the machine had substantial resources. It functioned as a welfare agency—coal in cold weather, food in hunger, were the machine's stock in trade.

If such assistance was available, it was hardly the rule. Among the many reports on the city's poor, none found households which had received help from local party leaders.

Nor could immigrants count on public employment. Most city jobs were given to native New Yorkers, largely of German and Irish origin, most of whom had moved to Brooklyn or upper Manhattan. Thus, 82 percent of the firemen were native-born, as were 80 percent of the mail carriers and 74 percent of the policemen. (Recall that the police commissioner had trouble finding officers who spoke "the Sicilian dialect.") Even a majority of the unskilled workers on the public payroll were native-born.

For all its cruelties and contrasts, New York in 1910 was entering its golden age. Out of its investment of lost or stunted lives grew the world's unrivaled city. Between 1910 and 1955, according to

Roger Starr, New York boasted "an unprecedented level of civic order." The violence of earlier years had abated; even the poorest streets were safe. Despite a diverse population, there was a tacit agreement on the rules and goals of urban life. This spirit survived the Depression, continued through World War II, and only began to wane during the first postwar decade.

Since that time remains a model for many people, it seems appropriate to ask what made the city work. To begin with, the poor enjoyed a promise of prosperity to come. Within a decade, the Lower East Side's residents were flocking to Brooklyn and Bronx, for airier apartments and more-inviting schools. Families no longer had to take in lodgers or send their children to work. Between 1910 and 1920, Manhattan began its population decline, and the other boroughs gained almost 1 million persons. If extending the subway system helped, rises in real wages were what made the moves possible. Indeed, soon after their arrival, immigrants began saving for a better life. Thus, as one report noted, "a great many people who are perfectly able to afford good housing nevertheless crowd into unsanitary dwellings in congested districts through the desire to save money to send home or for other purposes."

Assimilation was accelerated by World War I, which spurred a common patriotism. The war also cut off immigration, allowing the city to absorb its last waves. From 1910 to 1920, the 17.9 percent growth in New York's population—only half the rate of the previous decade—was due largely to the increase in surviving births, since the foreign-born cohort grew only 4.3 percent. The city did continue to attract Americans from other states, especially the South. The number of black New Yorkers advanced to 152,467, a 66.3 percent increase over 1910, anticipating future trends. The offspring of immigrants adopted New York accents, varying from borough to borough but carrying a characteristic tone. The rush and brashness of the city remained its distinctive qualities, renewed by the ambitions and energies of its latest citizens. Even so, the civic habits apparent in 1910 remained ingrained.

Throughout these decades, people's expectations remained relatively modest, and they seldom questioned the rules. They tended to confine their lives to their neighborhoods, where schools and churches and synagogues were instruments of control, emphasizing duties as much as rights. Moreover, class boundaries were recognized. Youths from poorer neighborhoods knew better than to venture into middle-class territory unless they had errands they could identify. Alcoholics and the homeless were allowed the Bowery but prodded with nightsticks if they turned up elsewhere. Racial segregation was the rule, embracing more than residence. Black faces were seldom seen in restaurants or department stores, and almost never in hotels. Crime in minority neighborhoods was modest compared with the rates of today. And constitutional safeguards seldom constrained the police.

History does not repeat itself, nor does it run in regular cycles. The New York that knew "civil peace" and "moral order" reflected conditions no policies can replicate. An "urban ego" that now pervades the population impresses New Yorkers of all classes with their own importance and entitlements. Seven million self-esteems are bound to clash a bit.

Yet this semianarchic clash has been accompanied by a reinvigoration of the city, due to new flows of immigrants. Earlier in this century, the Italians and Jews were infusing New York with a new spirit and energy, establishing it as an international center for business and the arts. It seems equally clear that current waves of arrivals are having a similar effect. In common with their earlier counterparts, they show an eagerness to work and save, to invest in enterprises that strengthen the city. Many of them arrive with middle-class values and have been allowed to assimilate into comfortable neighborhoods throughout the city. The immigrants of 1910 may have been equally aspiring, but they arrived at a less tolerant time. The epithets that greeted them—"alien in language, alien in modes of thought, and alien in tradition" from one public official—are seldom heard today. What these separate generations of newcomers have in common is that both have augmented the wealth of the city and changed its ambience in ways even the most prescient of experts never predicted.

The purpose of history is not to offer lessons, but to increase our understanding. By illuminating the past, history can show us what is truly new. The year 1910 tells us much about New York today as it enters the century's closing decade.

The poor, in 1910, were working poor. Women and children worked, as did many we today would consider disabled. So the problem of welfare dependency is new, because we offer people stipends so they may stay at home.

Education was effective because only a small minority of youngsters entered or finished high school. Even in the elementary grades, children from immigrant households learned how to speak and read standard English. The city supported more than a dozen daily newspapers. Today, New York is having a hard time duplicating what it did 80 years ago.

In 1910, the most general drug was distilled spirits. But the Irish, by then, were doing most of their drinking indoors, and alcohol was much less a public problem. Today's widespread use of drugs is new, as is the high incidence of crime. In the early years of the century, people lived under networks of controls. Among all classes, certain kinds of behavior simply were not countenanced. What is new is the extent to which a segment of the population now feels free to prey on others or to destroy themselves.

The dread disease of 1910 was tuberculosis, "the white death," which was passed along by packing too many people into confined living quarters. It declined as people moved out of lower Manhattan, to airier apartments in Brooklyn and the Bronx. Today's counterpart is, of course, AIDS. What is new is that AIDS has been transmitted largely by behavior that may be considered more voluntary. Using drugs is a matter of decision, as is sex without safeguards. In that earlier time, fewer people felt free to declare or act on their sexual inclinations.

The New York of 1910 was a city of classes. There was a small, bourgeois middle class, composed of the one in eight households who could afford a servant. And there was a large working-class, perhaps exploited and oppressed, but confident about a better future. Today there is simply a melange of economic levels and social styles, without solidarity, historic sense, or structure.

New York in 1910 was a vigorous two-party arena, with Republican strength concentrated among Protestants in the outer boroughs. Voters tended to be loyal to their parties and identified with them. Among those eligible to vote, turnout was high. Political life today is a shadow of its former self, not least because citizens set too exacting a standard and fault the system for failing to put on a better show.

Since the birth of the Republic, New York has been the nation's largest city. (Its 1790 population was 49,401.) By 1910, it had become its cultural and financial capital as well. Not only immigrants, but Americans from small towns and rural areas came to New York to make names and fortunes for themselves. Even so, in 1910, New York still stood third behind London and Paris as a center of worldly endeavor. Now that balance has changed. New York is less the nation's capital city—not because it has been supplanted by Dallas or San Diego, but because the country's resources and talents are

217

more widely dispersed. Yet coincidentally, New York has moved ahead of its European cousins to rank first as the place where things happen. New York is thus entered upon a new ascendancy at the same time as it experiences decline and decay. This duality is its fatal attraction, its vanity, and its charm.

INDEX